ENFORCING MORALITY

What parts of morality ought the law to enforce? What considerations justify its enforcement? What is the relationship between the legal and social enforcement of morality? Are there principled moral limits that constrain the enforcement of morality? How should we think about the pragmatic limits to the effective enforcement of morality? These are some of the main questions addressed by Steven Wall in this comprehensive and provocative study of a fundamental debate in jurisprudence and political theory. The book defends the practice of ethical environmentalism: the deliberate effort to improve the ethical character of the social environment of a society by political, legal and other means. The presumptive case for ethical environmentalism is presented and then assessed in light of a range of important considerations, including fair treatment, governmental neutrality, the value of personal liberty, rights to do wrongs and free expression.

Steven Wall is Professor of Philosophy at the University of Arizona, where he is also a member of the Philosophy, Politics, Economics and Law program. Among other publications, he is the editor of *The Cambridge Companion to Liberalism* (2015) and Oxford Studies in Political Philosophy (2015–).

T0382149

CAMBRIDGE INTRODUCTIONS TO PHILOSOPHY AND LAW

Series Editors

Brian H. Bix
University of Minnesota

William A. Edmundson
Georgia State University

This introductory series of books provides concise studies of the philosophical foundations of law, of perennial topics in the philosophy of law, and of important and opposing schools of thought. The series is aimed principally at students in philosophy, law, and political science.

Matthew Kramer, *Objectivity and the Rule of Law*
Larry Alexander and Emily Sherwin, *Demystifying Legal Reasoning*
Larry Alexander and Kimberly Kessler Ferzan with Stephen J. Morse, *Crime and Culpability: A Theory of Criminal Law*
William A. Edmundson, *An Introduction to Rights, 2nd edition*
Robin West, *Normative Jurisprudence: An Introduction*
Gregory S. Alexander and Eduardo S. Peñalver, *An Introduction to Property Theory*
Brian H. Bix, *Contract Law: Rules, Theory, and Context*
Liam Murphy, *What Makes Law: An Introduction to the Philosophy of Law*
Pablo E. Navarro and Jorge L. Rodríguez, *Deontic Logic and Legal Systems*
Alexander Somek, *The Legal Relation: Legal Theory after Legal Positivism*
David Lefkowitz, *Philosophy and International Law: A Critical Introduction*

Enforcing Morality

STEVEN WALL

University of Arizona

Shaftesbury Road, Cambridge CB2 8EA, United Kingdom

One Liberty Plaza, 20th Floor, New York, NY 10006, USA

477 Williamstown Road, Port Melbourne, VIC 3207, Australia

314–321, 3rd Floor, Plot 3, Splendor Forum, Jasola District Centre,
New Delhi – 110025, India

103 Penang Road, #05–06/07, Visioncrest Commercial, Singapore 238467

Cambridge University Press is part of Cambridge University Press & Assessment,
a department of the University of Cambridge.

We share the University's mission to contribute to society through the pursuit of
education, learning and research at the highest international levels of excellence.

www.cambridge.org
Information on this title: www.cambridge.org/9781009363792

DOI: 10.1017/9781009363808

© Steven Wall 2023

This publication is in copyright. Subject to statutory exception and to the provisions
of relevant collective licensing agreements, no reproduction of any part may take
place without the written permission of Cambridge University Press & Assessment.

First published 2023

A catalogue record for this publication is available from the British Library.

A Cataloging-in-Publication data record for this book is available from the Library of Congress.

ISBN 978-1-009-36379-2 Hardback
ISBN 978-1-009-36376-1 Paperback

Cambridge University Press & Assessment has no responsibility for the persistence
or accuracy of URLs for external or third-party internet websites referred to in this
publication and does not guarantee that any content on such websites is, or will
remain, accurate or appropriate.

Contents

Acknowledgments

I have been thinking and teaching about the topics in this book for well over a decade. I am grateful to Brian Bix and William Edmundson, the editors of this series, for giving me the opportunity to set my thoughts down on the issues addressed in the book in a systematic and comprehensive way. The book draws on several previously published papers, chief among which include "Moral Environmentalism," in C. Coons and M. Weber, *Paternalism: Theory and Practice* (Cambridge University Press, 2013) and "Enforcing Morality," in *Criminal Law and Philosophy* (2013). Thanks to Massimo Renzo for inviting me to contribute this latter paper to a symposium on the fiftieth anniversary of Hart's contribution to the Hart/Devlin debate.

I am grateful to David Schmidtz for organizing a reading group on an earlier draft of the book. That group brought together a stellar list of participants including, among others, Larry Alexander, Jason Brennan, Gerald Dworkin, Peter de Marneffe, Iskra Fileva, Harrison Frye, Michael Huemer and Dan Jacobson. In the fall 2020 term I taught a seminar on the topic of this book and benefited from discussions with the graduate students who attended. Special thanks to Andrew Lichter, Will Schumacher, Alex Motchoulski, Travis Quigley and Ritwik Agrawal.

Some of the ideas advanced in this book were first aired at various NOISE conferences. Thanks to David Shoemaker, who co-organizes these events with me, and to the other regular attendees including David Sobel, Dale Dorsey, Doug Portmore, Simon May, Justin D'Arms, Dan Jacobson, Connie Rosati, Mike Valdman, Jeff Moriarty, Rosa Terlazzo and Elizabeth Brake.

Writing this book at the University of Arizona has been a great pleasure, thanks in large measure to my terrific colleagues in moral and political philosophy, and especially to David Schmidtz, Michael McKenna, Tom Christiano, and the late Jerry Gaus. A penultimate version of Chapter 9 was presented at a seminar on free speech at Cornell run by Andrei Marmor and David Shoemaker. Comments from that seminar led to some last-minute revisions.

Thanks finally, and most significantly, to Lynn for her support and encouragement.

1

Introduction

Legal systems enforce morality. No one really denies it. "It cannot be seriously disputed," H. L. A. Hart observes, "that the development of law, at all times and places, has in fact been profoundly influenced both by the conventional morality and ideals of particular social groups, and also by forms of enlightened moral criticism urged by individuals, whose moral horizon has transcended the morality currently accepted."[1] From the fact that all legal systems enforce morality, it does not follow that they ought to do so. But no one really denies this either.[2] The legitimacy of legal prohibitions on a host of moral wrongs such as murder, rape and burglary is widely taken for granted and not subject to serious dispute. Since legal systems do and ought to enforce morality, the interesting question is not whether the law should enforce morality. The interesting questions concern what parts of morality the law ought to enforce, the considerations that justify its enforcement, how the law ought to enforce morality, the relationship between the legal and social enforcement of morality and whether there are moral limits that constrain the enforcement of morality – and, if so, the nature and justifications for these limits. These are the central questions explored in this book.

1.1 ENFORCING AND PROMOTING

The legal enforcement of morality is often taken to be an issue about the moral limits of the criminal law. This is understandable. Legal systems characteristically, even if not essentially, rely on the threat of punishment. In the world in which we live, legal efforts to regulate conduct and to guide it in morally desirable directions must impose criminal punishments to be effective. Still, the criminal law is but one

---

[1] Hart, *The Concept of Law*, 3rd ed., p. 185.
[2] Anarchists – more precisely, political (as opposed to merely philosophical) anarchists – may deny it. To the extent that they reject the legitimacy of legal systems, they will reject the legitimacy of enforcing morality through law. But for those who accept the legitimacy of legal systems, there is no serious dispute about the legitimacy of these systems enforcing morality. For the distinction between political anarchism and merely philosophical anarchism, see Simmons, "Philosophical Anarchism."

instrument for enforcing morality, albeit a particularly salient one. So, we do well to consider other ways by which the law can enforce morality.

The term "enforcement" connotes the use of force. The law enforces morality when it imposes sanctions on its subjects to increase their compliance with its norms. Classical writers in jurisprudence defined sanctions in terms of unpleasant consequences. Sanctions refer to "the evil which will probably be incurred in case a command be disobeyed."[3] Punishments, accordingly, were viewed as the paradigm case of sanctions. Nevertheless, as most writers have allowed, sanctions include more than punishments. For example, it is common to distinguish punishments from mere penalties. The former express the law's condemnation of the targeted conduct, whereas the latter may simply raise the costs of engaging in it.[4] If mere penalties count as sanctions, and if the law enforces morality whenever it imposes sanctions to do so, then the legal enforcement of morality extends beyond the criminal law.

The term "sanctions" can be understood even more broadly to include the withholding of benefits as well as the imposition of costs. Consider a mundane example. Suppose that I have been paying the rent for my friend's apartment while she looks for work. Over time I become concerned about her lack of effort in finding employment and announce that I will discontinue this support if she does not shape up soon. The expression of my intention to cease providing a benefit that I have been providing to my friend may function as a powerful incentive for her to do what I want her to do. Its influence on her conduct may be just as effective as a threat to harm her would be. Modern states provide their members with a wide range of benefits including retirement pensions, education, employment opportunities and health care. Modern states also extend tax credits and tax deductions to favored activities, such as a tax deduction for charitable giving or for making environmentally friendly renovations to one's home. These tax breaks too can be viewed as benefits, which can be extended or withheld. The state might withhold public money for art that was deemed to be offensive, thereby seeking to enforce community standards of decency, for example. By withholding this benefit, it would, in effect, sanction the artists who were producing the offensive art. If the withholding of a previously provided benefit qualifies as a sanction, then the difference between enforcing morality and promoting it is muted. Normatively speaking, it will not matter too much whether state action is classified as enforcement in virtue of the fact that a benefit is withheld or promotion in virtue of the fact that a benefit is extended.[5]

For this reason, in this book we will understand the enforcement of morality to include the use of carrots as well as sticks. It may be objected that when states

---

[3]   Austin, *The Province of Jurisprudence Determined*, Lecture 1.
[4]   Feinberg, "The Expressive Function of Punishment."
[5]   While the classification of state action does not have normative significance in itself, how it is perceived can make a difference. It often matters whether something is viewed as a gain or a loss. Perceived losses tend to produce greater pain or disutility than the pleasure or utility produced by equivalently sized gains. See Kahneman, *Thinking, Fast and Slow*, pp. 292–297 (discussing "the endowment effect").

promote morality, they always do so coercively, and so even when the state extends or withholds benefits to its members, it is exercising force over them. On this view, when the state is involved, there are no carrots without sticks. In reply, it can be said that coercion is not simply a function of the power of the coercing agent but also of how the use of this power affects the decision making of those subjected to it.[6] Some measures may be noncoercive, even though they are fully backed by the power of the state. These measures include extending recognition to certain institutions or practices (monogamous marriage) while denying it to others (polygamous marriage), providing subsidies for some activities (opera) while denying it to others (amusement parks), and using the law to express official support for some ideals or practices (religious toleration) while expressing official condemnation of others (recreational drug use).[7] Whether these noncoercive legal measures are themselves indirectly coercive need not detain us. We can include them with criminal law prohibitions under the general rubric of legal efforts to enforce morality.

1.2 MAIN ISSUES

Since nearly everyone agrees that harm prevention is an appropriate aim of the law, this idea is a natural place to begin our investigation. We can distinguish cases in which people harm others from cases in which they harm only themselves. A society, it is sometimes said, should concern itself only with preventing harm to others. Famously, John Stuart Mill expressed this view in his essay *On Liberty* by propounding what he described as "one simple principle" for governing the relations between society and the individual:

> [T]he sole end for which mankind are warranted, individually or collectively, for interfering with the liberty of action of any of their number, is self-protection. That the only purpose for which power can be rightfully exercised over any member of a civilized community, against his will, is to prevent harm to others. His own good, either physical or moral, is not a sufficient warrant. He cannot rightfully be compelled to do or forbear because it will be better for him to do so, because it will make him happier, because, in the opinion of others, to do so would be wise, or even right . . . .. The only part of the conduct of anyone, for which he is amenable to society, is that which concerns others. In the part which merely concerns himself, his independence is, of right, absolute.[8]

This principle, which has come to be termed the "harm principle," is not as simple as Mill advertised, as nearly every commentator on his essay has

---

[6] Schauer, *The Force of Law*, p. 129.
[7] Even in countries with a strong commitment to freedom of speech, such as the USA, the courts have generally held that there is no requirement that the government's own speech must be neutral with respect to different viewpoints. For critical assessment of this issue, see Alexander, *Is There a Right of Freedom of Expression?* pp. 82–102.
[8] Mill, *On Liberty*, pp. 223–224.

observed.[9] We will consider some of the complexities and puzzles it presents in Chapter 2. But whether we ultimately accept it or not, we should recognize that the harm principle is a moral principle. When society interferes with the liberty of some of its members so as to prevent them from harming others, it enforces (a part of) morality.

Mill's principle not only provides a justification for the enforcement of morality (prevention of harm to others) but it also identifies the limits to its enforcement. No enforcement of morality is justified beyond that which concerns preventing harm to others. Consider the following legal enactments.

- A legislative body passes a statute that fines anyone within its jurisdiction who is caught riding a motorcycle without wearing a protective helmet.
- A court refuses to uphold a contract between two adults on the grounds that the terms of the contract, while entered into freely, are grossly unfair.
- A judge sentences someone to prison for assisting another in their suicide.

The first of these enactments is an instance of *legal paternalism*. The legislative body interferes with the conduct of some people by imposing and by threatening to impose a fine on them, and it does so for their own good. The aim of the statute is to dissuade people from exposing themselves to the increased risk of serious injury that accompanies riding a motorcycle without protective headgear. The second of these enactments can be viewed as an instance of *legal moralism*. The court refuses to uphold the contract because its terms are grossly unfair. It is, in the language of the law, "an unconscionable contract." Does the upholding of contracts of this kind cause harm to others? Not necessarily, since if the contract is freely and voluntarily entered into by both parties, then any harm that results from it is self-imposed. Friends of the harm principle often register this point by invoking the Latin phrase "volenti non fit injuria" (to a willing person injury is not done). The third enactment can be viewed as a mix of legal paternalism and legal moralism. In criminalizing assisted suicide, the society may seek to protect its members from harming themselves with the assistance of others. Perhaps it worries that those who desire to end their lives typically suffer from forms of depression that impair their capacity to make free and voluntary decisions to do so. Such people need protection against themselves, and from others who would help them to end their lives. But the society may also view suicide as immoral, even when it is the result of a free and voluntary decision and is in the interests of the person who engages in it.

I shall have much more to say about both legal paternalism and legal moralism in subsequent chapters. For now, it need only be noted that Mill's principle excludes them both.[10] No legal enactment that involves either would be legitimate.

---

[9] Some writers have denied that Mill was, in actuality, committed to the harm principle. See Jacobson, "Mill on Liberty, Speech, and the Free Society." We will not take up this interpretive issue here.
[10] Mill's principle should not be confused with Mill's own views on the legitimate enforcement of morality, since while he accepted the principle, he also appeared to accept enforcements of morality that are in tension with it. Compare his principle with the applications he discusses in chapter 5 of *On Liberty*.

I have been focusing on the law (or the state[11]) as the agent of enforcement. But, at points, we will also consider societal, but nonlegal, instances of the enforcement of morality. This too was a pressing concern for Mill. His principle was intended to apply as much to "the moral coercion of public opinion" as to the physical force of legal sanctions. With this in mind, consider the case of controversial speech on college campuses and the efforts by some students to suppress it or interfere with it, not by legal means but by mobilizing resistance, including violent resistance, to it.[12] This too can be understood as an effort to enforce morality, even though the agent of enforcement in this case is not the state. To be sure, the state remains in the background. And those who wish to defend the rights to speak of those whose speech is targeted may try to enlist the power of the state to uphold these rights, thereby attempting to get the state to enforce that part of morality, as they see it, that concerns the protection of these rights.

The case of controversial speech reveals some of the complexity of our topic. For speech or expression may be wrongful, while being rightfully protected. Those who say false, dangerous or offensive things may not be in the right, even if they have a right to say it. We shall consider in Chapters 8 and 9 how to understand such purported rights to do wrong and how they bear on the enforcement of morality. Here we can simply note that if there are rights of this kind, then efforts to enforce one part of morality will block efforts, by the state and by others, to enforce other parts.

The idea that an important part of morality concerns the rights of individual people will be a familiar one to many readers of this book. Some think that individual rights exhaust the moral domain. This is not a plausible view. As the example of protected speech illustrates, if one has a right to do something, it remains a further question whether it is right for one to do it. But how exactly should the moral domain be characterized? Many have claimed that we need to distinguish a narrow from a broad conception of morality. The distinction has been drawn in various ways. Narrow morality, it has been claimed, refers to "a particular normative domain including primarily such duties to others as duties not to kill, harm, or deceive, and duties to keep one's promises."[13] Of special importance (for our purposes), these duties include requirements of justice and fair treatment. This normative domain, it is often claimed, engages "the sentiments of guilt and resentment and their variants."[14] Broad morality, by contrast, includes narrow morality but much more as well. Most generally, it concerns the question of how to live, "the precepts instructing people on what makes for a successful, meaningful, and

---

[11]   I will use the terms "legal enforcement" and "state enforcement" interchangeably.
[12]   The recent controversy over the alt-right speaker Milo Yiannopoulos at the University of California, Berkeley provides a good example. The controversy, and its background, is described in Marantz, "How Social-Media Trolls turned U.C. Berkeley into a Free Speech Circus," *New Yorker*, July 2, 2018.
[13]   Scanlon, *What We Owe to Each Other*, pp. 171–172.
[14]   Gibbard, *Wise Choices, Apt Feelings*, p. 6.

worthwhile life."[15] But, in addition, and more specifically, it includes self-regarding duties to develop one's talents and respect one's rational nature, ideals of character and duties to respect impersonal goods, such as perfectionist achievements and natural beauty, even when failure to do so would not contravene any duty to others.[16]

Drawing on the claims expressed in these statements, we can depict the distinction in the following rough-and-ready way.

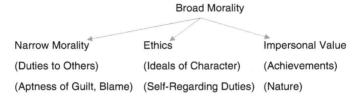

The divisions depicted here are not meant to be sharp. They are intended to map out characteristic features of different domains or compartments of morality. Consider self-regarding duties, for example. Perhaps we can appropriately blame people for failing to live up to them. If so, then the moral sentiment of blame will not be confined to narrow morality.[17] Or consider justice. A just or fair distribution of goods, I have emphasized, is a matter of narrow morality, but some have thought that justice has impersonal value. It is good for justice to be done, they say, even if it benefits no one.

There are, to be sure, other ways to mark a distinction between broad and narrow morality. Mill famously distinguished the morality of right and wrong from what he called "the art of life." The latter refers to the broader question of how to live. The former is characterized in terms of the appropriateness of punishment: "We do not call anything wrong, unless we mean to imply that a person ought to be punished in some way or other doing it; if not by law, by the opinion of his fellow creatures; if not by opinion, by the reproaches of his own conscience."[18]

On this proposal, narrow morality – the morality of right and wrong – just is the part of morality that is appropriately enforceable. The part of broad morality that extends beyond the narrow part should not be backed up by sanctions of any kind. In this way, Mill's view makes the claim that we should only enforce narrow morality true by definition (although it does leave open what parts of morality are

---

[15]   Raz, "Right-Based Moralities," p. 198.
[16]   Ibid.
[17]   Moral blame may have different senses. Blaming someone for failing to live up to a self-regarding duty may express a judgment of responsibility in one sense, while blaming someone for failing to honor their duty to another may express a judgment of responsibility in a different sense. If this were right, then the moral emotions that go with narrow morality could be understood as those that express the latter sense of responsibility. For discussion, see Watson, "Two Faces of Responsibility."
[18]   Mill, *Utilitarianism*, p. 14. Mill's position can be softened by replacing punishment with appropriate susceptibility to some non-punitive accountability-seeking reactive attitude. See Darwall, *The Second-Person Standpoint*, pp. 92–93.

appropriately subject to legal enforcement). But while Mill's characterization of narrow and broad morality could conflict with the characterization depicted earlier, it is not incompatible in substance with anything we need to say here. For we can investigate which parts of broad morality, as we have depicted it, are appropriately subject to enforcement and then, after concluding the investigation, characterize them as narrow or broad in Mill's terms.[19]

Nothing of substance, then, turns on the terminology we adopt to describe the different parts or domains of morality. The terminology depicted earlier, however, has the advantage of helping us to formulate clearly the questions that we want to ask. For example, some claim that legal officials should enforce only narrow morality. The part of broad morality that encompasses more than that encompassed by narrow morality should not be legally enforced. And, some hold in addition, that narrow morality is defined by the rights of individual people. Indeed, a proponent of Mill's principle could insist that each individual person has a fundamental right to live their life as they please, so long as they do not cause harm to others; and that the legal enforcement of morality should be confined to protecting this fundamental right for each person. Questions about the rightful exercise of this right could then be assigned to the broad conception of morality, which is not enforceable by law.

We shall be exploring the distinction between narrow and broad morality in more detail in Chapters 5 and 6. We will see that the distinction between these two conceptions or characterizations of morality is harder to sustain than it appears at first pass. If the distinction cannot be sustained, then it will no longer be credible to hold that only narrow morality should be legally enforced.

Whether morality is conceived narrowly or broadly, further questions about its nature invite consideration here. Should we speak of morality, as I have been doing so far, or should we speak instead of moralities? The latter course might seem to be more accurate, for there is, and has been, more than one morality practiced in the world. We speak of the morality of the ancient world or the morality of contemporary Christian culture, for example. At the same time, we often speak of morality as referring not to any moral code that is practiced by any particular society but instead as a set of critical principles or rules. As the opening quotation from Hart illustrated, morality can refer both to the conventional morality of a group and to the purportedly enlightened views of those who object to it (or endorse it). This ambiguity is important. If we are enjoined to enforce morality, then we need to clarify what kind of morality is in question.

Since the issue here is of central importance to our topic, a measure of clarification is in order. Let us stipulate that a social morality is a system of demands and aspirations that apply to and resonate with a particular group of people at a particular time. Let us add that this system of demands and aspirations is generally recognized

[19] Plainly, if we were to do this, then we would need to keep track of the different kinds of sanctions – legal, social, internal reproaches of conscience – that are appropriate for breaches of different parts of morality.

by the members of the group as a source of obligations, in the case of demands, and justifying reasons in the case of aspirations. The general recognition that these demands and aspirations have this kind of authority attests to their perceived importance by those who are subject to them.[20] So understood, social moralities are plural. Different groups have different social moralities. Yet while there exists a plurality of social moralities, each social morality arguably contains within itself the seeds of its own criticism. In virtue of the fact that social moralities are systems of demands and aspirations that purport to be authoritative for their members, it becomes possible to ask, both by their members and by outsiders, whether the purportedly authoritative demands and aspirations are in fact genuinely authoritative. While this question is sometimes raised by those who doubt that any system of social demands and aspirations could be authoritative, it is more often raised by those who wonder whether the social morality to which they are subject could be improved in ways that would make it more authoritative. When this latter group raises the question of the authority of social morality, they are appealing to a critical standard or set of critical standards. These standards are the standards of critical morality.[21]

Unlike social morality, critical morality is not something that must be established by particular groups at particular times. Like the canons of logical reasoning, it can exist solely as abstract standards or principles. Does this mean that critical morality is singular – that one standard, or set of standards, applies to us all? Perhaps, but perhaps not. The issue here is enormously complicated. Much depends on the substance or the content of critical morality. Some utilitarian writers have held that there is one fundamental critical standard of morality, one that enjoins the maximization of utility (or happiness). This critical standard applies to all societies. But a pluralistic account of critical morality can also be advanced, one that maintains that there is a plurality of critical standards. Such a view can allow that these standards can be ranked in different ways by different social groups and that no single ranking is optimal from the standpoint of critical morality. We will consider a pluralistic view of this kind in Chapter 6 when we discuss the value of tradition. However, for present purposes, we do not need to determine whether critical morality is pluralistic or whether there is a single enlightened morality that applies to us all. We can sidestep this issue by distinguishing the social morality of a group from the critical morality that applies to it, thereby leaving open the possibility that different critical standards apply to different groups.

With this distinction in hand, we can return to the enforcement of morality and take proper account of the ambiguity in the injunction to "enforce morality."

---

[20] This account of social morality draws on both Strawson's "Social Morality and Individual Ideal" and Fuller's "The Two Moralities" in his *The Morality of Law*.
[21] For this term, see Hart, *The Concept of Law*. Hart's distinction between positive and critical morality, which was influenced by Strawson's discussion, tracks the distinction drawn here between social and critical morality.

On one proposal, to enforce morality is to enforce the social morality of the group in question. This has been the view taken by many writers who have been described as communitarians. The British judge Lord Patrick Devlin, whose arguments will be considered in Chapter 3, provides a classic example. For him, the social morality of a society is a necessary ingredient in the glue that holds it together, and if this morality is not adequately enforced, the society will fall apart: "For a society is not something that is held together physically; it is held by the invisible bonds of common thought. If the bonds were too far relaxed the members would drift apart. A common morality is part of the bondage."[22]

Applying this communitarian view of the enforcement of morality to the matter of sexual morality in particular, Devlin argued that whether the law should aim to discourage prostitution or homosexuality turns on whether doing so is necessary for, or conducive to, the preservation of the public morality (i.e. social morality) of the society to which it applies. Devlin was responding to the recommendations advanced by The Report of the Committee on Homosexual Offences and Prostitution, a report commonly referred to as the Wolfenden Report, that was commissioned by the British government and published in 1957. A chief recommendation of this Report was that homosexual sex between consenting adults in private should no longer be subject to criminal sanction.

To the readers of this book, many of whom will have grown up in modern liberal societies, Devlin's focus on homosexuality may seem a little bizarre. Why would anyone want to criminalize conduct, such as homosexual conduct between consenting adults in private, if there is nothing inherently wrong with it? But this is precisely the point. For the society that Devlin was addressing – British society in the middle of the twentieth century – it was widely accepted that homosexuality was, in Devlin's words, "a miserable way of life" – one that could, if unchecked, corrupt the young. That judgment, which reflected the settled and dispassionate assessment of the British people at that time, was an important part of the social morality of this society. And Devlin's point is that it is proper and necessary for a society to support and uphold its social morality.[23]

The proposal that we are now considering, that illustrated by Devlin's response to the Wolfenden Report, is subject to a devastating objection. How could a society have an unqualified right to enforce its social morality? For suppose that the social morality of a given society sustains the institution of chattel slavery. If the proposal we are considering were accepted, then it would follow that this society would have a right to uphold this evil practice. But this cannot be right. The objection brings us back to the interdependence of social morality and critical morality that was noted earlier. The claim that a society has the right to enforce its social morality is not itself

---

[22] Devlin, *The Enforcement of Morality*, p. 10.
[23] Devlin's own position on the issue of the criminalization of homosexual sex was complex. On the one hand, he personally favored decriminalization. On the other hand, he insisted that his society had the right to criminalize it, if it judged that doing so was necessary to protect its social morality.

a claim of social morality. Devlin makes plain that he thinks that societies, not just his own society, have the right to uphold and enforce their social moralities. This right, then, must be a right of critical morality. But now it can be asked, how could a society have an unqualified critical moral right of this kind?

Devlin was sensitive to the interdependence of social and critical morality, and he struggled to account for it: "There are, have been, and will be bad laws, bad morals, and bad societies. Probably no law-maker believes that the morality he is enacting is false, but that does not make it true."[24] Nonetheless, Devlin insisted that the lawmaker's job is not to enforce the morality that they think is true but rather to enforce the social morality of their society. Their task is to ascertain not "the true belief, but the common belief" of their society. It is a good question why we should think that this is indeed the correct description of the lawmaker's job.

Devlin hints at an answer. His refined view goes beyond the simple thought expressed by the metaphor of the glue holding a society together. The lawmaker must enforce the common moral beliefs of their society not only because doing so helps to hold the society together but also because they have a duty to defer to the views of those they serve. This refined view thus connects the right of a society to enforce its social morality to the value of popular self-rule. We shall examine the arguments for this view more fully in Chapter 3, but here a few preliminary remarks can be made about it.

On Devlin's refined view, the lawmaker in a democratic society has a duty, a moral duty, to uphold the moral judgments of their constituents so long as they are consistent with democracy. This moral duty is a duty of critical morality but it directs the lawmaker to enforce not what they, the lawmaker, believe is right or wrong but rather what their society believes is right or wrong.[25] The duty in question is a democratic duty, since it is grounded in the claim that each citizen in a democracy has an equal claim to define the social morality of the society to which they belong. Admittedly, the democratic duty referenced here is a little obscure. Its content goes beyond the demand to extend formal political rights (to vote, to run for office, to organize in support of political causes, etc.) to the adult citizens in one's society. The duty in question lies on the lawmaker and the judge, and it instructs them to recognize that their judgment of right and wrong has no greater authority than those over whom they govern. By granting that all citizens have an equal claim to discern right from wrong, the office-holder must honor the common morality, the established social morality of their society, rather than seek to replace it with their own understanding of what a more enlightened morality would require.

Several comments about this refined proposal can now be ventured. First, the appeal to democratic values obviously restricts the reach of the argument for the

[24] Devlin, *The Enforcement of Morality*, p. 94.
[25] Similar claims are sometimes made about the role of a constitutional judge in a democratic society. See Bickel, *The Morality of Consent* and Bork, *The Tempting of America*.

enforcement of social morality. A nondemocratic society could not justify the enforcement of its social morality on these grounds. Second, while the refined proposal is a proposal to enforce the social morality of a society, the argument appeals to critical morality, to wit the critical moral democratic duty that it invokes. Third, the democratic duty, if it is indeed a duty of critical morality, is plausibly but one such duty. Other duties of critical morality are likely to conflict with it. Suppose, for example, that a lawmaker believes that it is wrong from the standpoint of critical morality to impose cruel and excessive punishment on an offender for a minor crime, such as public caning for an act of vandalism;[26] but they also know that this punishment for this type of crime is widely viewed as acceptable in their society. If they accept the democratic duty to honor the social morality of their society, then they will need to balance this duty against their perceived duty to avoid supporting unjust punishments. The refined proposal, in this kind of case, must hold that the democratic duty takes precedence over any conflicting duties of critical morality. Accordingly, one could reject the refined proposal either by denying that there is any such democratic duty or by holding that it is frequently overridden by other requirements of critical morality.

Let us turn now to a second proposal concerning the enforcement of morality, one that drops any reference to social morality. On this proposal, the law ought to enforce critical morality. More precisely, the law ought to enforce the critical morality that applies to the society over which the law has jurisdiction. Of course, it is possible that the critical morality that applies to a society will coincide with its social morality. But even in this very fortunate circumstance, it is the fact that the morality is sound by critical standards, and not the fact that it is socially established, that is crucial.

Now, critical morality is one thing; a lawmaker's or judge's beliefs about its contents are another. No legal official is infallible. Legal officials make mistakes all the time. Should we say, then, that on the second proposal the law should enforce critical morality or that the law should enforce the lawmaker's beliefs about critical morality? The question is ill formed in one way. Barring unusual circumstances, a lawmaker can only enforce critical morality by acting on their beliefs about what its contents are. In intending to enforce or promote critical morality, the lawmaker must act on their beliefs about its contents. There is really no other way for them to do so.[27] Notwithstanding this point, if the lawmaker is clearheaded, then they will acknowledge that their judgments are fallible and that their efforts to promote critical morality are justified only if the beliefs on which they act are correct.

---

[26] Public caning for crimes of vandalism is currently legal practice in Singapore, as well as a few other countries. In 1994 an American, Michael Peter Fay, was convicted of vandalism while visiting Singapore and was given a sentence of caning, which was subsequently carried out. The incident provoked international attention and protest from the US government.

[27] A lawmaker might not act on their own beliefs but instead defer to the beliefs of someone they trust, such as a religious official. But even in this kind of case the lawmaker would be acting on their belief that the religious official had trustworthy judgment on the matter in question.

Their intention is to promote critical morality, not to promote their beliefs about critical morality irrespective of their truth.

The recognition of the fallibility of legislative judgment should not paralyze the lawmaker. For failure to enforce what they consider to be sound critical morality can have bad consequences itself. But it should give them pause. The lawmaker should want to ensure that their judgments are formed under social conditions that allow for their correction when they are mistaken, and that allow them to have warranted confidence in them when they are correct. The social conditions that do well in this regard play an important role in justifying a right to free expression, especially free and open debate on matters of public, political concern. We will explore these issues in some detail in Chapter 9.

For now, I want to highlight two distinct ways by which one might criticize a proposal to enforce critical morality by law or by other means. One could argue that the portion of the critical morality that is being targeted for enforcement is not properly subject to enforcement. Alternatively, one could argue that the proposal rests on mistaken beliefs about the morality or immorality of what is being targeted. To take an example: consider a proposal to criminalize prostitution. A critic of the proposal might contend that it is none of the law's business to interfere with prostitution. Their view might be that prostitution, so long as it is consensual, does not cause harm to others and that the harm principle should regulate the legal enforcement of morality, for example. Alternatively, a critic might grant that it would be permissible for the law to criminalize prostitution, if prostitution were immoral, but then go on to deny that it is immoral. To be sure, a critic could have both of these thoughts at the same time, believing that prostitution is not wrong and also that, if it were wrong, it would still be none of the law's business to enforce it. But while both thoughts are compatible and can sit in the mind of the same person at the same time, they remain distinct thoughts, and it is important to appreciate the difference between them, as they represent different ways of arguing about the legitimacy of various proposals to enforce critical morality.

Bringing together two of the distinctions we have introduced – that between narrow and broad morality and that between social and critical morality – we can now consider a view that resembles Devlin's view in holding that the law ought to enforce broad as well as narrow morality, but departs from his view in giving critical morality rather than social morality pride of place. A view of this kind will be considered in detail in Part II of this book, but a few preliminary points can be made about it here. The view in question assigns the state, and the legal officials who run it, a general duty to promote the welfare of those who are subject to its authority. It then argues that in order to adequately discharge this duty, the law must enforce morality, including broad morality. Thus, like Devlin's view, this view recognizes that the welfare of people is deeply influenced by the social environment in which they live, but unlike Devlin's view, it assesses the quality of that social environment from the standpoint of critical morality. In one respect, then, the language of enforcing morality, on this view, is a little inapt. It holds that the moral norms of a society should be enforced when they are sound, and when they are not sound, they should not be enforced. Indeed, on the view we are now considering, one function of the law is to improve the social morality of the society in which it holds sway.[28]

No doubt caution is in order here. There are substantial limits that apply to any legal effort to improve the social morality of a group. Morality, whether social or critical, is not subject to deliberate change. As Hart explains, "standards of conduct cannot be endowed with, or deprived of, moral status by human *fiat*, though the daily use of such concepts as enactment and repeal shows that the same is not true of law."[29] When the law undertakes to improve morality, it aims to bring the social morality of those who are subject to it closer to the standards of critical morality. But for this to work, the process of change must be gradual. By changing legal rules and norms, the state can attempt to shape social morality indirectly. The fact that some conduct is made illegal, or the fact that some conduct, such as homosexual sex, is decriminalized, may over time affect societal attitudes about its permissibility.

There are opportunities here for the reformer, but also dangers. A more conservative version of the view we are now considering accentuates the dangers. By attempting to improve social morality, the law might weaken its authority and loosen its bonds. As one writer cautions, "It would be a mistake to make the perfect the enemy of the good-enough, especially when the good-enough actually exists and is an environment that gives structure and meaning to people's lives, while the perfect is just somebody's theory."[30] The conservative version of the view, accordingly, centers on preserving rather than reforming the social morality of a society. According to it, the law ought to enforce morality only if two conditions are jointly met. The morality to be enforced (i) must be part of the actual social morality of those who are subject to the law and (ii) must be judged to be sound or at least acceptable from the standpoint of critical morality.

This view neatly avoids the objection that many have pressed against Devlin's view and that we took brief note of earlier. Even if it were granted that society has a right to use the law to enforce its social morality, this right could not be unqualified. As Delvin himself acknowledged, "Societies in the past have tolerated witch-hunting and burnt heretics: was that done in the name of morality? There are societies today whose moral standards permit them to discriminate against men because of their colour: have we to accept that?"[31] Devlin's posing of these rhetorical questions reveals his ambivalence about his own view. But the conservative view we are now considering harbors no such ambivalence. Society, it holds, has no right to enforce false or misguided morality.

---

[28] For discussion of this point, with special emphasis on the law's role in improving sexual morality, see Green, "Should the Law Improve Morality?"
[29] Hart, *The Concept of Law*, 3rd ed., pp. 175–178.
[30] Green, "Should the Law Improve Morality?" p. 489.
[31] Devlin, *The Enforcement of Morality*, p. 91.

A new issue arises at this point. I have been proceeding on the assumption that social morality and critical morality are distinct in the sense that the former is a matter of descriptive fact, whereas the latter is a matter of critical prescription (of what moral code ought to be established as opposed to what moral code is actually established). As such, the former is investigated by the methods of the sociologist or the anthropologist, while the latter is investigated by methods of rational argument, such as those employed by the ethicist, the moral philosopher or the theologian.[32] But this assumption backgrounds something important. Social morality, like other artifacts, is subject to interpretation. And methods of interpretation can, and often do, appeal to critical standards. For example, suppose that there are two rival interpretations of a given rule of social morality and that each interpretation fits the facts of established practice well. In choosing between them, one needs to appeal to something other than common beliefs about them, since each does equally well on this score; and here, it may be thought, it is appropriate, perhaps necessary, to appeal to standards of critical morality. The best interpretation of the rule in question, one may think, is the one that puts it in the most attractive light.[33]

The proper interpretation of social morality, like that of law, is contested terrain. We cannot investigate this matter here. The point for present purposes is modest: to the extent that one comes to believe that the interpretation of the content of social morality requires some recourse to the standards of critical morality, it will not be possible to say with Devlin that in attempting to enforce the social morality of one's society one does not need to attend to its goodness or truth. This modest point also complicates the conservative version of the argument for the enforcement of critical morality that we just reviewed, since, if the point is accepted, then the line between conserving existing social morality and reforming it will not be a sharp one.

Reconsider now the general form of the argument for enforcing critical morality that has been sketched here. Whether this argument is understood on either the reformist or conservative version, it appeals to a general duty, purportedly one that applies to the state, and the legal officials who run it, that directs the state to promote the good of those who are subject to its authority. This duty, as we have seen, requires the state to attend to the moral environment, or, as I will later call it, the "ethical environment," that its laws and policies shape and sustain. The claim that state officials have a general duty of this sort can be challenged in a variety of ways.

Legal measures designed to shape the moral environment, whether by means of the criminal law or by means of milder legal measures that are not directly coercive, aim to favor some ways of life over others on the grounds that they are better ways of life. This position, it may be thought, runs afoul of a key desideratum of a modern

---

[32] Some identify the standards of critical morality with the teachings of revealed religion. For them, the method for identifying its content will center on techniques for accurately interpreting these teachings.

[33] For an imaginative and powerful development of this general thought, see Dworkin, *Law's Empire* (discussing the idea of constructive interpretation).

liberal state; namely, that it should remain neutral between different conceptions of the good life. The neutralist position has a number of influential proponents in contemporary political philosophy,[34] and its spirit informs objections to the legal enforcement of morality that ordinary citizens often voice. A full defense of the kind of legal enforcement of critical morality that we have been discussing, accordingly, must address the concerns that stand behind and motivate this neutralist critique.

An initial response to the critique is tempting. Neutrality is only a desideratum if it is genuinely possible. But, as was noted at the outset of this chapter, no one seriously denies that the law should enforce morality. And, if it enforces morality, then it will perforce favor some ways of life over others. (If a rapist or a thief were to object to laws that criminalize their preferred activity on the grounds that they are non-neutral and discriminatory toward their way of life, no one should be impressed.) But this tempting response is too quick. More sophisticated versions of the neutralist position can be articulated. The idea of neutrality invites two basic questions. Who is supposed to be neutral, and to whom or what is neutrality supposed to be shown? We have been speaking loosely of the state, or the legal order, as the entity that is supposed to be neutral. But to whom or what is this neutrality owed? Not to any and all activities or ways of life that people may take up. This much is clear from the example of the rapist or the thief. How then to circumscribe the scope of neutrality? Here we can help ourselves again to the distinction between narrow and broad morality. Whether or not there is one true broad morality, there are certainly many conceptions or rival understandings of its content. Some of these conceptions will conflict with the requirements of narrow morality, but many will be consistent with them. Working with these distinctions, the neutralist can now present a more promising version of the view. The state, or legal order, should be neutral with respect to all conceptions of broad morality that are consistent with the requirements of narrow morality.[35] The rapist or the thief has a way of life that is flatly incompatible with narrow morality and so their way of life is not owed neutral treatment. But there are many ideals of conduct that are consistent with narrow morality and the neutralist can insist that the state should not take sides between them.

We will take a closer and more critical look at the neutralist position in Chapters 5 and 6. We will be interested in identifying and evaluating the considerations that purport to justify it. Still, even from the sketch provided here, it should be clear how the neutralist position challenges the moral environmentalist view that we have been associating with the legal enforcement of critical morality. For, in attempting to shape the moral environment of the society in which it claims jurisdiction, the law

[34] For a survey of views on state neutrality in contemporary political philosophy, see Wall and Klosko, *Perfectionism and Neutrality: Essays in Liberal Theory.*
[35] Some friends of the neutralist position hold that the state need only be neutral among conceptions of broad morality (more precisely, the part of broad morality over and above that of narrow morality) that are actually held, or adhered to, by those who are subject to its authority. See Larmore, *Patterns of Moral Complexity*, p. 67.

will almost certainly favor some conceptions of broad morality over others, and this
favoritism will not be limited to favoring conceptions of broad morality that honor
the requirements of narrow morality over conceptions of broad morality that do not.

1.3 PRINCIPLES AND PRACTICE

The foregoing discussion introduced some of the main issues, and alluded to some
important lines of argument, that will occupy our attention in this book. Along the way it
introduced some key distinctions, in particular those between narrow and broad morality
and between social and critical morality. Before proceeding, a few more notions need to
be explained, all of which relate to the difference between defending an enforcement
proposal as in-principle permissible and defending it as in-practice advisable.

Principles are general directives.[36] They tell us what we ought to do or what we
ought to refrain from doing in a range of situations. They inform practical decisions.
But principles do not always tell us all we need to know to make practical decisions.
Sometimes principles do not apply to a case; sometimes they apply but are overridden; and sometimes they direct us elsewhere to make the decision. Return to the
harm principle. This principle, as it is standardly construed, states a necessary
condition for justified interference with the actions of another. Its content can be
stated negatively. It is always wrong to interfere with the actions of another who is not
causing harm to anyone else.[37] From this statement of the principle it does not
follow that if X is causing harm to Y, then X ought to be interfered with. This
inference does not follow because there are costs to interference, and these costs may
render interference ill advised. As Mill explained, "it must by no means be supposed,
because damage, or probability of damage, to the interests of others [harm], can
alone justify the interference of society, that therefore it always does justify such
interference."[38] Mill had an elegant way of expressing this point. Conduct that did
not cause harm to others was "self-regarding" and none of society's business, whereas
conduct that caused, or risked, harm to others could in principle be interfered with if
doing so was in the general interests of society.

This point is especially important to bear in mind when thinking about proposals
to enforce morality through criminal law. Using criminal law to enforce morality is
expensive, liable to mistake and abuse and certain to impose hard treatment on
convicted offenders. Accordingly, the good that it does, and the bad that it deters,
may not be enough to justify the costs it imposes. Consider a proposal to criminalize
the use and sale of cocaine. This proposal could be rejected on the grounds that it is
ruled out by the harm principle. If someone is harmed from consuming this drug,

---

[36] There are different kinds of principles and reliance on them can serve different purposes. See Nozick,
      The Nature of Rationality, pp. 3–40. The principles I have in mind here are moral or normative
      principles that purport to apply to legal officials, or others in a position to enforce morality.
[37] This is one formulation of the harm principle. In Chapter 2 we will consider other formulations.
[38] Mill, *On Liberty*, p. 292.

the resulting harm is self-imposed and so not properly considered a "harm" under the harm principle. This proposal could also be rejected on the grounds that the costs of criminalization in this case would exceed its benefits and so, on balance, criminalization would not be in the general interests of the society. Both responses could be sound. But if the first response is sound, then it is unnecessary to consider the merits of the second.

Many of the principles we will consider in this book take this form. If accepted, they foreclose the need for investigation into the costs and benefits of the proposals they rule out. Alternatively, if they do not foreclose the need for such investigation, the principles establish a strong presumption against the proposals they rule out – a presumption that could be overridden only if the cost/benefit calculation weighed greatly on the other side.[39] Eitherway consideration of the principles engages issues in moral and political philosophy, whereas investigation into the costs and benefits of various enforcement proposals must draw on empirical analysis informed by the methods of the social sciences.

However, this way of putting matters, while substantially accurate, threatens to cover up something important. Philosophers who write on the legal enforcement of morality sometimes claim that "all practical reasoning involves the application of principles to facts."[40] No doubt this is an overstatement. One does not have to be an ethical particularist to appreciate that practical reasoning is more complex than this. Nevertheless, this principles-first approach provides support for a tempting picture of the order of inquiry in practical thinking. First, determine which principles are sound and how they should be understood; next, ascertain the relevant facts; and then apply the principles to the relevant facts to reach a judgment about what ought to be done. Whatever its merits, this way of proceeding can blind us to the ways by which the principles themselves can depend on facts. Call a principle that depends on facts a fact-dependent principle and a principle that does not depend on any facts a fact-independent principle.[41]

The principles that we will be considering in this book are fundamental principles. But they are also fact-dependent in various ways. So, in assessing them, we cannot ignore facts. But this need not cause trouble for our order of inquiry. Fact-dependent principles, we can say, have conditions that determine their domain of application. These application conditions refer to various facts, such as general facts about human nature that are presupposed by a principle, or facts about the state of

---

[39] Philosophers speak of the stringency of a principle. On one end of the spectrum, a principle could be maximally stringent or absolute in that it could not be overridden by any balance of costs and benefits. At the other end, a principle could be minimally stringent, serving as a mere tie-breaker when the cost/benefit assessment of rival options is equally balanced. We shall be considering principles that purport to be very stringent, if not maximally, then substantially so.

[40] Feinberg, *Harm to Others*, p. 16.

[41] For a searching discussion of the relation between facts and principles, see Cohen, *Rescuing Justice and Equality*, chapter 6. Cohen argues that the most basic or fundamental normative principles are fact-independent.

technology that a principle takes for granted. To investigate the plausibility of a given fact-dependent principle, we do not need to know if its application conditions obtain in this or that circumstance, but we do need to attend to them. For if we do not attend to them, we may mistakenly infer that certain examples count against the principle when in fact they fall outside its domain of application.

To give an example: some writers propose the harm principle for some types of societies, but not others. The harm principle, they contend, applies to societies that do not have the means to target for legal sanction certain morally bad, but (non-)harm-causing, options with precision. In these societies "there is no practical way of ensuring that the coercion will restrict the victim's choice of repugnant options but will not interfere with their other choices."[42] This practical limit is thus part of the principle. It restricts its domain of application. It is no counterexample to the principle, accordingly, to point out that it would permit interference with people's (non-)harm-causing choices in circumstances in which the means for such targeted precision were available. Reflection on imagined counterexamples of this kind, while not refuting the principle, may be illuminating in other ways, however. For they may help us to understand better the normative considerations that purportedly justify the principle in question. So long as one is careful to keep in mind the different roles played by the normative considerations that purportedly support a principle and the factual considerations that purportedly determine its range of application, no confusion should result.

It remains the case that principles do not tell us what to do. To reach practical decisions, we still need to apply them to the facts. But now it is fair to ask: apply them to what *sort* of facts? A complete answer to this question will not be provided in this book, although some discussion of it will be ventured in Chapter 10. Here it will be useful to single out two types of facts that are plainly relevant to the principles that we will be discussing and to propose some guidelines for thinking about them.

> *Society-specific facts.* Principles that concern the legal enforcement of morality can apply to one society and not others in virtue of certain facts unique to that society.

> *Concessive facts.*[43] Principles that concern the legal enforcement of morality can be indexed to circumstances in which it is anticipated that more fundamental principles would be incorrectly applied, or would lead to bad consequences.

The principles that we are concerned with in this book are neither society-specific nor concessive. The fact that a society has a particular legal constitution that would make an otherwise acceptable principle legally ineligible should not be taken to show that the principle does not apply to it. The principle, after all, might provide a justification for changing the constitution, even if the prospects for such change

---

[42]   Raz, *The Morality of Freedom*, p. 419.
[43]   The term "concessive" is taken from Estlund. See his general discussion of concessive principles and requirements in *Utopohobia*, pp. 149–172.

were not high. More generally, in seeking to identify sound fundamental principles that apply to the legal enforcement of morality, we do not want to hold that each society has its own set of fundamental principles. The principles we are interested in are more general than that.[44] Likewise, we should not limit the domain of application of a principle to circumstances in which the principle will be well administered. If we were to do so, then the responsibility of legal officials to apply otherwise sound principles would diminish as they became more inclined to misapply them.[45]

Nevertheless, while society-specific facts and concessive facts should not be taken to limit the domain of application of fundamental principles, they are certainly relevant to the question of what kind of legal measures a society should undertake. Mill claimed that "the strongest of all the arguments against interference of the public with purely personal conduct is that, when it does interfere, the odds are that it interferes wrongly and in the wrong place."[46] If Mill was right about this, then legal interference with purely personal conduct should not be undertaken. Indeed, it might be good strategic policy to hold that such interference should never be undertaken. But Mill's claim, if true, does not show that it is in principle wrong for legal officials to interfere with purely personal conduct. It establishes only that it is always inadvisable for them to attempt to do so.

Indirect consequentialists may object to this way of putting matters. Mill's point, they may say, is that in-general inadvisability is what distinguishes a principle from a mere policy. As one commentator on Mill explains, "Mill's argument is that utility itself demands the adoption of a weighty (but not infinitely weighty) side-constraint principle [which is the harm or liberty principle defended in *On Liberty*]."[47] The view adopted in this book is that this way of thinking about fundamental principles exaggerates the obstacles and dangers of promoting the good directly. The propensity of legal officials to make mistakes in their efforts to enforce morality almost certainly varies from place to place. We should not turn policies that are prudent to adopt in some (or even most) circumstances into fundamental principles that limit the enforcement of morality in all circumstances.[48]

Recognition of this point should not lead us to undersell the seriousness of worries about the competence of legal officials to enforce morality. These worries are undoubtedly important and must be confronted by anyone seriously concerned with the issue. The main line of argument in this book does not put the spotlight on these worries, however. The focus is on the general theoretical principles that have

---

[44] In saying this, I do not mean to deny that societies can have their own sound practice or tradition-dependent principles. See Chapter 6, Section 6.4, but these principles, while no doubt important, are not fundamental in the sense indicated here.

[45] See Tadros, *Wrongs and Crimes*, pp. 94–95.

[46] Mill, *On Liberty*, p. 283.

[47] Gray, *Mill on Liberty: A Defence*, p. 60.

[48] The principles favored by rule consequentialists are often both society-specific and concessive. See, for example, the view christened "wary rule consequentialism" defended by Hooker in *Ideal Code, Real World*, pp. 114–117.

engaged the attention of philosophers who have debated the nature and limits of the enforcement of morality. The concluding chapter corrects this neglect. It turns from principle to practice and argues for a comparative and piecemeal approach to addressing practical worries about the legal enforcement of morality. We will see that this approach – including the limits on the enforcement of morality that it supports for particular societies – is fully consistent with the theoretical case for the legal enforcement of morality that emerges from the discussion that precedes it.

PART I

Background Controversies

Philosophical discussions of the legal and social enforcement of morality have a history. They are often initiated by political events and anxieties over social change – events and anxieties that in turn provoke reflection on the controversies in question. The first part of this book critically reviews the writings of Mill, Hart, Devlin and Feinberg, among others. These writers were the most influential contributors to the modern debate over the legal enforcement of morality, at least in the English-speaking world. Some historical background is provided but the purpose of these chapters is not primarily historical or interpretive. The critical discussion of the authors and the controversies that engaged them allows us to introduce a number of key distinctions and to clarify the nature of, and limitations to, a range of important arguments for justifying and limiting the enforcement of morality.

The critical discussion pursued in this part has a constructive purpose as well. By marking the limits of many popular arguments for restricting the reach of criminal law, it prepares the ground for the positive defense of critical legal moralism that is proposed and defended in the second part of this book.

2

Mill's Principle

In the previous chapter we introduced Mill's principle for regulating the enforcement of morality. We will continue to refer to this principle as the harm principle. The harm principle is a harm-to-others principle. It does not apply to self-harming acts, nor does it apply to harms between consenting adults. This chapter aims to further clarify the content of this principle and to assess its plausibility. Our discussion begins with Mill's own views but it is not limited to them. The interpretive question of how Mill understood his own principle and how it can be reconciled with his other philosophical commitments is a fascinating and challenging one.[1] But our interest in his principle is not primarily interpretive. We want to explore the plausibility of the harm principle in general, and so we will draw freely on other discussions of it.

2.1 MILL'S PROJECT

Mill proposed and defended the harm principle in his classic essay "On Liberty," published in 1859. For Mill, the harm principle is, first and foremost, a principle of liberty. The animating idea of his essay is that individual people should be at liberty to lead their lives on their own terms, free from both legal oppression and the social oppression that enforces conformity of thought and action. In addition to being a principle of liberty, the harm principle, as Mill understood it, is a principle of progress. By giving the widest possible scope to its members to go their own way, society will benefit and move forward as new ideas are proposed and new ways of life are tried out. To be sure, many of these new ideas will prove to be foolish and many "experiments in living" will turn out to be utter failures.[2] But the prospects for social progress depend on people introducing "good things which did not exist before."

---

[1] For contrasting interpretive discussions of Mill's principle, see Berger, *Freedom, Morality and Happiness*; Gray, *Mill on Liberty: A Defence*; and Jacobson, "Mill on Liberty, Speech and the Free Society."

[2] Mill's attitude toward centralized socialism is instructive here.

These innovators are "the salt of the earth." They prevent a society from "becoming a stagnant pool."[3]

Progress and liberty thus go together, at least for the modern world. They are both advanced by granting individual people the "freest possible scope" for liberty of thought and action. But this proposal is not as simple as it at first appears. For it may suggest that legal and societal interference with the liberty of individuals should always be minimized. This is not an attractive idea, and it was not one that Mill himself embraced. Indeed, regarding legal interference in his own society, Mill held that it is about as likely that it will be improperly condemned as improperly recommended.[4] What is needed, then, is some standard or principle to determine when such interference is appropriate and when it is not. A society that respects and celebrates individual liberty is not one that minimizes societal interference in the lives of individuals *tout court* but one that minimizes improper societal interference.

The harm principle is Mill's answer to the question of how to determine when such interference is proper and when it is not. Famously, it holds that "the sole end for which mankind are warranted, individually or collectively, in interfering with the liberty of action of any of their number is self-protection. That the only purpose for which power can be rightfully exercised over any member of a civilized community, against his will, is to prevent harm to others."[5]

The reference to members of a civilized community, which is jarring to the contemporary ear, is significant. For Mill proposes the harm principle not just for any society but only for societies, such as his own (nineteenth-century Victorian England), that have attained a sufficiently high level of moral development. Thus, the harm principle is a principle of progress not only because it will promote progress but also because it applies only to societies that have progressed enough.[6]

The harm principle, then, is quite clearly a fact-dependent principle. Its conditions of application depend on social facts that reflect the role Mill envisions it playing in the progressive development of humanity. These social facts are of two general kinds. The first, which I have just mentioned, refers to the level of development of the society to which the principle applies. The test here is whether the members of a society have reached a point where they are "capable of being improved by free and equal discussion." For societies that have not reached this point, benevolent despotism, not individual liberty, is what is needed. The second kind of facts refers not so much to the applicability of the principle as to its urgency and stringency. Mill cautioned that "the tendency of all the changes taking place in the world is to strengthen society and diminish the power of the individual."[7]

---

[3] *On Liberty*, p. 267.
[4] *On Liberty*, p. 223.
[5] Ibid.
[6] The principle also applies only to "human beings in the maturity of their faculties." Children and persons with severe cognitive impairment lie outside its scope.
[7] *On Liberty*, p. 227.

The growth and spread of commerce, innovations in modern communication, the centralization of education and the rise of democracy all contribute to the power of society over the individual, especially over the individual whose tastes are their own and whose way of life does not follow custom or conform to mass opinion. In these circumstances, which are the circumstances of the modern world, the harm principle assumes great importance, which is why Mill insists that it must be viewed as an absolute principle, one that is not overridden by other considerations.

Democracy and mass opinion in particular pose grave threats to individual liberty, and these threats are not going away. Indeed, they can be expected to intensify as the democratic idea takes root and spreads across the developed world. Like Alexis de Tocqueville, whose work influenced him, Mill welcomed democracy but warned against a new form of tyranny that it makes possible – "the tyranny of the majority."[8] This tyranny, if not checked, will stifle the freedom and independence necessary for social progress. For the tyranny of the majority is in some respects more insidious than other forms of tyranny. It extends beyond the legal penalties that can be imposed by the state to include social sanctions that penetrate "much more deeply into the details of life, enslaving the soul itself."[9]

Against this backdrop, Mill's essay intervenes. Its purpose is to contribute to the erection of "a strong barrier of moral conviction" against this new form of tyranny. The articulation and defense of the harm principle are central to this project. For the harm principle, as Mill conceives it, both carves out a space for individual spontaneity and self-development and provides a necessary corrective to the democratic cast of mind.

2.2 FIXING THE CONTENT OF THE PRINCIPLE

Appreciating the motivations behind Mill's principle can help us to assess its plausibility. The principle, as we have seen, was put forward in response to perceived dangers. To the extent that those dangers seem less real to us than they did to Mill, or if other dangers seem to be more real or more pressing to us, then we may be less inclined to accept the principle or give it the kind of priority Mill assigned to it. We will return to this point when we discuss hate speech in Section 2.4. But first we need to try to get clearer on the content of the principle, which will occupy us in this section, and then on the grounds that support the principle, which will occupy us in the following section.

Identifying the content of the harm principle might appear to be a straightforward matter. It is not. Characterizing the key notion of harm is a challenging task, and Mill had very little to say about the matter himself. He appears to have assumed that the meaning of harm is transparent, and that what counts as a harm to another

---

[8] The phrase itself is from de Tocqueville. See his *Democracy in America*, volume 1, part 2, chapter 7.
[9] *On Liberty*, p. 220.

person is not an especially controversial matter. This is unfortunate. Elucidating the concept of harm raises difficult theoretical issues, and the extension of the term "harm" is far from settled by ordinary speech. Consider risk imposition, for example. Presumably, you can impose a risk of serious harm on someone without harming them. But the harm principle clearly targets risk impositions as well as harms. Perhaps risk impositions as such do not harm,[10] but proponents of the harm principle will want to hold that some risk impositions are harmful. Next, consider offense. Is offense harmful? Many have resisted this possibility. Harm is one thing, offense another.[11] But the pain or anguish that is caused by an offensive utterance, in principle, could be greater than that caused by a physical assault, even if many offensive utterances have no such consequence.

An initially tempting response to this possibility is to distinguish "mere offense" from "harmful offense." The latter, but not the former, involves harm, and so only harmful offense should be subject to restriction. But this argumentative move requires recourse to an independent notion of harm, and this is precisely what Mill has not provided. There is a further problem here as well. If we distinguish "mere offense" from "harmful offense," then should we not also distinguish "mere physical intrusions" from "harmful physical intrusions" on one's body? After all, some physical intrusions on one's body, such as a nonconsensual pulling of one's hair, are merely annoying or hurtful. Like "mere offenses," they do not damage us or set back our interests in any significant way. Yet most supporters of the harm principle have wanted to include them under the rubric of harm.

A good characterization of harm should be both descriptively accurate and morally appealing. The problem is that these two desiderata can pull in different directions. This is particularly true if one holds, as Mill did, that preventing harm to others is the "sole end" for which interference with others is justified. The appeal to "mere offense" and "mere physical intrusions" instantiates one strategy for defining harm. The setback of not just any interest, but of important or enduring interests, is necessary to harm. But while this account of harm is descriptively accurate, it is not morally appealing when it is factored into the harm principle. Sometimes it is appropriate to interfere with a person's liberty of action when they intrude upon and hurt another, even when their action falls short of harming them.

Some proponents of the harm principle err in the other direction. They sacrifice descriptive accuracy for moral appeal. This is accomplished by moralizing the notion of harm. Harm occurs, it is said, only when there is a wrongful setback of an interest.[12] Each of us has an interest in not being hurt, or not being subject to the

---

[10]   For a powerful defense of the claim that risk impositions as such do not constitute harms, see Perry, "Risk, Harm and Responsibility."

[11]   One writer observes, "in the context of racist utterances or utterances glorifying sexual violence against women, people often use the word 'offense' as a way of trivializing what others would call a 'harm.'" Schauer, "The Phenomenology of Speech and Harm," p. 652 note 32.

[12]   Feinberg, *Harm to Others*.

physical intrusion of others, but if these setbacks to our interests were consented to by us, then no harm would result. It is only when hurts and intrusions are wrongly imposed on us that harm eventuates. Such a view neatly handles "harms" in so-called competitive contexts. If you open up and run a better restaurant than me, then you may put my restaurant out of business, bankrupting me in the process. But there is no harm here, since you have not wrongly set back my interests.

Moralizing harm in this way has clear attractions. Still, it is important to appreciate what is lost when this path is taken. We might have hoped that an appeal to harm could help us determine when someone had acted wrongly and so when it would be appropriate to interfere with them. Compare the following two statements:

(1) It is wrong for you to break my leg, without my consent, because this harms me.
(2) It is wrong for you to break my leg, without my consent, because this wrongs me.

The first statement is more informative than the second. It explains why it is wrong for you to break my leg by appealing to harm. But if harm is moralized, then wrongfulness is already built into the notion of harm. And the first statement begins to look like the second. To be sure, not all explanatory information is lost. If harm is construed in terms of the wrongful setback of interests, then there can be no harms without setbacks of interests. So, the first statement will not reduce to the second.

Return to the harm principle. If the principle holds that only acts that cause harm to others can be rightfully interfered with, and if harm is moralized to refer to a wrongful setback of interests, then wrongs to others, which are not also harms to others, should not be interfered with. That is a contentful claim. But is it plausible?

Consider the case of easy rescue. X can save Y from drowning at little cost to themselves and there is no one else around who could do so. Suppose that X refuses to help. Should they be subject to interference from others because of their refusal to aid? Mill thinks the answer is "yes." By failing to rescue Y, X has harmed them. But now it seems as if the notion of setting back a person's interests is being stretched too far. Failing to benefit a person is not the same thing as harming them. Not every wrongful action is an action that causes harm, and the harm principle, on the interpretation we are now considering, holds that it is only wrongful harm-causing actions that are appropriately subject to interference.

Perhaps Mill was wrong to judge that in cases like easy rescue X harms Y. But friends of his principle have proposed a promising way to reconcile this judgment with the harm principle. This involves an appeal to "distinct and assignable obligations."[13] To get a feel for this idea, consider an ordinary contract. X agrees to pay Y a sum of money in exchange for Y's services. Y provides the services. X is now under a distinct and assignable obligation to Y to pay them the agreed-upon sum of money. Further, X's failure to pay Y harms Y in virtue of the fact that they were obligated to pay them.

---

[13] See the discussion of this idea in Rapaport's introduction to the Hackett edition of *On Liberty*, pp. xvii–xviii.

This example shows that the harm principle needs supplementation. It needs to be supplemented with an account of obligation (more precisely, it needs an account of when, and under what conditions, people have distinct and assignable obligations to others) in order to distinguish mere failures to benefit from failures to benefit that cause harm. With this account in hand, one could then argue that failure to aid in easy rescue cases counts as a harm because we have obligations to aid others in those circumstances.

It is an attractive line to take. But worries about the informativeness of the harm principle now resurface. Consider a third statement:

(3) It is wrong for you to break my leg, without my consent, because you have a distinct and assignable obligation not to do so.

This statement does not tell us much more than the second statement earlier. Introducing an account of obligation threatens to trivialize the notion of harm as harming becomes hard to distinguish from wronging.

We have been trying to fix the content of the harm principle by defining the key notion of harm. Descriptive adequacy pushes us to accept a relatively narrow construal of harm. We can wrong others by harming them but we can wrong them in other, non-harm-causing ways as well. Moral appeal then pushes us to broaden the notion of harm to include more conduct that intuitively seems to be wrongful and appropriately subject to interference. But as Mill himself foresaw, this can easily get out of hand. Consider a doctrine that Mill refers to as "social rights."[14] This doctrine holds that we have rights to live in a social environment that protects us from bad options. Invasions of these rights impede our "free moral and intellectual development by surrounding [our] path with dangers and by weakening and demoralizing society, from which [we] have a right to claim mutual aid and intercourse."[15] So understood, social rights correlate with obligations on others to uphold and sustain them. Accordingly, if the doctrine of social rights were accepted, and if it were true that we harm others when we act contrary to our obligations to them, then the harm principle would permit an enormous amount of interference into our lives.

Mill takes this consequence to reveal the absurdity of the doctrine of social rights. But his dismissal is too quick, for he too appeals to an account of our social obligations to others. While "society is not a contract," Mill insists that each member "who receives the protection of society owes a return for the benefit."[16] This requirement extends beyond the duty not to harm others to include the duty to bear one's share "of the labors and sacrifices incurred for defending the society or its members from injury or molestation."[17] Thus Mill's real objection to the doctrine of social rights seems to

[14] *On Liberty*, p. 288.
[15] Ibid.
[16] Ibid., pp. 224–225.
[17] Ibid., p. 276.

have more to do with its substantive content than with the need for some such doctrine to account for the obligations we owe to fellow members of our society.

The inclination to stretch the meaning of harm to cover wider and wider ranges of conduct, encompassing both actions and omissions, results from the fact that the harm principle, as Mill presents it, is very restrictive. Recall that, for Mill, the *only purpose* for which power can be rightfully exercised over another, against their will, is to prevent harm to others. However, one could accept the harm principle but drop its restrictiveness. One could hold that the harm principle justifies the exercise of power over another without holding that it provides the only justification.[18] For instance, one could hold that the *primary purpose* for which power can be rightfully exercised over another is to prevent harm to others. With this less restrictive version of the harm principle in hand, one could then resist the overinflation of the notion of harm. For conceding that an act was not harmful to anyone would not settle whether it was appropriate to interfere with it. In this way, one could formulate a notion of harm to function in the harm principle that was both descriptively adequate and morally appealing.

This way of proceeding brings its own costs. The harm principle, so construed, loses a good deal of its critical force. After all, very few people would deny that harm prevention can justify interference. In response, friends of Mill's principle can shift the focus back to some of its restrictive features. While granting that harm prevention is not the sole purpose for which power can be rightly exercised over another, they can insist that certain purposes never justify it. This fits Mill's text well, for directly after he articulates the harm principle he emphasizes that a person's good, "either physical or moral," is not a legitimate ground for interfering with them.[19] To invoke the terminology introduced in Chapter 1, Mill's principle excludes both legal paternalism and legal moralism.

We need to consider Mill's justification for the harm principle to see whether it coheres well with an unyielding stance against using power to promote people's good against their will. But before turning to Mill's arguments on this front, one further clarificatory point about his principle is in order. Mill speaks of the need to interfere with actions that cause harm to others and of the importance of harm prevention. These two notions are different, and reflection on the differences between them reveals an interesting ambiguity in the harm principle.[20] Does the harm principle justify only interference with actions that cause harm to others (first formulation) or does it justify in addition interference with actions for the purpose of harm prevention (second formulation)?

To appreciate the difference here, consider the case of legal restrictions on the possession of dangerous chemical compounds such as cyanide. Some people who

---

[18]   For general discussion of the distinction between restrictive and justificatory principles, see Tadros, *Crimes and Wrongs*, chapters 6–7.

[19]   *On Liberty*, p. 223.

[20]   See Lyons, "Liberty and Harm to Others" and Brink, *Mill's Progressive Principles*, pp. 183–187.

desire to acquire these substances would use them safely for innocent purposes, presenting no significant threat of harm to anyone. Under the first formulation of the harm principle, restrictions on the ability of these people to possess these substances would be excluded, but on the second formulation such restrictions could be justified. After all, for the purposes of harm prevention, it may be best to prohibit all individuals from possessing these substances with possible exceptions being made for business enterprises that use them for beneficial purposes.[21]

One reason to favor the second formulation of the harm principle over the first invokes what are sometimes called accumulative harms.[22] These harms result when the actions of a group of people bring about a harmful outcome and there is no way of determining how much each individual member of the group contributed to it or even whether their action made any difference to the outcome at all. Environmental harms provide good examples. The air pollution that results from the uncoordinated action of millions of people may cause harm to others, but each of these actors taken individually may have harmed no one. If the harm principle justifies interference with harm-causing actions only, then it may not justify interference to stop the air pollution in this example, but if it justifies harm prevention as well, then this interference can be justified under it.

Might it be said that if an action contributes in some way, however small or remote in time, to a harm that eventuates, then it should be classified as a harm-causing action? This response would allow friends of Mill's principle to hold onto the view that it targets only actions that cause harm to others, while maintaining that it can adequately handle cases involving accumulative harms. The problem with this response is plain enough. Far too many actions contribute in some way to harmful outcomes. For this reason, Mill stressed that harm-causing actions should be understood as those that result in direct harm to others. As he observed, no one is an isolated being. Most of our actions affect the interests of others in some way, however indirect and remote those effects may be.

Some have argued that while many polluting acts harm no one, some such polluting acts would "trigger" a substantial harm by pushing the level of pollution beyond a harm-causing threshold.[23] And since each individual polluter cannot know whether they will be the trigger, each should be taken as imposing a risk of substantial harm on others. Hence, restrictions on all the polluting acts would be consistent with the first formulation of the harm principle. But now suppose that I am one of the polluting agents and I know that my act of pollution will not be the triggering act.

---

[21] Mill's own brief discussion of the sale and possession of poisons evinces a concern for the liberty of those who would use them for innocent purposes. He suggests that sellers of poisons could be required to keep a record of the transactions but buyers should be free to acquire them (*On Liberty*, p. 295). This is in the spirit of the first formulation of the harm principle. By contrast, Feinberg's discussion of the related issue of restrictions on gun ownership (*Harm to Self*, pp. 194–198) is more congenial to the second formulation.

[22] Feinberg, *Harm to Others*, pp. 225–232.

[23] Kagan, "Do I Make a Difference?"

I know this since the other potential polluters have made it plain that, while they would prefer to pollute, they will not do so if there is any prospect that the triggering threshold will be crossed. Having no such scruples myself, I go ahead with my polluting activities, which, given the behavior of others, result in no harm to anyone. Still, or so many friends of the harm principle will want to say, it would be permissible under the harm principle to restrict my pollution. Yet to render this verdict, the harm principle must be understood along the lines of the second formulation, whereby it could justify restricting my polluting activities, along with those of the relevant others, on the grounds that doing so serves the goal of harm prevention.[24]

It seems best, then, to interpret the harm principle, including Mill's version of it, as a principle that justifies interference for the purpose of harm prevention. So interpreted, the harm principle targets actions that cause direct harm to others *and* actions that contribute, or are appropriately related, to harmful outcomes, even if these actions are not themselves harm-causing actions. The worry persists, however. Is not harm prevention too broad? Would it not license or permit too much interference? One writer objects: "the harm principle is often thought to rule out criminalization of conduct that some think is wrong, but which does not cause harm to others – gay sex is an obvious example. But [the harm principle] does not rule out criminalization of gay sex. Criminalizing gay sex may prevent a few people getting involved in harmful relationships."[25]

This example is instructive in a number of ways. First, the conduct in question must refer to consensual gay sex, since it is plain that the harm principle does not rule out criminalization of nonconsensual gay sex. But then any relationship harms that result from gay sex are not the kind of harms targeted by the harm principle. As we have explained, the principle targets nonconsensual harms only. Second, harm prevention is not a sufficient condition for justified interference. The harm principle is a filter. Any conduct that is not harm-causing or related to harm in an appropriate way should not be interfered with, but conduct that passes through the filter is only eligible for interference. A key reason for this is that interference itself is an evil and this evil can be greater than the good of harm prevention that it yields. This presumably is the case with gay sex. Any harm that would be prevented by criminalization here would be outweighed by the evil of interference.

---

[24] Reflection on this example reveals the difficulty of adhering to the harm principle, while steadfastly abjuring legal moralism. For in the example as I have presented it, no legal restriction is, strictly speaking, necessary to prevent the harm in question. If I am not restricted from polluting, other potential polluters will refrain from doing so out of concern for others or the public good, thereby preventing my polluting activities from being harmful. Still, my polluting behavior looks to be unfair, even if it is not harmful. And the need to prevent this unfairness may provide the principal reason to impose a legal restriction in this context. If so, we have something close to "a free-floating evil" [Feinberg's phrase]; and the use of the law to prevent free-floating evils is a form of legal moralism.

[25] Tadros, *Wrongs and Crimes*, pp. 103–104. Tadros is here criticizing a principle that he refers to as HC2. It holds that "it is wrong to criminalize conduct unless criminalizing that conduct prevents harm."

Bearing these points in mind, Mill's harm principle can escape the charge that it is too permissive. To be sure, work remains to be done to figure out how to balance in a principled way the evils of interference against the goods of harm prevention. But so long as harm prevention is not presented as the sole justification for interference with the liberty of individual people, then proponents of the principle can sidestep a number of important counterexamples to it. Further, the principle, so understood, continues to exclude legal paternalism and legal moralism.

2.3 GROUNDING THE PRINCIPLE

We have been trying to fix the content of the harm principle. But no specification of its content can be adequate without attending to its underlying justification. This underlying justification – I will refer to it as the grounding of the principle – not only explains why we should accept the harm principle in the first place but also guides us in applying it in contexts where its implications are not clear.

Since there is more than one possible grounding of the principle, it might be better to speak of harm principles as opposed to the singular harm principle. Nevertheless, we can aim here to identify the strongest or most promising justification for the principle. Our task is made somewhat more manageable by distinguishing good-centered from right-centered groundings of the principle. The former justify the harm principle by explaining how its observance in a society promotes the good of its members, whereas the latter justify it by appealing to the fundamental rights of the parties to which it applies. In this chapter, we focus on good-centered groundings of the principle, leaving the discussion of right-centered groundings for later chapters.

Now, the casual reader of Mill's essay can be forgiven for thinking that Mill proposes a rights-centered justification for his principle. After proposing it, he announces: "The only part of the conduct of anyone for which he is amenable to society is that which concerns others. In the part which merely concerns himself, his independence is, of right, absolute. Over himself, over his own body and mind, the individual is sovereign."[26] But Mill is quick to correct the impression that his case for the harm principle rests on an appeal of the rights of individual people. Famously, he writes: "I forego any advantage which could be derived to my argument from the idea of abstract right as a thing independent of utility."[27] When Mill claims that individuals have rights, he means that they have certain vital interests that are so important to their well-being that they ought to be considered as rights.[28] We must attend to these vital interests to unearth the good-centered grounding for the principle that he provides.

---

[26]   *On Liberty*, p. 224.
[27]   Ibid.
[28]   Ibid. See also Mill's discussion of rights in his *Utilitarianism*, pp. 247–248.

Recall from Section 2.1 that Mill was concerned to advance both the liberty of the individual and the progress of his society. He believed that these two goals were compatible. By securing an extensive sphere of liberty for each individual, we thereby establish social conditions conducive to societal advance. The reason for this is that individual liberty, and the social conditions that sustain it, create space for experimentation in thought and action. And, since human beings have much to learn about the world and how to live well, this experimentation is necessary for them to progress.

Experimentation promotes the good of human beings, accordingly, by generating new discoveries about how to live well. The state facilitates this learning process not only by refraining from exercising power over its members in ways that contravene the harm principle but also by serving as "a central depository" that actively circulates and diffuses the experience that is gained from the many trials that it permits. Let us call this the *social learning argument* for the harm principle. As we shall see, this is not the only, or even the most important, argument that Mill advances to ground the harm principle. But it is vulnerable to a telling objection. It makes the value of liberty entirely a function of our ignorance.[29] As we learn more about what Mill calls the "art of life," its importance diminishes. Even if it is countered that there will always be a need to interpret what we have learned in new ways and adjust what we have learned to new circumstances, the social learning argument implies that once we have learned that a certain practice or way of life is misguided, the reason for allowing people to engage in it is undercut. Indeed, if the social learning argument is sound, then we must be able to learn from trial-and-error experimentation, and this learning, in turn, reduces the scope of liberty that the argument can justify.

The lesson to draw here generalizes. An adequate grounding of the harm principle must provide a secure defense of the liberty the principle protects. The grounding should establish that the liberty in question is valuable in itself, and not merely as a means to some other good, such as the good of social progress. Mill is aware of this point. For the central argument that he presents in defense of the harm principle purports to show that individual liberty is an essential element of a good life. The argument appeals to an ideal of character that Mill refers to as "individuality." This ideal is an amalgam of two component ideals – self-development and autonomy. Those who realize the ideal of individuality pursue their own way of life on their own terms (autonomy) and by so doing develop and perfect their faculties and capacities (self-development). It is a doubtful that Mill would have allowed that one of these components could be adequately realized in the absence of the other. He maintained that "the human faculties of perception, judgment, discriminative feeling, mental activity, and even moral preference are exercised only in making a choice."[30] If one simply does what others do and thinks what others think, then one will fail to develop a character of one's own and fail to develop as a human being.

[29] Gray, *Mill on Liberty: A Defence*, pp. 114–116.
[30] *On Liberty*, p. 262.

Now, it does not follow from these claims that people cannot achieve self-development unless they live in a society regulated by the harm principle. That inference would imply absurdly that no one had ever achieved a significant measure of self-development in the vast number of societies that do not honor this principle. Mill's claims about the connection between the harm principle and self-development, accordingly, should be interpreted as holding that conditions of liberty are conducive to self-development rather than necessary for it. But this more modest claim too can be challenged. Mill's nineteenth-century critic James Fitzjames Stephen objected that the formation of strong and independent characters requires restraint, not freedom from restraint: "If you wish to destroy originality and vigour of character, no way to do so is so sure as to put a high level of comfort easily within the reach of moderate and commonplace exertion."[31]

Both Mill and Stephen almost certainly overstate their claims on this matter. Determining the optimal social conditions for the self-development of individual people would be a daunting social scientific project, and sweeping appeals to liberty or restraint do not go very far in advancing understanding. Presumably, some kinds of restraint are beneficial to self-development and others are detrimental to it, and figuring out which kinds of restraint benefit most people in this regard and which do not is no easy matter. Proponents of Mill's principle thus do well to not rest too much on the purported connection between the harm principle and self-development. That leaves the other component of individuality: autonomy. If the realization of autonomy is an essential element of a good life, and if the harm principle secures a sphere of liberty that facilitates its realization, then a promising good-centered grounding for the harm principle comes into view. Let us refer to it as the *autonomy argument* for the harm principle.[32]

The autonomy argument has considerable appeal. Many people find compelling the claim that to live well we need to lead our lives on our own terms, in line with what we consider to be valuable and meaningful. Few today would disagree with Mill's claim that "no one's idea of excellence in conduct is that people should do absolutely nothing but copy one another."[33] Moreover, autonomy plausibly is furthered both by liberty of action and what Mill calls "a variety of situations."[34] The harm principle secures an extensive sphere of liberty, as we have explained; but it also, if Mill is right, encourages people to try out different pursuits and to establish

---

[31] Fitzjames Stephen, *Liberty, Equality and Fraternity*, p. 31.
[32] Mill's term "individuality" is sometimes contrasted with autonomy insofar it celebrates eccentric lifestyles. An autonomous life, it is pointed out, can be an utterly conventional one. This is true. But Mill's endorsement of eccentricity is probably best explained by his sense that the pressures of conformism, at least in the milieu in which he was writing, were the primary threat to freedom and self-development.
[33] *On Liberty*, p. 262.
[34] Ibid., p. 274. (Achieving autonomy also requires other conditions and capacities, such as the ability to plan one's life and to take charge of one's affairs, but for present purposes we do not need to provide a complete account of the ideal.)

different patterns of living, thereby generating a wide range of options for people to choose from.

Notice that, in calling attention to the importance of "a variety of situations," Mill embraces a version of what we referred to in Chapter 1 as moral or ethical environmentalism. In order to live well and to realize the good of autonomy, people need to live in a supportive social environment – one that provides them with a wide range of options or models of how to live.[35] In this environment people can fashion their lives on their own terms by selecting among the options available to them. Good societies, in this way, cultivate good characters.

To sum up the autonomy argument: the foundational good is the good of individual people. An essential component of a good life, at least for people in developed societies, is the realization of autonomy, but autonomy requires, or at least is best cultivated by, certain social conditions. Chief among these social conditions are an extensive sphere for free thought and action, one that is not unduly confined by either legal or social penalties, and the availability of a wide variety of different options. The set of these options is augmented by the free experimentation of individuals and groups that is made possible by the extensive sphere of liberty that is afforded to them. The harm principle defines the necessary sphere of liberty and thus conformity with it is vital to establishing the social conditions that advance the good of individual people.

We now have identified two distinct arguments for grounding the harm principle: the social learning argument and the autonomy argument. The autonomy argument is the more fundamental argument, since it purports to establish that the liberty safeguarded by the harm principle is an essential component of an intrinsic good. The autonomy argument also corrects for the defect in the social learning argument that we highlighted earlier, to wit that the case for liberty is undercut as we learn more about how to live. It corrects for this defect since even if we come to know that some practice or option is a mistake, its availability in our social environment could enhance our autonomy and efforts to foreclose it could diminish our autonomy. We have also seen that the free experimentation that observance of the harm principle makes possible serves both social progress and the autonomy of individual people.

Yet the two arguments provide distinct grounds for the harm principle, and while they supplement each other in various ways, they also stand in some tension. This is best appreciated by reading Mill's interesting discussion of the Mormon practice of polygamy. Mill's disdain for this practice is unequivocal.

> No one has a deeper disapprobation than I of this Mormon institution; both for other reasons and because, far from being in any way countenanced by the principle of liberty, it is a direct infraction of that principle, being a mere riveting of the chains

---

[35] For a contemporary defense of this Millian idea, although one that construes autonomy differently than Mill, see Raz, *The Morality of Freedom*. Raz's views will be discussed in Chapter 7.

of one half of the community, and an emancipation of the other from reciprocity of obligation toward them.[36]

Despite this severe indictment of the practice, Mill insists that it must be tolerated. It is a voluntary institution, or at least as voluntary an institution as monogamous marriage in Mill's day tended to be, and, as such, it can be viewed as an experiment in living that is protected by the harm principle.

It is fair to ask: how can this be? If polygamous marriage, as practiced by the Mormons of Mill's time, is indeed a "direct infraction" of Mill's principle, then how can that very principle demand that it be tolerated? Mill, who was also the author of *The Subjection of Women*, was not one to sell short the lives of women. If he is concerned that they, as much as men, lead good lives, then how could he think that a principle that is grounded on the ideal of autonomy is properly invoked to defend it?

The question can be answered if we shift attention from the autonomy argument to the social learning argument. For polygamous marriage of the sort practiced by the Mormons is an experiment in living. And, if Mill is right, then social progress depends on tolerating such experiments, so long as they do not harm others. At this point, it may be countered that the verdict is in on this particular experiment. Mill is right. Polygamous marriage is a failed path, one that frustrates rather than promotes human flourishing. However, even if this is conceded, the proponent of the social learning argument has a response. The best bet for social progress, they can insist, is a principled commitment to noninterference rather than an approach that aims to distinguish failed from promising experiments. Blanket toleration best promotes social learning, since the alternative requires societies to make judgments that they cannot reliably make.

This best-bet supplement to the social learning argument captures Mill's ambivalence toward the polygamy case. A concern with social progress recommends toleration, but a concern for the autonomy of those involved, especially the women, speaks in favor of suppression of this practice – if not by law, then by social pressure. Thus, reflection on this case not only illustrates how Mill's arguments for the harm principle can pull in opposing directions but also suggests that, when push comes to shove, Mill is prepared to put social progress above individual autonomy. The "riveting of the chains" of the Mormon women is a cost that must be endured for the sake of the progressive development of the society to which they belong.

2.4 SPEECH AND HARM

There is much more to be said about the tension between social progress and individual autonomy in Mill's thought. His examples are always illustrative, but they do not always teach the same lesson. Later in this book we will consider the

---

[36] *On Liberty*, pp. 290–291.

alternative position of giving priority to individual autonomy over the demands of social progress. But we conclude this chapter by considering what is arguably the most important application of Mill's principle. This concerns the purportedly self-regarding domain of thought and discussion.

The free expression and discussion of ideas is crucial to social learning. Progress depends on the discovery of new truths, and virtually unrestricted debate and discussion best serves the discovery of such truths. This, at any rate, was Mill's contention. But is it believable? Might a less free, but more civil, discussion of ideas better serve the aim of truth discovery? Further, shouldn't a society be as concerned about the diffusion of dangerous falsehoods as it is about the circulation of important truths? The worries expressed by these rhetorical questions point to a more general concern. Mill may be too optimistic about the deliberative competence of ordinary people. As one recent commentator explains,

> In Mill's vision, intellectual or moral authority commands freely given respect and spontaneous assent, by citizens who may lack relevant competence or knowledge, but can recognize it when they see it. A common objection to this ideal of democratic intellect (perhaps nowadays more often felt than formulated) is that it assumes unrealistically high standards of integrity and disinterested rationality from too many people on too many subjects.[37]

Recall Mill's view that the harm principle is not meant to apply to all societies but only to societies whose members have reached a point where they are "capable of being improved by free and equal discussion." Some critics of Mill's defense of free speech, accordingly, can be interpreted as denying that the bulk of citizens in modern societies have indeed passed this mark.

A more common line of criticism accepts Mill's optimistic assumption that citizens can be improved by free and equal discussion but contends that restrictions on free expression are necessary to improve its truth discovery function. For instance, consider restrictions on campaign financing, an issue that has loomed large in the USA since the US Supreme Court's 1976 decision in *Buckley* v. *Valeo*.[38] By restricting the amount of money that people can donate to political campaigns, well-crafted laws may be able to improve the quality of debate over whom to elect. Going further, some have recommended public financing of political campaigns, supplemented by strict controls on political commercials.[39] If such measures make sense for political speech, might they be applied more generally? The goal would be to improve the quality of debate in the area in question. In some contexts, the unregulated free exchange of ideas will best serve the discovery of truth, but in other contexts restrictions may further, rather than set back, this goal.

[37] Skorupski, *Why Read Mill Today?* p. 60.
[38] *Buckley* v. *Valeo*, 424 U.S. 1 1976 (striking down the Election Act Amendment of 1974, which had placed limits on private expenditures to political campaigns).
[39] Dworkin, *Is Democracy Possible Here?* pp. 150–154.

There is a ready reply available to the friend of Mill here. Restrictions that aim to improve the truth discovery function of thought and discussion are content-neutral. They are not intended to take sides on disputed questions or favor some points of view over others. Mill's case for the liberty of thought and discussion, it now can be said in reply, is not intended to exclude content-neutral restrictions. It is meant only to exclude content-based restrictions on speech and expression.

This brings us to the issue of hate speech. Restrictions on hate speech target its expressive content. Let us define hate speech as the expression of words or ideas that are (i) motivated by hatred and/or (ii) (reasonably) experienced as hateful by those who are targeted by them, especially when these victims belong to a vulnerable minority group.[40] (On a narrow reading of this definition, both (i) and (ii) must be satisfied. On a broad reading, either (i) or (ii) alone would suffice.) So defined, hate speech is protected speech under the harm principle.

Hate speech is offensive. But offense, even harmful offense, is not an eligible basis for restricting speech on Mill's view. Indeed, Mill suggests that offensive speech, far from harming us, often benefits us. It does so by forcing us to consider the basis for our own convictions, thereby making these convictions more adequately justified and more authentically our own. To illustrate: suppose that a book is published that attacks Islam as a dangerous religion. This religion, the book contends, makes its adherents ungovernable and tends to the dissolution of society. Muslims, upon becoming aware of the book, understandably may be offended, viewing it as hateful speech. But if the attack the book mounts presents arguments, then it also offers Muslims an opportunity to defend their commitments. And that opportunity benefits them insofar as it leads them to a better understanding of their own creed.

Caution is in order here, however. The term "hate speech" encompasses a broad range of expression and expressive acts. This type of speech can have different purposes and multiple effects. A hateful utterance, or an utterance reasonably perceived to be motivated by hate, either spoken or written, can do any of the following:

   (i) provoke violence
  (ii) harass
 (iii) cause offense and hurt feelings
 (iv) degrade
  (v) challenge beliefs and convictions.

Mill's defense of offensive speech spotlights (v), as the Islam example illustrates. But what about (i)–(iv)?

---

[40] Legal restrictions on hate speech are currently part of domestic law in Canada and a large number of European countries including Germany, France, the Netherlands, Sweden and the United Kingdom. For discussion of some of the more illiberal aspects of these laws and how they have been applied, see Alexander, "Illiberal Europe," *The Weekly Standard*, April 10, 2006.

Mill allows that "even opinions lose their immunity when the circumstances in which they are expressed are such as to constitute their expression as a positive instigation to some mischievous act."[41] Speech that incites violence, for example, can be restricted, since, in the circumstances in which it is uttered, it results in clear and direct harm to others.[42] Likewise, speech in the workplace that constitutes harassment of an employee can be restricted on Millian grounds. Even staunch advocates of free speech grant "that conduct that infringes on the right to equal educational (or employment) opportunities, regardless of gender (or other invidious classifications) should not be condoned simply because it includes expressive elements."[43]

Speech or expression that provokes violence or constitutes harassment can also be restricted on content-neutral grounds. Hateful speech directed at vulnerable racial or gender groups need not be singled out for special treatment. That is why, in the remarks just quoted, the phrase "regardless of gender (or other invidious classifications)" is inserted. The same cannot be said – or at least it is common to deny that the same should be said – about speech that degrades its victims. Degrading speech targets members of vulnerable minorities. It aims to undermine their dignity or standing in society. This is the type of hate speech that many today aim to suppress. As Jeremy Waldron explains,

> Dignity . . . is precisely what hate speech laws are designed to protect – not dignity in the sense of any particular level of honor or esteem (or self-esteem), but dignity in the sense of a person's basic entitlement to be regarded as a member of society in good standing, as someone whose membership of a minority group does not disqualify him or her from ordinary social interaction. That is what hate speech attacks, and that is what laws suppressing hate speech aim to protect.[44]

Waldron's dignity-based defense of hate speech restrictions is subtle, and it will be instructive to consider briefly how it relates to Mill's position on free speech.

Waldron rests his case for hate speech restriction on the distinction between offensive speech (iii) and degrading speech (iv). Restrictions on the former can be applied in a content-neutral manner, treating hate speech directed at vulnerable minority groups no differently than other types of speech that cause offense. Waldron, however, agrees with Mill in rejecting these restrictions out of hand.[45] No one has a good claim to be protected from being offended by what others say. But Waldron parts company with civil libertarians, who are guided and inspired by

---

[41] *On Liberty*, p. 260.
[42] Restrictions on speech that provoke or instigate violence fall under the so-called fighting words doctrine (under American constitutional law). For sensitive discussion of this doctrine, see Greenawalt, *Fighting Words*, pp. 50–58.
[43] Strossen, "Regulating Racist Speech on Campus: A Modest Proposal," *Duke Law Journal* (1990), p. 499.
[44] Waldron, *The Harm in Hate Speech*, p. 105.
[45] See Waldron, "Mill and the Value of Moral Distress."

Mill's work, when it comes to the issue of degrading speech. Waldron favors such restrictions, or at least certain instances of them, and these restrictions violate content-neutrality insofar as they target categories of speech and modes of expression directed at some groups but not others.

In thinking about the debate between Millian civil libertarians and Waldron-style proponents of hate speech restriction, we need to ask whether degrading speech can be adequately distinguished from offensive speech. To focus the discussion, it will be helpful to introduce and contrast two cases.

> **Burning Cross.** A group of white teenagers in Minnesota burn a cross in front of the house of a black family.
> **Cartoon.** A Danish newspaper publishes a cartoon that depicts the prophet Muhammad as a terrorist.

Both of these cases depict real events. *Burning Cross* resulted in an important US Supreme Court decision on the constitutionality of hate speech restrictions[46] and *Cartoon* provoked controversy around the world, leading many to call for the editors of the newspaper to be fired, or at least punished.[47] Both cases involve speech that targets a racial or religious group and can be reasonably judged to be offensive and hurtful. But can the two cases be distinguished on grounds that the first constitutes degrading speech, whereas the second does not? That is the distinction that Waldron needs, since, on his view, the speech in *Burning Cross* should be restricted as hate speech, whereas the speech in *Cartoon* should not.[48]

Degrading speech attacks the dignity of those it targets. This dignity or social standing is not, in the first and primary sense, a matter of individual psychology. It is a matter of living in a supportive social environment; namely, one that provides one with the public assurance that, as one goes about one's daily life, "there will be no need [for one] to face hostility, violence, discrimination, or exclusion by others"[49] and that one will be respected as a full member of one's society. *Burning Cross* no doubt offends and wounds but, more fundamentally, it degrades its victims insofar as it denies them this public assurance of security and respect.

Might the same be said of *Cartoon*? True, in this case there is not the element of direct intimidation present in *Burning Cross*. But threats and intimidation can be restricted on content-neutral grounds. And Waldron's defense of the distinction between degrading and merely offensive speech does not appeal to this feature. He is more concerned with the printed word, or the posted image on the internet, which is a more permanent part of the social environment than the spoken word or

---

[46]   R.A.V. v. *City of St. Paul*, 505 U.S. 377 (1992).
[47]   Smith and Fisher, "Temperatures Rise over Cartoons Mocking Mohammad," *The New York Times*, February 3, 2006.
[48]   Waldron discusses neither case in much detail. But it seems clear from his general discussion that this is the position he holds. See his brief remarks on the Danish cartoon controversy in *The Harm in Hate Speech*, pp. 125–126.
[49]   Ibid., p. 4.

physical demonstration.[50] *Burning Cross* was an ephemeral expressive act, whereas the image expressed in *Cartoon* endures.

A more promising effort to distinguish the two cases puts the accent on the difference between attacking a person's identity and attacking their beliefs. After all, one's race, or the social perception that one belongs to a certain race, is not a question of what one believes. It is a social fact. But one's religion is a matter of conviction. Unlike *Burning Cross*, *Cartoon* does not attack people. It attacks their beliefs.

This response is sustainable only if a line of the right sort can be drawn between a person and their beliefs. It is a familiar liberal platitude that we owe respect to people, not to their beliefs. But people's social identity is bound up with their beliefs. The beliefs in question in *Cartoon* are central to the self-understandings of millions of Muslims. Further, and perhaps more importantly, if Islam is viewed as a religion that is inseparable from terror and violence, then its adherents will be subject to distrust and stigma from others. Their social standing, in this way, may be compromised.

The distinction between degrading speech and offensive speech is a good one. Speech can degrade without offending (its victims may have thick skins, for example), and speech can offend without degrading. The problem is that speech often has more than one effect. *Cartoon* likely, all at once, offends (iii), degrades (iv) and challenges beliefs and convictions (v). This presents real dangers. In practice, Waldron's defense of hate speech restrictions would likely extend beyond its dignity-based rationale, targeting speech that should be protected in a free society. By the same token, Mill's efforts to show how offensive speech can benefit its targets ring hollow when applied to many expressions of hate. Does anyone seriously think that the airing of derogatory racial epithets contributes to the discovery of truth or helps people better understand their own beliefs? Moreover, while Mill considered the pain caused by offensive speech, he did not consider the dignity-based costs of speech that Waldron highlights. Some even contend that these costs themselves set back the goal of free and open discussion by preventing the views of those whose standing has been compromised from being heard or receiving a fair hearing.[51]

A natural approach to the issue of hate speech, albeit one that is not as precise as one might hope, is to argue that we need to balance the benefits against the costs of restriction. The expressive value of the speech in *Burning Cross* is very small, whereas the threatening message it sends to its victims is profound. Here restriction of expression seems reasonable, as the costs exceed the benefits. In *Cartoon* the value of the speech has greater value. The offensive cartoon, as Waldron allows, contributes, "in its twisted way, to a debate about the connection between [Muhammad's] teachings and the more violent aspects of modern jihadism."[52] Here the restriction

---

[50]   Ibid., pp. 37–38.
[51]   For a moderate version of the view that hate speech silences its victims, see Brink, "Mill's Liberal Principles and Freedom of Expression," p. 141 note 37.
[52]   Waldron, *The Harm in Hate Speech*, p. 125.

of speech is less reasonable as it poses a greater threat to the free speech values that Mill champions.

Notwithstanding these remarks, speculation about how Mill himself would have come down on the issue of hate speech restriction is of limited value. While some commentators have argued that he would have approved narrowly crafted restrictions on hate speech,[53] it is important to remember that Mill was rejecting a balancing approach to the benefits and costs of speech. Thought and discussion as well as the expression of ideas fall squarely within the protected sphere defined by the harm principle. To understand why Mill adopted such an uncompromising approach to the issue of free speech, we need to return to the anxieties that motivated his defense of the harm principle. The dangers that concerned Mill, as we noted in Section 2.1, were conformity of thought and the majoritarian suppression of individual creativity and spontaneity. In his mind these dangers were nourished by the democratic mindset that was taking root in the more advanced societies with which he was concerned. Offensive and even intemperate speech was a valuable corrective to "the deep slumber of decided opinion."[54]

Contemporary readers of Mill's essay are likely to be less animated by the threat of conformism and more concerned with the dangers of division and polarization. Many of these readers now favor a legal order and a social environment that is considerably more restrictive of expression than Mill's ideal, but one that aims to be more supportive of social equality and mutual respect. Even if they accept the Millian arguments for social learning and autonomy, they will be inclined to interpret the harm principle, and its application to particular issues, differently than Mill in light of their different concerns. Surely they are right to do so. How much Mill's argument for free expression must be revised, and indeed whether it should be rejected outright, are matters that require further investigation. We will return to them in Chapter 9.

2.5 SEXUAL MORALITY

Recall that the harm principle, at least in Mill's hands, is a limiting principle. It holds that harm to others provides the sole ground for legal interference. One can reject this as a general rule but accept it for some domains of human interaction. One might hold, for example, that people's sex lives are their own business. Whatever general doubts one might have about drawing the line between self-regarding and other-regarding conduct, we might be confident that the line can be drawn here. Furthermore, the notion that there is no harm between consenting adults may seem to be particularly applicable to sex. What counts as genuine

---

[53]   Brink, "Mill's Liberal Principles and Freedom of Expression."
[54]   *On Liberty*, p. 250.

consent to sexual interaction raises a host of tricky issues, but once it is secured, it may be thought, no further moral issue remains.

In fact, most people do not feel this way. All societies have regulated sex, and the regulations go beyond harm prevention. Certain sexual practices are often judged to be deviant or abhorrent, and therefore appropriate targets for legal restriction. Consider, to take just one example, necrophilia – the practice of having sex with dead bodies. Here the question of harm seems not to be in play, and the question of consent inapplicable. Mill's principle, or so it would seem, would protect it from interference. But many legal systems make necrophilia a criminal offense, nonetheless. Perhaps there are good reasons to criminalize this conduct, but is it, or could it be, a good reason for a society to criminalize this practice because most people in the society condemn it? More plausibly, could the fact of widespread abhorrence of a sexual practice be a part of such a reason? To address these questions, we turn now to the Hart/Devlin debate.

3

The Hart/Devlin Debate

The highwater mark of the modern debate over the enforcement of morality was reached in the UK in the late 1950s and early 1960s. It consisted of an exchange of essays and lectures between Patrick Devlin, a distinguished sitting judge, and H. L. A. Hart, a professor of jurisprudence at Oxford University, and it centered on the legal regulation of sexual morality.[1] Both participants in the debate were familiar with Mill's defense of the harm principle and both made some effort to explain how their own views differed from Mill's. The debate introduced some important distinctions and propounded some novel arguments. Of particular interest is the distinction pressed by Hart between legal paternalism and legal moralism. A careful study of this debate can be illuminating, even for those who are no longer exercised by the particular issues of sexual morality that provoked the whole discussion.

3.1 THE WOLFENDEN REPORT

Before turning to substantive matters, some brief historical background is in order. The Hart/Devlin debate was occasioned by concerns over sexual morality, in particular issues relating to the legal regulation of homosexuality and prostitution. At the time in the UK consensual sex between adult men and prostitution between adults were both criminal offenses, but pressure to reform the law was gaining steam.[2] Several high-profile prosecutions of homosexuals had brought these issues to the forefront of the public's attention. In response, the British government in 1954 commissioned a Committee on Homosexual Offences and Prostitution to study whether and how the law on these matters should be reformed. The report issued by the Committee three years later came to be known as the Wolfenden Report, after

---

[1] Devlin's contributions are collected in his *The Enforcement of Morals* and Hart's are presented in his *Law, Liberty and Morality*.

[2] Gay sex between adult men remained a criminal offense in the UK until the Sexual Offences Act of 1967. Homosexuality between adult women had never been a crime.

the name of its chairman, Sir John Wolfenden.[3] A summary of the Report's position was presented.

> [The function of the criminal law on these matters], as we see it, is to preserve public order and decency, to protect the citizen from what is offensive or injurious, and to provide sufficient safeguards against exploitation and corruption of others, particularly those who are specially vulnerable because they are young, weak in body or mind, inexperienced, or in a state of special physical, official or economic dependence. *It is not in our view, the function of the law to intervene in the private lives of citizens, or to seek to enforce any particular pattern of behavior, further than is necessary to carry out the purposes we have outlined.*[4]

The Report then proceeded to recommend that neither homosexual conduct nor prostitution between consenting adults should remain criminal offenses.

The publication of the Report was an important political event. Not surprisingly, it sparked a good deal of public discussion over the role of the criminal law in enforcing morality, which prompted Devlin to present a public lecture on the topic to the British Academy in 1959.[5] This lecture, in turn, provoked a forceful response from Hart a few months later,[6] and the debate between the two men continued for another six years.

Devlin rejected the Report's understanding of the function of the criminal law, while Hart in the main defended it. For this reason, Devlin's position is associated with conservatism and Hart's with liberalism. But Devlin's own views on these issues were complicated. He was not an opponent of reform. He had, in fact, testified before the committee that the law criminalizing homosexuality should be changed. Devlin's objections were not directed at the specific recommendations advanced in the Report but rather at the background justifications it offered for them. These justifications were restricted to the subject matter with which the Report was concerned, but, as Devlin observed, "there seems to be no reason why, if they are valid, they should not be applied to the criminal law in general."[7] And it was the implications of the generality of the Report's position that concerned Devlin.

At the heart of the Report's position, as Devlin understood it, was the vague but sweeping principle that "no act of immorality should be made a criminal offence unless it is accompanied by some other feature such as indecency, corruption, or exploitation." If this principle were consistently applied to existing British law, it would have striking consequences. Devlin explained: "Euthanasia or the killing of another at his own request, suicide, attempted suicide and suicide pacts, dueling,

---

[3] At the time, Wolfenden was vice chancellor of the University of Reading.

[4] "Report of the Committee on Homosexual Offences and Prostitution," paragraph 13 (1957). Cited by Devlin, *The Enforcement of Morals*, p. 2 (italics added).

[5] The Maccabaean Lecture, "The Enforcement of Morals," printed in *Proceedings of the British Academy*, vol. xlv (1959).

[6] Hart, "Immorality and Treason," *The Listener*, July 30, 1959.

[7] Devlin, *The Enforcement of Morals*, p. 3.

abortion, incest between brother and sister, are all acts which can be done in private
without offence to others and need not involve the corruption or exploitation of
others."[8]

While the Report's principle justified its recommendation that homosexual sex
between consenting adults in private should not be a criminal offense, it also
appeared to imply that the law should not criminalize *any* consensual activity that
does not injure, offend, exploit or corrupt others. This opened the Report up to
Devlin's criticisms, and in particular to his observation, seemingly damning, that it is
no defense to murder or assault that the victim consented to it.[9] From this observation Devlin drew a general lesson. The criminal law must be concerned with the
protection of society, over and above its concern to protect individuals from injury
and offense.

Now, exactly what Devlin meant by the protection of society is not immediately
clear. We will examine this interesting idea in more detail in Section 3.3. For now,
we can note how Hart positioned himself in relation to the Report's principle and
Devlin's critique of it. Hart agreed with Devlin that the Report's principles and
justifications have wide application, noting that they bear a striking similarity to the
position defended by Mill.[10] But Hart's own views were considerably less radical
than Mill's, and perhaps less radical than the views expressed in the Report.

Hart contended that Devlin was not entitled to draw the general lesson he drew
from his damning observation about the Report's principle. For, as Hart pointed out,
Devlin overlooked the possibility that "the rules excluding the victim's consent as
a defence to charges of murder or assault may perfectly well be explained as a piece
of paternalism, designed to protect individuals from themselves."[11] This possibility
was important to the Hart/Devlin debate. For, in contrast to Mill, Hart was prepared
to accept the legitimacy of legal paternalism. And by doing so he was able to defend
the recommendations of the Report on the issues it dealt with while avoiding the
least tenable implications that Devlin drew from its general justifying principle. By
embracing legal paternalism, Hart put himself in a stronger position to reject legal
moralism out of hand, thereby sharply distinguishing his view on the enforcement of
morality from Devlin's view.

3.2 LEGAL MORALISM EXPOUNDED

The meaning of legal moralism, and the extent to which it genuinely contrasts with
legal paternalism, call for analysis, however. Let us start with Devlin's own views and
then consider some other formulations of the idea.

[8] Ibid., p. 7.
[9] Devlin's position on this matter is affirmed in the Model Penal Code sections 2.11(1) and 2.11(2)a.
[10] Hart, *Law, Liberty and Morality*, p. 14.
[11] Ibid., p. 31.

For Devlin, the central error of the Wolfenden Report was its misguided attempt to find "a single principle to explain the division between crime and sin."[12] We have seen that the principle it settled on is not very simple, for it encompasses the disparate notions of injury, offense, exploitation and corruption. No matter. We can define a *public wrong* as any action or activity that injures, offends, exploits or corrupts another without their consent. And we can say that a *private wrong* is a wrong that is not a public wrong. With these stipulated definitions in place, we can present an initial formulation of legal moralism.

(LM): It is a proper function of the criminal law to regulate and restrict private wrongs.

Consider one of Devlin's examples – (consensual) incest between siblings. This is, Devlin maintains, a private wrong; but it is one with which the criminal law in principle ought to be concerned. That doesn't mean that there should be a law that criminalizes incest, for it might be the case that such a law, in the circumstances being considered, would cause more harm than good. Legal moralists are committed only to the idea that it is a proper function of the law to consider whether the benefits of criminalizing private wrongs exceed the costs of doing so.

Now, (LM) targets private wrongs. But, as we saw in Chapter 1, private wrongs can be indexed to either social or critical morality. Start with social morality. On this understanding, a private wrong is an action or activity that is widely judged or perceived to be wrong in the society in question. As Devlin allows, a society could be mistaken in its judgment or perception that some action or activity is truly wrong, but the fact that it passes this judgment or has this perception is a fact nonetheless; and it is this latter fact that is crucial to legal moralism, as Devlin understands it. We now can present a sharpened formulation of Devlin's understanding of legal moralism.

(LM^{social}): It is a proper function of the criminal law to regulate and restrict actions and activities that are widely judged or perceived to be private wrongs in the society over which it has jurisdiction.

If incest is widely abhorred in a society, then it is a proper function of the criminal law in that society to suppress it, or at least to consider the costs and benefits of doing so, on this formulation of legal moralism. It is not necessary to establish that this abhorrence is justified or rightful.

This last claim points to a tension in legal moralism. Standardly, we do not cite the fact that we believe that something is wrong as a reason for opposing it. It is rather the fact that it is wrong, or the fact that it has certain wrong-making features, we think, that provides the reason to oppose it. A society that abhors incest is a society

---

[12] Devlin, *The Enforcement of Morals*, p. 22.

whose members, on the whole, believe that incest is, in fact, wrong. In their minds their abhorrence of it is justified.

Devlin sees the tension and tries to massage it. Discussing the role of the legislator in enforcing morality, he writes: "Naturally he will assume that the morals of his society are good and true; if he does not, he should not be playing an active part in government. But he has not to vouch for their goodness and truth."[13] On this view, the legislator should themself believe that the morals they are enforcing are good and true. But their job is to enforce the morals of their society, whether or not they are good and true. The view is puzzling. Why does Devlin insist that the legislator themself should believe that the morals they are enforcing are good and true if their job does not really concern what they believe but rather what their society believes?

Devlin's legislator could believe that it is *not* a proper function of the criminal law to restrict and regulate actions and activities that are widely perceived to be private wrongs in their society but that, in reality, are not private wrongs. Such a legislator would reject LM^{social}, but they could still accept a different formulation of legal moralism, one that appeals to critical morality.

(LM^{critical}): It is a proper function of the criminal law to regulate and restrict actions and activities that are private wrongs in the society over which it has jurisdiction.

It would be an interesting feature of Devlin's position on the enforcement of morality if it turned out that his ideal legislator must reject Devlin's own position, embracing LM^{critical} and rejecting LM^{social}. In all likelihood, Devlin did not intend anything so paradoxical. He may have thought simply that a legislator will not do a good job of enforcing their society's social morality unless they are committed to it themself.

Let us now try to get a clearer understanding of the notion of private wrongs understood in terms of critical morality. A private wrong, we have stipulated, is a wrong that is not a public wrong in the stipulated sense. It is a wrong that does not injure, offend, exploit or corrupt another without their consent. Devlin gives the example of dueling. This practice is immoral, and that is sufficient ground to consider it an appropriate candidate for criminalization. But is dueling a good instance of immorality as such?

Recall Hart's claim that legal paternalism is distinct from legal moralism. By outlawing the practice of dueling, the law may be seeking to protect people from harming themselves. This would constitute legal paternalism. And if laws that prohibit dueling can be justified on grounds of legal paternalism, then an appeal to legal moralism is unnecessary to their justification. Devlin has an interesting reply. Paternalism can be understood narrowly or broadly depending on whether our interests in being moral or upright are included in the calculus of what is good for us. In rejecting paternalism, Mill had asserted that a person's own good, physical or moral, is not a sufficient warrant for interfering with them. But Hart seems to have overlooked the possibility that a person's good has a moral as well as a physical dimension. People's lives may be made worse for them because of the wrongdoing they engage in, and not solely because wrongdoing can bring with it costs to their (nonmoral) personal interests.[14] If it is morally wrong for a person to exploit others, then doing so will set back that person's moral good. And, if a person's moral good is part of their personal good, then the distinction between legal paternalism and legal moralism becomes harder to draw.

Moral paternalism – and the legal enforcement of moral paternalism, which we can refer to here as "moralistic legal paternalism" – presupposes that some things are and some things are not part of our moral good. But what exactly is meant by our moral good? We can be harmed by setbacks to our bodily, psychological and economic interests. Call these standard harms. But can we be harmed also by setbacks to our moral character? Commenting on this possibility, Joel Feinberg, whose work we will consider more fully in the next chapter, allowed that "a bad or worsened character is, in itself, an evil thing" but rejected the notion of a moral harm as dubious.[15] A bad character is bad, but it does not follow that it is bad *for the person* whose character it is. Indeed, it is possible that a person could profit from their bad character, as it may enable them to advance their overall interests more effectively.

It is worthwhile to pause and consider whether the notion of a moral harm is indeed dubious. For if it were, then Hart and Feinberg would be in a strong position to reject the kind of moral paternalism that Devlin invoked. Feinberg allows that if you care very much about your own character, then if you do things that worsen your character, you harm yourself. Moral harms, he thinks, are conditional on you caring about the state of your character. There is nothing dubious about this. The same is true of standard harms. If you care a great deal about your bicycle, then if someone damages it, they will harm you; but, if you do not care at all about your bicycle, then they will not harm you by damaging it.[16]

Moral paternalism gets a grip, then, to the extent that people care about the state of their characters. If most people care a lot about their character, then moral legislation that aims to protect them from vice has the potential to benefit them by shielding them from moral harms. There are subtleties to consider here, to be sure. If someone avoids prostitution out of fear of legal sanction, then they may avoid vice,

---

[14] Tadros presents a nice question that bears on this issue. Suppose you learned that your child, or someone whose well-being you cared very much about, was involved in an interaction that was seriously wrongful, but you did not know whether they were the perpetrator or the victim. What would you wish for? (Imagine the harm that resulted from the wrongdoing was serious, but short of death or serious brain injury.) Would you want your loved one to be the victim or the perpetrator? To the extent that you prefer that your loved one be the perpetrator, or even that this is at least a hard call, then your response likely reflects the judgment that a person's moral good is an important part of their personal good. (See *Wrongs and Crimes*, pp. 1–2.)

[15] Feinberg, *Harmless Wrongdoing*, pp. xx and 22–23.

[16] Ibid., p. 22.

but for the wrong reason. And good character may require not only that one avoid vice but also that one do so for the right reasons.

Does this present a serious problem for moralistic legal paternalism? Yes and no. There is a standing danger that legal efforts to promote good character will lead people to act on the wrong reasons, thereby not improving, and perhaps worsening, their character.[17] But the danger, while real, does not settle the matter in all cases. Sometimes legal means can promote good character by strengthening or supporting good motives that people already have, and sometimes they can do so by engendering good motives that they did not have prior to the legal intervention. Good character is a matter of having good habits, and laws that promote virtue or deter vice can help people to sustain or form good habits and so can promote their good in this way.

Moralistic legal paternalism then will be a viable option in some cases and in some contexts. And the notion of a moral harm, which legal moral paternalism targets, does not seem to be a dubious notion. It might be countered that most people in fact do not care much about the state of their characters. For most people, it might be said, a moral harm is no harm at all. It is doubtful that this is true, but it is a possibility. Another view of moral harm is available, however. Virtue may be an objective prudential good and vice an objective prudential bad. On so-called objective list views of well-being, certain goods, such as knowledge, achievement and friendship, contribute to our well-being but not in virtue of our caring about them. The fact that they are good for us explains why we have reason to care about them. Now suppose that an objective list view of well-being is correct. Then it could be maintained that virtue is on the list of objective goods and that moral harms set back well-being by compromising virtue. Indeed, on such a view, it would be natural to hold that caring about the state of one's character is itself a virtue, and that for people to lead lives that are good for them, they need to have this virtue. Once again, the notion of a moral harm is not dubious at all.

Hart says nothing about how he understands well-being, and Feinberg is committed to a broadly subjectivist understanding of this notion. But if an objectivist account of well-being is correct, then Devlin's position looks to be much more credible. We will have more to say about objective and subjective conceptions of well-being in Chapter 5. For now, let us grant the plausibility of an objectivist understanding of well-being. On this supposition, and on the further supposition that virtue is an objective prudential good, does it follow, as Devlin suggests, that granting the legitimacy of moral paternalism would "make all morality the law's business?"[18] The answer is clearly "no," given Devlin's embrace of LM^social. From the fact that most people in a society abhor some activity, such as homosexual sex, it does not follow that it is a moral harm for those who engage in it. To establish this,

[17] Incentives that the law creates sometimes engender motivations that crowd out or displace other more virtuous motivations for acting. See Frey and Jegen, "Motivating Crowding Theory: A Survey," *Journal of Economic Surveys* 15 (2001): 589–611.
[18] Devlin, *The Enforcement of Morals*, p. 137.

one would need to establish that the activity is in fact a vice, and not merely that it is widely perceived to be a vice.

Return now to Hart's distinction between legal moralism and legal paternalism. We have argued that the possibility of moral paternalism complicates this distinction. But we have also seen that Devlin is committed to a form of legal moralism that does not imply, at least not straightforwardly, moral paternalism. LM^{social} is a thesis about the moral ideals and principles that must be enforced if a society is to perdure and function effectively. As we saw in Chapter 1, Devlin viewed the common moral beliefs of a society as the glue that holds it together. As he explains, "For society is not something that is kept together physically, it is held by the invisible bonds of common thought. If the bonds were too far relaxed the members would drift apart. A common morality is part of the bondage. The bondage is part of the price of society; and mankind, which needs society, must pay its price."[19] This passage ties the enforcement of morality to the protection and preservation of society. But it also suggests that the protection of society serves the interests and needs of its members. If so, then in protecting society, the enforcement of morality also protects individual people. Once again, the distinction between legal paternalism and legal moralism blurs. Efforts to enforce moral principles could be viewed as efforts to protect people from undermining the social conditions that promote their well-being.[20]

Was Hart mistaken, then, to insist on distinguishing legal moralism (what he called "enforcing morality as such") from legal paternalism? Put otherwise, are there good examples of pure legal moralism? We will see in Section 3.4 that indeed there are, but understanding them requires us to move from LM^{social} to $LM^{critical}$. Our present task is to investigate Devlin's case for legal moralism, even if it does not, under close analysis, qualify as a pure form of legal moralism.

3.3 TREASON AND DEMOCRACY

Devlin draws a striking analogy between treason and immorality. The former threatens a society from without (by aiding a foreign enemy), while the latter threatens it from within (by disintegrating the bonds that hold it together). No serious person denies that a society can punish treason; but if a society has the right to defend itself from without, surely it has the right to defend itself from within.

The analogy is revealing, and it has an important implication that Devlin did not see but to which Hart is sensitive. A society's right to defend itself may not be absolute. It may depend on the kind of society it is, and it may not extend to all

---

[19] Ibid., p. 10.
[20] Defenders of the harm principle commonly allow that it is permissible to restrict the liberty of members of a group in order to promote the public good of the group. (For discussion, see Feinberg, *Harm to Others*, pp. 221–225.) Accordingly, a defender of Devlin's society-centered argument for legal moralism could hold that it is justified on harm-prevention as well as paternalist grounds.

measures deemed to be useful to its self-defense. As Hart observes, if the society is sufficiently wicked, then its destruction may be better than its continued existence, and if a society could defend itself only by employing wicked means, such as torture, then it may not have the right to do so.[21]

Devlin's society-protection argument, accordingly, rests on the presupposition that the society under consideration is worthy of protection. And this presupposition, Hart contends, is not itself validated by the society's own morality. It can be validated only from the standpoint of critical morality. Further, Hart argues that the claim that a society, even one that is worthy of social protection, has a right to protect itself is not a claim that is validated by its own social morality. It purports to be a general principle of critical morality.[22]

Devlin appears to believe that all societies have a right to defend themselves. He affirms the following proposition:

(P) "Society is entitled by means of its laws to protect itself from dangers, whether from within or without."[23]

But does Devlin hold that (P) is a principle of critical morality, as Hart suggests? Perhaps not. Devlin could hold that every society, in fact, has a social morality that recognizes that it has a right to defend itself from dangers. This universally instantiated fact, and not any judgment of critical morality, stands behind the social protection argument.

We can distinguish a claim that is true or correct from a claim that is universally accepted. If (P) is presented as a true or correct claim of morality, then Hart's point is secure. But if (P) is presented merely as a proposition that is universally accepted (i.e., accepted from within every existing social morality), then Devlin's argument is not committed to any general principle of critical morality.

Whatever the status of (P), we can accept it for the sake of argument. Building on (P), Devlin writes:

Societies disintegrate from within more frequently than they are broken up by external pressures. There is disintegration when no common morality is observed and history shows that the loosening of moral bonds is often the first stage of disintegration, so that society is justified in taking the same steps to preserve its moral code as it does to preserve its government and other essential institutions.[24]

Hart objects. From the fact that a society's morality changes it does not follow that the society disintegrates or ceases to exist. Moral change, like legal change, is consistent with a society's continued existence.

Hart is certainly correct on this point. But how damaging is it to Devlin's argument? As Devlin explains in a footnote to his lecture, "I do not assert that *any* deviation from

---

[21]   Hart, *Law, Liberty and Morality*, p. 19.
[22]   Ibid., pp. 18–19.
[23]   Devlin, *The Enforcement of Morals*, p. 13.
[24]   Ibid.

a society's shared morality threatens its existence any more than I assert that *any* subversive activity threatens its existence. I assert that they are both activities which are capable in their nature of threatening the existence of society so that neither can be put beyond the law."[25] This passage makes plain that it is only some changes to a society's common morality that threaten its existence. Others do not. So, Devlin can agree with Hart that a society's common morality can change without destroying the society.

Devlin's argument, put more precisely, is that some changes to a society's morality threaten its existence, that a society has a right to protect itself against those changes and that it is legitimate for it to use criminal law as a method for doing so. At this point it is worth recalling the issues that initiated the whole debate between Devlin and Hart: those of sexual morality concerning prostitution and homosexual sex. Devlin holds that society has a right to criminalize these activities, but it is now clear that, on his argument, society has this right *only if* these activities, if unchecked by law, would threaten the existence of the society. And Devlin provides no evidence or argument that this is indeed the case.

Given that the use of the criminal law is costly and that it imposes hard treatment on people, we need a positive reason to criminalize an activity. The burden of proof lies with those who favor criminalization. And this is a burden that, at least on the issues of sexual morality that were being considered, Devlin failed to meet.

The society-protection argument, accordingly, needs supplementation. On its own, it cannot justify the claim that a society has a right to criminalize prostitution or homosexual sex between consenting adults. But a charitable reading of Devlin reveals that he does offer supplementation. His argument is directed at legislators and judges. He is trying to persuade them that it is a proper function of the criminal law to enforce their society's common morality, including that part of it that applies to acts between consenting adults. Legislators and judges may protest that they should only enforce their society's morality if they judge it to be correct or sound. But this stance, Devlin contends, misconceives the role of the legal official in a democratic society. The judge or legislator in a democratic society should not substitute their own judgment of morality for the judgment of those over whom they rule. "A free [democratic] society is as much offended by the dictates of an intellectual oligarchy as by those of an autocrat."[26]

Let us for the moment set to one side the role of a judge in a democratic society and focus exclusively on the role of the legislator in such a society. Legislators should represent their constituents. This much is uncontroversial. But how exactly should they do so? It is common to distinguish a delegate from a trustee conception of the legislator's role.[27] On the former conception, the legislator should act as a conduit for the views of those they represent. They strive to determine the dominant

[25] Ibid.
[26] Ibid., p. 93.
[27] The distinction goes back to Edmund Burke. For his classic defense of the trustee conception, see his "Speech to the Electors of Bristol." For a general discussion of the role of a representative in a democratic society, see Pitkin, *The Concept of Representation*.

sentiment among their constituents on the issues they must vote on, and then vote in line with that sentiment. By contrast, on the trustee conception, the legislator listens and attends to the views of those they represent, but they are prepared to depart from them when they judge them to be misguided. They aim to advance the interests of their constituents, including their interests in doing the right thing, rather than deferring to their expressed views about where those interests lie.

Devlin's supplementary argument, which reflects what I referred to as his considered position in Chapter 1, clearly assumes the delegate conception. Democratic government rests on the conviction that while people vary in intelligence and virtue, all adult citizens have "the faculty of telling right from wrong," and it is this equality of capacity that underlies their claim to equal rights to govern.[28] But a proponent of the trustee conception of representation could push back on this very point. Equal rights to govern are established when all adult citizens are given an equal vote in legislative elections. If they do not like how their representative is representing their interests, then they can recall them at the next election and replace them with someone more to their liking.[29] Still, Devlin has a point about the elitism suggested by the trustee conception. The elitism is not that of an intellectual autocracy but of a milder form. It is the elitism suggested when it is held that the views and sentiments of the ordinary person – "the man on the Clapham omnibus," to use Devlin's colorful phrase – are in need of correction and refinement by the more educated members of society who represent them. This kind of elitism, while not strictly incompatible with democratic government, stands in some tension with it.

Reconstructing Devlin's position, then, we arrive at the following line of argument.

  (i) In principle, a society has the right to protect itself from dangers, including internal dangers.
 (ii) Certain immoral activities, including consensual immoral activities between adults, can destroy a society.
(iii) It is permissible for a society to use the criminal law to suppress or discourage those immoral activities that threaten its existence.
 (iv) When adult citizens disagree over whether an activity, such as prostitution or homosexuality, threatens the existence of their society, in a democratic society the majority sentiment should prevail.[30]
  (v) The role of the legislator in a democratic society, accordingly, is to follow the majority sentiment of their constituents on these matters.

[28] Devlin, *The Enforcement of Morals*, p. 100.
[29] As Hart observes, representatives may have a strong incentive to defer to the views of their constituents rather than do what they think is right, for the former course may help them stay in office. But the issue of how a representative should do their job is different from the issue of what they are motivated to do. See *Law, Liberty and Morality*, p. 81.
[30] At points Devlin suggests that majoritarian sentiment is insufficient for the enforcement of moral standards. Something approaching a consensus is required. (See *The Enforcement of Morals*, p. 90, for example.) But this kind of consensus requirement is in tension with his general appeal to democracy.

The first three of these claims recapitulate the society-protection argument. Claim (iv) introduces a democratic norm that applies to a society's efforts to protect itself, which licenses the inference about the role of the legislator expressed in claim (v). The democratic norm explains why a society, or more exactly a democratic society, can protect itself from merely perceived dangers – dangers that may not be real but are perceived to be real by enough of its members.

We have explained how a proponent of the trustee conception of representation could block the transition from (iv) to (v). But a different and more subtle response is also available. The argument we have reconstructed refers to the majority sentiment of a society, but this notion is a little unclear. Sentiment is ambiguous between judgment and feeling. In a thoughtful critique of Devlin's position, Ronald Dworkin distinguishes the moral convictions of the members of a society from their prejudices, aversions and rationalizations. The former reflect considered judgments, whereas the latter do not. This distinction, in turn, allows Dworkin to argue that a legislator need only defer to the moral convictions of their constituents. They should not defer to their prejudices and rationalizations, since these do not reflect, and may even betray, their moral judgments.

Dworkin's response neatly allows him to accept a version of the delegate conception of the role of a representative in a democratic society while denying that if a majority of a representative's constituents disapprove of an activity, then they should defer to this majority sentiment. If a majority of their constituents disapprove of homosexuality, but can offer no reasons for their disapproval, then the representative need not defer to them.

But why, it may now be asked, should a representative in a democratic society privilege the judgments of their constituents over their feelings? Why must a delegate defer to the judgments, but not the feelings and prejudices, of those they represent? To this, Dworkin has an intriguing answer. It is, he claims, part of our social morality that you cannot justify restricting the freedom of people without offering reasons and arguments. Appeals to feelings and prejudice, however widespread, are insufficient. "A conscientious legislator who is told a moral consensus exists," Dworkin concludes, "must test the credentials of that consensus."[31] To justify its enforcement, they must assure themself that it represents the genuine convictions of their constituents and not merely their a-rational inclinations.

Dworkin's claim here is one that is made within the social morality of the societies with which he is principally concerned, namely those of the UK and the USA. In these societies, he is alleging, people, at least in the main, think that the legitimate restriction of freedom requires reasoned justification. He thus counters Devlin on Devlin's own terms. But, whether or not Dworkin is right on this matter, his claim raises a larger issue. The content of a society's social morality at any given time, as we pointed out in Chapter 1, requires interpretation, and the standards of interpretation

---

[31] Dworkin, *Taking Rights Seriously*, p. 254.

are not themselves a matter of social morality. In testing the credentials of a purported moral consensus on some matter, the legislator is attempting to interpret their society's moral judgment on the matter. But their interpretation will be sensitive to their own sense of what a moral consensus consists in. And, for all that has been said by Devlin, this interpretive sense may need to be guided by the legislator's own understanding of the demands of morality.[32]

To see this point more clearly, it will be useful to shift attention now to the role of judges in enforcing social morality. Unlike legislators, judges, as the slogan goes, should apply the law, not make it. To be sure, the slogan is misleading insofar as judges need to make law when the law they are applying is vague or inconsistent, but it is uncontroversial that the role of a judge differs significantly from the role of a legislator. In applying the law, the judge must interpret it. Now suppose that the law contains moral provisions and that the judge must interpret these provisions. Should they attempt to do so in light of their own moral convictions, or should they instead attempt to do so in light of their own understanding of the social morality of their society?

Devlin's general position suggests the latter course. Consider as an example the Eighth Amendment to the US Constitution, which proscribes "cruel and unusual punishments." On one view, the judge must draw on their own best understanding of what are, in fact, cruel and unusual punishments in order to interpret this constitutional provision. On a rival view, the judge must do their best to discern what the authors and ratifiers of this provision thought were cruel and unusual punishments in order to interpret it.[33] Does Devlin's appeal to democracy help in deciding between these two approaches? He claims that "in a democracy educated men cannot be put into a separate category for the decision of moral questions."[34] This provides a measure of support for the view that judges should interpret moral provisions in light of the social morality of their society. They should not attempt to put their own purportedly enlightened morality above that of their fellow citizens. But the issue here is complicated by the fact that Devlin acknowledges that in a democratic society it is appropriate for there to be constitutional limits on majority rule. These limits are by design counter-majoritarian, and so it is not obvious, to put it mildly, that they are best interpreted in light of the majority's understanding, either past or present, of their content.[35]

---

[32] As Dworkin notes, Devlin comes close to acknowledging this point himself. Devlin allows that a legislator can properly dismiss the patently "irrational beliefs" of their constituents when enforcing the social morality of their society. But this means the legislator will need to engage in a measure of critical interpretation (ibid., p. 254 note 3).

[33] See the spirited exchange on this very issue between Justice Antonin Scalia and Dworkin in Scalia's *A Matter of Interpretation*. A friend of Devlin's view might reject both Scalia's and Dworkin's approaches. What matters, they might say, is not the society's original understanding of "cruel and unusual punishment" but rather its current understanding of what this encompasses. But such a view sits uneasily with the affirmation of the value of counter-majoritarian constitutional constraints.

[34] Devlin, *The Enforcement of Morals*, p. 94.

[35] Not obvious, but not obviously incorrect either. On Dworkin's own positive account of law, the judge must interpret the law in light of the judgments of justice of others in their society as well as their own

We cannot here resolve the complex issue of how judges should interpret moral provisions in the law, including, and especially, counter-majoritarian constitutional constraints. The point for now is only that this issue pulls us beyond simple appeals to democracy. Like other normative ideals, democracy is contested terrain. Different conceptions of democracy have been proposed, and some of these conceptions fit better with Devlin-style legal moralism than others.[36] To address the question of which conception of democracy is best or most reasonable, we need to leave behind the perspective of the judge or the legislator in a particular legal system and take up the more general perspective of political philosophy. Devlin's case rests on a particular understanding of democracy, one that assumes that democracy is compromised when the majority do not get to decide whether to enforce a moral view, such as the view that homosexuality is wrong and destructive of society. Even if this view is well considered and based on arguments and not mere prejudice, it may be illegitimate for a democratic society to enforce it. This would be the case if citizens have general moral rights – rights that rule out this kind of legal moralism – that must be respected for the society to be genuinely democratic. General moral rights are counter-majoritarian constraints, and respect for these constraints may be a precondition for democratic rule rather than a compromise with it.

We will return to the issue of moral rights, and how they bear on the debate over the enforcement of morals, in later chapters. The Hart/Devlin debate, as it has been reconstructed here, ends with a dispute over the best understanding of democracy. Devlin's position rests on a majoritarian conception of democracy. This is a conception that he does not defend, and his critics insist is mistaken. It is, the critics maintain, a fundamental error to "believe that loyalty to democratic principles entails acceptance of what may be termed moral populism: the view that the majority have a moral right to dictate how all should live."[37]

3.4 PURE LEGAL MORALISM

Hart framed his debate with Devlin in terms of critical morality. He was right to do so, for the debate bottoms out in a disagreement over the nature of democracy and the limits of the majority's right to rule. And this debate is plainly a matter of critical morality, and not a matter of the content of the social morality of any particular society. But Hart erred, as we pointed out earlier, in thinking that matters of sexual morality must be viewed as matters of morality as such – ones that do not engage issues of harm and benefit, whether to self or to others. The possibility of moralistic

judgments of justice. The former is required by "fairness," and is a clear nod in Devlin's direction. See *Law's Empire*, pp. 249–250.

[36] On this point, compare what Dworkin terms the "majoritarian" with the "constitutional" conception of democracy in *Freedom's Law*, pp. 1–38.

[37] Hart, *Law, Liberty and Morality*, p. 79.

legal paternalism makes it harder to delimit a special class of moral legislation that qualifies as pure legal moralism.

To discuss examples of pure legal moralism, it will be helpful to make a couple of assumptions. Let us assume first that the examples involve genuine immorality and are not merely believed to be immoral by the members of some society. The examples we seek should be pure cases of LM^{critical}. Let us assume second that participation in immoral activities does not necessarily set back people's interests. Either the participation does not set back their interests because they do not have an interest at all in having a good moral character or it does set back their interests in having such a character but provides benefits to them that adequately compensate for that setback. This second assumption enables us to hold the line between legal moralism and moralistic legal paternalism.

With these assumptions in place, consider now the case of evil fantasies, such as the pleasure a person gets from thinking about evil activities. The enjoyment derived from viewing pornographic materials that depict and celebrate acts of violence and rape against women provides a good example. Standard arguments against pornography target either its production (arguing that people were wronged in producing it) or its effects (arguing that its consumption causes acts of sexual violence or leads men to objectify women in ways that are harmful to them). But, for the sake of argument, let us assume that the materials were produced cleanly and that their consumption would not contribute in any way to sexual violence or harm to women. The case for legal regulation must now take a moralistic form. One must claim that the enjoyment of such pornographic material debases its consumers, and that this debasement, while not itself a setback to their interests, nonetheless is sufficiently bad to justify enforcement measures against it. Occurrences of the debasement, one must claim, are "free-floating evils"[38] of sufficient gravity to warrant legal action.

The case against the legal enforcement of morality in this kind of example will strike many as compelling. They will ask: even if it is bad for people to take pleasure in evil fantasies, and even if it is regrettable that they do, if no one is harmed and no one's interests are set back, then why bring the law into it at all?[39] It is a good question. Some things that occur are intrinsically bad. But, if the intrinsically bad things that occur really do not set back anyone's interests, then the law should not try to suppress them. Call this the *person-affecting restriction*.[40] Is there good reason to accept it?

We should note first the possibility that we could have good reason to prevent an intrinsically bad state of affairs from occurring, even if doing so did not benefit anyone. To see this, consider an admittedly far-fetched example.[41] There are two

---

[38]   The term is from Feinberg, *Harmless Wrongdoing*, pp. 18–19.
[39]   This question paraphrases Feinberg's own response to this kind of example. Ibid., p. 328.
[40]   The term is from Parfit, *Reasons and Persons*, p. 394.
[41]   The example is modeled on considerations presented by Temkin in "Equality, Priority and Leveling Down" and "Justice and Equality: Some Questions about Scope."

groups of people living in different worlds with no knowledge of each other and no possibility of communication between them. The first group of people are saints and faring well while the second group are sinners and faring less well. Now imagine that there is a bundle of life-improving resources that will fall from the heavens on the second group, gratuitously increasing their well-being level significantly above the first group, unless you intervene to harmlessly destroy it. You decide to intervene. You might think that you have a reason to do so, since it would be unfair and undeserved for the sinners to fare better than the saints. This reason could not be explained by appealing to benefits, for no one is benefited if the bundle of resources is destroyed. You could say, however, that you have a reason to prevent an intrinsically bad occurrence, and it would be an intrinsically bad occurrence if the sinners were to fare better than the saints.

While far-fetched, the example bears directly on the practice of punishment. For many people think that it is intrinsically good for wrongdoers to be punished, but punishing wrongdoers in some circumstances may not benefit anyone. In such circumstances, if punishment is justified, then it must be justified on the grounds that it would be intrinsically bad for the wrongdoers to go unpunished.

The view of punishment that holds that there is reason – one of fairness or desert – to punish those who are guilty of wrongdoing, even if doing so serves the interests of no one, is called retributivism; and, while this view is accepted by many, it is a controversial view.[42] But if it were accepted, then one could reject the person-affecting restriction, and having rejected this restriction, one could then argue that it is appropriate to use the criminal law to suppress other occurrences that were intrinsically bad, such as those implicated in cases of pure legal moralism. Hart anticipates this line of argument from retributivism to legal moralism. He notes plausibly that the retributive theory of punishment is most plausible when there is not only a wrongdoer but also a victim.

> [The persuasive force of the retributive theory] is surely dependent on there being a victim as well as an offender; for where this is the case, it is possible to conceive of the punishment as a measure designed to prevent the wrongdoer from prospering when his victims suffer . . .. But where there is no victim but only a transgression of a moral rule, the view that punishment is called for as a proper return for the immorality lacks even this support.[43]

Hart's view in this passage has considerable appeal. But it stands in tension with our example of the saints and the sinners. For in the example, the sinners have not prospered at the expense of the saints. Perhaps the sinners are sinners because of their evil thoughts and fantasies, taking delight in the suffering of others, while not causing this suffering themselves.

---

[42] Compare Moore, *Placing Blame: A Theory of the Criminal Law* with Shafer-Landau, "The Failure of Retributivism," *Philosophical Studies* 82 (1996): 289–316.

[43] Hart, *Law, Liberty and Morality*, pp. 59–60.

In the saints and sinners example you intervene to prevent the sinners from undeservedly benefiting, while in the case of punishing those who engage in activities that are immoral as such, but do not harm anyone, the punisher harms the wrongdoer. This is a difference, but not one that seems particularly significant. After all, from the standpoint of what would have happened to the sinners if you had not intervened, your intervention looks harmful. It might be thought that punishment in the service of pure legal moralism would always be disproportionate. Punishment involves hard treatment and condemnation, and inflicting these evils on people requires not just a reason but a weighty reason.[44] Still, while generally correct, this thought seems too absolute. By varying the gravity of the harmless wrongdoing and the severity of the punishment, one likely can arrive at proportionate responses.

If so, then unless retributivism is rejected, there does not seem to be an ironclad case against using the criminal law to address pure cases of legal moralism. However, in practice, Hart's skepticism is well founded. The case for enforcing morality is much stronger when harms are involved, whether the harms are self-imposed or imposed by others.

One feature of Devlin's position remains to be considered. Moral responses, he claims, are as much a matter of feelings as of judgments. Disgust and indignation, if sincere and considered, should be given their due. Consider how he describes the case of homosexuality: "We should ask ourselves in the first instance whether, looking at it calmly and dispassionately, we regard it as a vice so abominable that its mere presence is an offense. If that is the genuine feeling of the society in which we live, I do not see how society can be denied the right to eradicate it."[45]

Yet familiarity with a practice once felt to be abominable can make it seem innocuous. Some contemporary readers of Devlin will be puzzled by his remarks on homosexuality. They may struggle to find intelligible the general abhorrence that was once felt toward it in their countries. But there are practices that these readers too will feel to be an abomination. On this point, Devlin is surely right. There are practices and activities that are simply felt to be beyond the pale, even if they do not cause harm to self or to others.

Here is one gruesome example.[46] In 2001, a German man advertised on the internet for someone who would agree to let him kill and eat them. The advertisement was answered, the two people met, and the man proceeded to kill and then eat his victim. The victim had consented, and the consent was recorded. But under German law, as Devlin noted was true of English law, consent to a crime is no

---

[44] Some retributivists, however, deny that deserved punishment is any evil at all, and so not one that must be outweighed. See Gardner and Tanguay-Renaud, "Desert and Avoidability in Self-Defense," *Ethics* 122/1 (2011): 111–134.

[45] Devlin, *The Enforcement of Morals*, p. 17.

[46] "Victim of Cannibal Agreed to Be Eaten," *The Guardian*, December 4, 2003 (www.theguardian.com /world/2003/dec/04/germany.lukeharding).

defense. The man was eventually charged with murder and sentenced to life imprisonment.

What made this crime shocking, of course, was not just the murder but the cannibalism. The fact that the victim was killed pulls this case outside the domain of pure legal moralism. Even if the victim's consent were valid (something that might be doubted in this case), his interests were set back by the killing; and, as Hart noted, there are legal paternalist grounds for refusing to allow consent as a defense to charges of murder. But the outrage and shock engendered by the case was focused on the cannibalism. Indignation and disgust seem appropriate here, if they are appropriate anywhere.

Consider next the case of cannibalism without murder. Imagine that this is practiced on the dead who had given their full consent while they were living. People could arrange to acquire human flesh and consume it without setting back the interests of anyone involved in the practice. But many people would continue to regard this practice as an abomination, viewing its mere presence as an offense. If you think the law should take steps to prevent this kind of cannibalism either through criminal sanctions or in other ways, then you favor a measure of pure legal moralism.[47]

Devlin took feelings of disgust seriously. So too do most people. Social psychologists have documented a familiar pattern to people's moral judgments. We often immediately find an activity or practice to be disgusting or disturbing. We form the judgment that it is wrong, and then we search for justifications for the judgment that we have formed.[48] This should give us pause. Perhaps the judgment prompted by our initial feelings of disgust will not survive rational scrutiny. Genuine moral judgments, as Dworkin noted, are not mere prejudices. They are not arbitrary. They can be explained. The explanation for why something is wrong must point to some reason or value, not the gut feeling or mere perception that it is wrong. Still, even if the justification for the judgment that something is wrong comes after the fact, it would be a mistake to conclude that it must be nothing more than a mere rationalization.

The challenge for the defender of pure legal moralism, accordingly, is to identify the values and reasons that underlie judgments that some activity or practice is wrong, such as the judgment that human cannibalism is wrong, that may have been prompted in the first place by feelings of disgust or indignation. The values and reasons must not be confined to considerations of harm to others or harm to self, for then, even if sound, they would not provide support for pure legal moralism. And, even if considerations could be identified that explain the wrongness of the activity

---

[47] For example, in the USA cannibalism as such is not illegal. But "most, if not all, states have enacted laws that indirectly make it impossible to legally obtain and consume the body matter" (www .law.cornell.edu/wex/cannibalism).

[48] Haidt, "The Emotional Dog and Its Rationalist Tail: A Social Intuitionist Approach to Moral Judgment," *Psychological Review* 108/4 (2001): 813–834.

in question without appealing to harms, these considerations, once they were assessed in a calm manner, would need to be weighty enough to justify the hard treatment and condemnation that result from criminalization.

There may be no general, exceptionless, principle that rules pure legal moralism out of court. Even so, the clearheaded defender of it will find that they confront a formidable challenge. One possibility that we will explore in Chapter 5 is that respect for various kinds of impersonal goods, such as natural beauty or artistic excellence, can ground legal restrictions on conduct that could not be justified by appealing to the interests or claims of persons. Legal restrictions of this kind, whether justified or not in the end, would provide another, albeit non-standard, example of pure legal moralism.

3.5 CONCLUSION

The Hart/Devlin debate centered on criminal law. But the issues that provoked it – homosexual sex and prostitution – raise broader questions about the legal and social enforcement of sexual morality. These activities have been subject to legal regulations that are not part of criminal law. Recent debates over the legal recognition of same-sex marriage can be understood as debates over whether the law should actively favor heterosexual relationships over same-sex relationships with the implication that the former merit legal support in a way that the latter do not. And those who argue for the decriminalization of prostitution often couple their arguments for decriminalization with support for various legal regulations and restrictions designed to discourage the practice.[49]

Those who believe that there is nothing wrong with engaging in homosexual sex or nothing wrong with prostitution will not rest content with their decriminalization. They will demand that the law not be used to discourage these activities or contribute to the stigmatization of those who engage in them. Nor will they be content until there is broad social acceptance of the activities in question, and they may seek to enlist the law in support of their efforts to bring about the desired social acceptance.

The movement from decriminalization to tolerance to acceptance of a once disfavored practice is a matter of critical morality as well as societal change. The movement can be one of progress or corruption. Most readers of this book will view the change in societal attitudes regarding homosexuality to be one of progress. The verdict on evolving attitudes toward prostitution is likely much more divided. The challenge for those who hold that a certain practice, such as prostitution, is appropriately discouraged by society, but not appropriately criminalized by it, is to hold the line at tolerance and stop the slide to full acceptance.

---

[49] For a good discussion of the different legal options that can be pursued on this matter, see de Marneffe, *Liberalism and Prostitution.*

The social morality of the societies Hart and Devlin confronted has changed dramatically over the past seventy-five years. But the fundamental issue their debate raised remains with us, even for matters of sexual conduct. When is it appropriate for a society to use its law, including the criminal law, to discourage practices that are degrading or harmful to those who engage in them? One answer to this question attracts many. So long as the disfavored conduct secures the free consent of those who engage in it and are directly affected by it, the law must leave it alone. We turn now to examine this line of thought and its limitations.

4

Sovereignty and Consent

In the previous chapter we considered one type of harmless wrongdoing. This concerned acts that are impersonally wrong. These are properly described as "victimless crimes." If there are such crimes, and if they are wrong, then they do not wrong anyone. Might there also be instances of harmless wrongdoing that are harmless but not victimless? Many have thought so. The following kind of example is often presented.

> Unbeknownst to Jill, Jack breaks into her house when she is at work. He takes a short nap in her bed and leaves. He is careful not to damage her house or her bed in any way. He leaves everything as he found it, and he is careful to make sure that she or anyone else never discovers his trespass.[1]

Most people think that Jack wrongs Jill in this example. But does he harm her? Suppose that he does not. No interest of hers is set back, and so Jill is not a victim in virtue of the fact that she has been harmed. But she remains a victim nonetheless.

Perhaps, then, Jack does harm Jill. He violates her property, even though he does not damage it, and he invades her privacy. If Jill has interests in her property and in her privacy, then Jack's trespass may harm her by setting back these interests. We will investigate this line of argument in the next section. But, even if it succeeds in explaining why Jack harms Jill, other apparent examples of harmless wrongdoing with victims will prove to be harder to account for in this manner. Consider a second example, one that involves a measure of altruistic sacrifice.[2]

> After much thought and careful deliberation, Alvin decides to participate in a dangerous clinical trial, one designed to test a risky experimental drug for a disease that Alvin suffers from and for which there is no known cure.[3] The drug presents a substantial risk of serious harm to trial participants. It will not benefit

---

[1] This version of the example is presented by Ripstein, "Beyond the Harm Principle," *Philosophy and Public Affairs* 34/3 (2006): 215–245.

[2] For discussion of self-sacrifice in the context of harmless wrongdoing, see Tadros, *Wrongs and Crimes*, p. 203.

[3] High-risk HIV cure and remission studies present recent real-world examples of this kind of trial. See Eyal, "How to Keep High-Risk Studies Ethical: Classifying Candidate Solutions," *Journal of Medical Ethics* 43/2 (2017): 74–77.

Alvin, and he knows this, but he wishes to participate in the trial in order to help future victims of the disease. The trial is shut down before it begins by an ethics review board, which rules that the trial imposes too high a risk of harm on its participants.

In this example, Alvin freely consents to participate in the trial, knowing full well that doing so is not in his best interests. But he is motivated to do so out of genuine altruistic concern. When he is prevented from participating in the trial, he is not harmed. Nonetheless, he may be wronged. He will be wronged if the ethics review board was wrong to shut down the trial. For in wrongly shutting down the trial, they would wrongly frustrate one of his aims, an aim that is important to him. He thereby would become a victim of harmless wrongdoing.

This result, on reflection, should not be all that surprising. Friends of the harm principle, as we saw in our discussion of Mill, standardly oppose paternalism. But genuine paternalism succeeds in promoting the interests of, or at least preventing the setback of the interests of, those who are interfered with.[4] So, if genuine paternalistic interference is wrong, the reason why it is wrong cannot advert to the harmfulness of the interference. What then explains the wrongfulness of the interference? Mill suggested that each of us has a sphere or domain of self-regarding conduct in which each of us should be sovereign. If I am sovereign over a decision in my life, and you interfere with me with regarding it and without my consent, then you wrong me by usurping my legitimate control over my life. Let us now look more closely at this notion of sovereign control.

4.1 FROM HARM TO SOVEREIGNTY

Proponents of the harm principle often appeal to a notion of personal sovereignty in articulating their position. After introducing the harm to others principle, Mill concluded that "Over himself, over his own body and mind, the individual is sovereign."[5] Likewise, the philosopher Joel Feinberg, who sought to update and defend the harm principle as it applies to criminal law, invoked a distinctive notion of personal autonomy to support it. This notion he described as "sovereign self-rule applied to individuals."[6]

The connection between the harm principle and the notion of personal sovereignty is intuitive as well. For it would seem that in order to apply the harm principle, one needs to have an understanding of people's entitlements. You harm

---

[4] To clarify: genuine paternalism is paternalism that succeeds in its aim. If carried out, it promotes the well-being of its intended targets. Nongenuine or false paternalism purports to benefit its targets but does not succeed in doing so.

[5] Mill, *On Liberty*, p. 9.

[6] Feinberg, *Harm to Self*, p. 52. ("The politically independent state is said to be sovereign over its own territory. Personal autonomy similarly involves the idea of having a domain or territory in which the self is sovereign.")

me when you invade my domain (without my consent), but what exactly determines my domain? Plausibly, our entitlements do, as one writer explains: "Each of us is entitled to govern the domains of our own minds and bodies, free from coercive intrusion. We are entitled to determine what takes place in our minds, what happens to and in our bodies, and how to use our minds and bodies for our own benefit."[7] If this is right, then a conception of personal sovereignty stands behind the harm principle. It helps to fix its content and guides its application. Feinberg, for example, attempts to identify the boundaries of personal sovereignty by discussing harm and offense. We are entitled to use our bodies as we please so long as we do not transgress the boundaries that these notions establish. In addition, we are entitled to our privacy – what Feinberg construes as "a certain amount of 'breathing space' around our bodies" – as well as our property. These entitlements of privacy and property, like our entitlements over our bodies, are part of the domain over which we enjoy sovereign control.

By appealing to entitlements to fix the boundaries of personal sovereignty in this way, proponents of the harm principle may appear to be in a strong position to handle examples of the kind introduced earlier. Cases of undetected, and apparently harmless, trespass can be described as "harmful" in virtue of the fact that they invade the sovereignty of their victims – likewise for cases of unjustified paternalistic interference. Yet, if this is the move that is made with respect to these cases, then it is natural to wonder whether the appeal to harm could be dispensed with altogether. Rather than stretching the meaning of harm to cover such cases, one could go straight to the notion of sovereignty. Undetected trespass is wrong because it invades the sovereignty of its victims, whether or not it harms them in doing so.

Some critics of the harm principle seize on this point. Efforts to include boundary incursions as harms, they contend, rescue the harm principle only "by turning it into an empty format in which the sovereignty principle is stated."[8] When proponents of the harm principle appeal to a principle of sovereignty to articulate their position, the appeal to sovereignty can do all the work that needs doing. Appeals to harm become otiose, or so the critics contend.

To assess this critique, we need to take a closer look at how the sovereignty principle has been understood. One possibility to bear in mind is that just as the articulation of the harm principle may need to appeal to some notion of personal sovereignty, the articulation of the sovereignty principle may need to appeal to some notion of harm to others. We should not assume, in other words, that we must choose between the two principles, for it may turn out that they are complements to each other.

The sovereignty principle is concerned with the relations that obtain between persons, or how they stand with respect to one another. A person is sovereign in their

[7]   De Marneffe, "Self-Sovereignty and Paternalism," in *Paternalism: Theory and Practice*, eds. Coons and Weber (Cambridge: Cambridge University Press, 2013), p. 56.
[8]   Ripstein, "Beyond the Harm Principle," p. 219.

domain if no one else rules over them in that domain. On a strong formulation, the principle holds that "the only legitimate restrictions on conduct are those that secure the mutual independence of free persons from each other."[9] So understood, the sovereignty principle has two parts. The first part identifies the content of what it means to be an independent person. This will consist in a set of entitlements to use one's body and mind as one sees fit so long as doing so is compatible with respecting the corresponding entitlements of others. The second part holds that the only valid reason for interfering with a person's conduct is that doing so is necessary to respect or safeguard the entitlements of others. The remainder of this section will address the first part of the principle and the next section will consider the second part.

Your sovereign entitlements limit my sovereign entitlements. I can use my fist as I see fit, but I can't use it to break your nose. For when I break your nose, without your consent, I use my body to violate your entitlement to decide what happens to your body. Each person's entitlements to their body and mind are limited in this way by the like entitlements of others. This example is not controversial, but it is more complex than it first appears.

Mutual independence between persons can be secured either by limiting people's entitlements to use their bodies or by limiting their entitlements not to have their bodies damaged. If I can use my fist to break your nose, then, so long as you have the corresponding entitlement to use your fist to break my nose, our respective entitlements remain equal. In this scenario, each of us would enjoy greater control over the use of our fists and lesser control over what happens to our noses. In reply, it is no good to say that our respective entitlements to use our fists must be limited, for if not, then we would both be liable to harm from each other. This is no good, since we are now considering the sovereignty principle as an alternative to the harm principle.

To see this point more clearly, consider a simplified situation. There are only two persons to consider. Suppose that both prefer to have greater control over what happens to their bodies in exchange for lesser control over what they can do with their bodies. Then, by appealing to their preferences about how to use their bodies, we could arrive at the result that the sovereignty principle requires that neither person has the entitlement to use their fist to break the other's nose. But preferences can change, and the result here, at any rate, is contingently fortuitous. What does the sovereignty principle require when preferences conflict, as they almost certainly will in more complex cases?

A defender of the sovereignty principle could respond that its requirements should not be ascertained by looking at the preferences and purposes of the people involved. Instead, we should put the focus on people's power or abilities to form preferences and settle on purposes. "Part of the reason freedom is important," it has been claimed, "is that it allows each person to decide what purposes to pursue."[10]

9 Ibid., p. 229.
10 Ibid., p. 231.

However, the focus on powers and abilities just brings us back to the problem of how to specify the entitlements to use our powers and abilities in the first place. To get determinate results, the sovereignty principle needs supplementation that takes us beyond the formal requirement that the entitlements of each are limited by the entitlements of others.[11]

Rather than appealing to the preferences and purposes of people, the needed supplementation could advert to important human interests. We have important interests in controlling our lives in certain ways and in being protected from various setbacks to our well-being. We can refer to these as generic agency and welfare interests, since they are not interests that depend on the particular preferences and purposes of individual people. A generic interest is an interest (nearly) all of us have, or perhaps (nearly) all of us in a certain society have. We have a generic interest in bodily integrity but no comparable interest in having the freedom to use our bodies to damage other people's bodies.

On this approach, the sovereignty principle incorporates or presupposes a set of generic interests. In this spirit, consider the following proposal.

> A government violates a person's sovereignty over themselves in prohibiting them from making a choice if and only if (a) this choice involves an important form of discretionary control over their own mind or body, (b) there is no evident and substantial reason of welfare for someone (possibly them) to want them not to make this choice that has much greater weight than their reasons to make it and (c) prohibiting this choice is not necessary to ensure that someone (possibly them) has adequate control over their own mind or body.[12]

In our terms, clauses (a) and (c) advert to agency interests, whereas (b) adverts to welfare interests. The significance of these respective interests is not a function of how much they are valued by particular people. Their weight and significance are an objective matter. We will have more to say about agency interests in Section 4.5. For now, we can focus on the welfare interests referred to in (b). The proposal continues: "A reason of welfare for A to want B not to make a choice is substantial if and only if it identifies a way in which A is substantially worse off if B makes this

---

[11] In discussing Kant's view, Ripstein writes that independence from others must start with "your person as your body," and he claims further that "if another person interferes with your body, he thereby interferes with your ability to set and pursue your own purposes by interfering with the means that you have with which to set them, namely your bodily powers or abilities" (Ripstein, *Force and Freedom*, p. 41). None of this addresses the issue being pressed here. Your body can be interfered with when others limit how you can use it as well as when others do things to it. Expanding entitlements that protect you from the latter restrict entitlements that protect you from the former. The issue is particularly thorny when risk is introduced into the picture, since entitlements that maximally protect our bodies from exposure to the risk of harm from others would severely constrain what we could do with them. For an imaginative discussion that squarely confronts the problem that risk poses to setting sovereign boundaries between persons, see Nozick, *Anarchy, State and Utopia*, pp. 57–87.

[12] De Marneffe, "Self-Sovereignty and Paternalism," p. 58.

choice, typically by being at much higher risk of harm."[13] Here the appeal to welfare and risk of harm play a crucial role in specifying the entitlements of sovereign control.

Is this a promising approach? The attentive reader may suspect that we are now arguing in a circle. We began by saying that you cannot apply the harm principle until you specify the entitlements of the relevant parties. To do so, we said that one needs to invoke a prior principle – the sovereignty principle. But then we suggested that the sovereignty principle itself lacks determinate content, and to give it content we need to appeal to generic human interests, paying attention in particular to what makes people substantially worse off or risks harming them. But now, it seems, we have come back to the harm principle.

Some circles are worse than others, however. What is needed is an account of sovereignty and an account of harm that are independently plausible and mutually supporting. Neither has to be normatively prior to the other. If this is correct, then proponents of the sovereignty principle overstate their case when they present it as an alternative to the harm principle, one that supersedes it. However, they do not err in holding that the harm principle cannot explain all wrongful incursions into our lives. Our interests in controlling our lives, even when no substantial harm is in prospect, remain, and these interests are not well expressed by stretching the meaning of harm to cover them.

4.2 STRINGENCY

Fixing the content of the sovereignty principle does not settle its stringency. We may know what is required for people to be mutually independent, and we may know the boundaries of the sovereign domain in which each person rules themself and is not ruled by others. But boundaries can be crossed, and the question of stringency addresses whether, and when, such boundary crossings could be or are justified.

The strong formulation of the sovereignty principle introduced in the previous section is maximally stringent. Recall that it holds that the only valid reason for interfering with a person's conduct is that doing so is necessary to respect or safeguard the entitlements of others. On this formulation, interference with people is justified when it protects the boundaries of sovereignty. Otherwise, it is unjustified. As Feinberg noted, this understanding of sovereignty fits how many have understood the notion as it applies to nation-states: "Only a nation's own sovereignty (in the guise, say, of 'self-defense') may ever be placed on the scales and weighed against another nation's acknowledged sovereignty, for sovereignty decisively outweighs every other kind of reason for intervention."[14] In actuality, this is a particular conception of state sovereignty, one that is often referred to as the Westphalian conception of sovereignty after the Treaty of Westphalia in 1648 that established the

---

[13] Ibid.
[14] Feinberg, *Harm to Self*, p. 55.

modern international order of nation-states. Feinberg acknowledges that this understanding of sovereignty does not capture how nation-states actually behave toward one another, as they often cross one another's boundaries in pursuit of political objectives. But the Westphalian conception is not descriptive. It is normative. Nation-states *should* only interfere with the sovereignty of other nation-states if doing so is necessary to protect and enforce their own sovereignty.

There are obviously all sorts of disanalogies between nation-states and persons. Even if one were attracted to the Westphalian conception of sovereignty for nation-states, why think it should be applied to persons as well? Feinberg offers one reason. If personal sovereignty is absolute, if it is an all-or-nothing concept, then any infringement of it is unjustified. By contrast, if personal sovereignty is not maximally stringent, then infringements of it can be justified by other values. The disvalue of infringements would now need to be balanced against the goods secured by them. But we may not have a good method or reliable procedure for doing the balancing. If so, then our sovereign control over ourselves would be left in a precarious position.

Maximally stringent views of sovereignty, however, can have crazy consequences. Take a trivial infringement, such as the seizure of a hair from my head that was not consented to, and place it against a very large benefit that could be secured by doing so, such as the discovery of a cure for cancer. Do not focus here on how the infringement is supposed to secure the benefit. (Perhaps the hair on my head contains a rare enzyme that can be synthesized to develop the needed cure.) The point is that, *if* the infringement could secure the benefit in this example, then it would seem crazy to hold that the infringement was unjustified.

For the proponent of stringent personal sovereignty, a strategy is available that responds to this kind of example. We can call it the adjustment strategy. The adjustment strategy is to adjust the boundaries of personal sovereignty so that the embarrassing counterexamples no longer apply. Personal sovereignty remains as stringent as ever. It is just that it no longer covers the example at hand. If curing cancer would secure a huge benefit for millions of people, thus preventing this disease from harming them, then a proponent of personal sovereignty could hold that our sovereign control over our bodies does not extend to failures to massively aid others at little cost to ourselves.[15]

The adjustment strategy enables the proponent of personal sovereignty to hold firm to their absolutism. Personal sovereignty should never be balanced against other values. It trumps all competing considerations. But notice that it succeeds only by doing the balancing at an earlier stage, as it were. In adjusting the boundaries of personal sovereignty, the theorist aims to give due regard to the values that potentially compete with it. Of course, this kind of adjustment need not be done once and for all. It can be an ongoing process, as new considerations emerge or different challenges are presented.

---

[15] This is the strategy employed by Feinberg. See his discussion of failures to prevent harms (*Harm to Others*, pp. 126–186).

The strong formulation of the sovereignty principle holds that the only valid reason for interfering with a person's conduct is that doing so is necessary to respect or safeguard the sovereign entitlements of others. A less strong, or moderate, formulation allows that the principle can be legitimately overridden by other values. Reflection on the adjustment strategy suggests that there may not be an important difference between the two formulations. To secure its plausibility, the strong formulation must sacrifice scope for stringency, whereas the moderate formulation can do so by preserving scope but reducing stringency.

4.3 PATERNALISM AND ITS VARIETIES

Personal sovereignty, on either the strong or the weak formulation, is often thought to stand in tension with paternalism and especially legal paternalism. It is easy to see why. The paternalist interferes with the freedom of other people to promote their well-being. Such interference can betray a busybody mentality, and it often provokes resentment. "It is none of your business how I lead my life so long as I do not harm anyone else," many are inclined to say. If we are indeed entitled to make foolish or reckless self-regarding decisions, then this is well explained by the sovereignty principle. Part of having sovereign control over our lives is the control we exercise when we mess them up.

Yet sometimes we engage in self-harming behavior that does not manifest sovereign control over our lives. Suppose that I am intoxicated and you intervene to prevent me from stepping in front of a bus. This is paternalistic interference, as you are intervening to protect me from harming myself. But you do not impose your purposes on me. Your intervention, or so it seems, will not infringe at all on my sovereign control over my life. If anything, it will further my control over my life, as it is no part of my plans to step in front of the bus.

Cases of this kind are referred to as "soft paternalism." The paternalism is soft in virtue of the fact that it does not interfere with the voluntary will of the person interfered with. Various factors, such as ignorance, duress, extreme anxiety, impairment by mind-altering drugs and so on, can undermine our voluntary control over our lives. Interventions to promote our good that do not frustrate our voluntary will, it is thought, do not compromise our sovereignty because our sovereign control over our lives concerns our power to make voluntary choices about how to lead our lives. Indeed, some writers question whether soft paternalism is aptly described as paternalism at all: "the soft paternalist points out that the law's concern should not be with the wisdom, prudence, or dangerousness of [a person's choice], but rather with whether or not the choice is truly [the person's]. Its concern should be to help implement [the person's] real choice, not to protect [the person] from harm as such."[16]

---

[16]   Ibid., p. 12.

This is broadly correct, but still a little misleading. The proponent of soft paternalism does not countenance just any interference with people's nonvoluntary choices. Interference is justified only if it is necessary to prevent people from harming themselves by their nonvoluntary choices. To this extent, the law insofar as it engages in soft paternalism must be concerned with the prudence or dangerousness of the choices that are targeted.

Now we can ask: is it really true that soft paternalistic interference, including legal forms of it, do not infringe on our personal sovereignty? We suggested earlier that sovereign control over our lives concerns our power to voluntarily direct our lives as we see fit, not our power to do things that we do not really want to do. But this can be challenged. Notice, to start with, that on the Westphalian conception of state sovereignty, nation-states are not permitted to interfere with the internal governance of other nation-states on soft paternalist grounds.[17] If Canada is about to implement a very foolish piece of legislation, one that would not be implemented if Canadians knew more than they do about its effects, then it is not permissible for the United States to intervene to prevent Canada from its destructive nonvoluntary decision. "We are just protecting you from a decision that you do not really want to make" is no defense to outside interference in the internal governance of a state on the Westphalian conception of sovereignty. There are doubtless many reasons for this, but it seems true that if a nation-state has protection against outside interference, even when it is making decisions that do represent what it wants to do, it has greater sovereign control over its territory than if it did not have this protection. If our bodies are like territories, then the analogy suggests that we would have greater sovereign control over our bodies if interference on soft paternalist grounds were not permitted than if it were. Perhaps, on this understanding, our sovereign control over our bodies should be overridden for soft paternalistic reasons, but it is overridden nonetheless.[18]

Most proponents of the sovereignty principle resist this line of thought, however. They contend that soft paternalistic interference, at least when it is justified, does not compromise our sovereignty. One argument for this understanding of the principle links soft paternalism to the harm principle. Consider a case involving two people. The first person is impaired. Knowing this, the second person gets them to sign up for a risky investment scheme, from which the second person will profit. The harm to the first person here is financial, but it is harm that is caused by the second person. Accordingly, on the harm principle, interference is justified in order to prevent the second person from harming the first. Can this idea be applied to a case involving only one person? Return to the bus example. When I step in front of the bus, I will most certainly be harmed. The cause of the harm is not my voluntary decision to engage in risky behavior but rather some internal distortion that subverts

---

[17]   Arneson, "Joel Feinberg and the Justification of Hard Paternalism," *Legal Theory* 11 (2005): 259–284, at 267–268.

[18]   For fuller discussion, see Wall, "Self-Ownership and Paternalism," *Journal of Political Philosophy* 17/4 (2009): 399–417.

my will – in this case, the impaired state that is caused by my intoxication.[19] Just as I need protection from harm from others, I need protection from harm from internal factors that run counter to my sovereign will.[20]

This argument further highlights the difficulties of determining the boundaries of the sovereign self. The body of a person is a natural analogue to the territory of a nation-state. But bodies, at least on the argument we are now considering, contain alien elements from which we need protection. The idea is also strained. If my impaired will is not my will, then those will is it? Better to say that my impaired will is indeed my will but that it does not demand respect in the way that my unimpaired will does.

Soft paternalist interference, at least in the single-person case, often takes the form of restraint that is intended to ascertain my genuine will. In a famous example from Mill, a person physically prevents another from walking across a bridge with rotten planks.[21] There is no time to warn them, and it is reasonable to presume that they would not want to cross the bridge if they knew its condition. Mill believes that the interference here is justified. But suppose now that the person, having been stopped and duly warned of the dangers of crossing the bridge, still desires to do so. On Mill's view, it now would be wrong to intervene. Their decision to cross the bridge would be reckless, but it is theirs to make.

The contrary view holds that, providing our decisions are foolish and dangerous enough and the means of interference are effective and proportionate, it can be permissible to intervene in order to protect us from harming ourselves. This is hard paternalism. It is hard insofar as it overrides people's decisions to harm themselves even when those decisions are not impaired but reflect their real or genuine wills.

Does hard paternalism necessarily infringe on personal sovereignty? Many have thought so. They insist that when the law overrides our judgment and our will about how we should lead our lives so as to protect us from our imprudent choices, it imposes its purposes on us and diminishes our sovereign control over our bodies and minds.[22] There is a further worry that is often expressed. If hard paternalism is countenanced, then where will it all end? Recall from the previous chapter that Hart was prepared to embrace legal paternalism – and we can now add hard legal paternalism – to rebut Devlin's claim that an appeal to legal moralism is necessary to explain why the law does not permit consent as a defense to murder. But having let

---

[19]   Does it matter if at an earlier point in time I voluntarily decided to ingest the substance that now impairs my will? Perhaps; but if so, then the example can be clarified by stipulating that at the earlier point in time I accidentally and unknowingly ingested the substance.

[20]   Compare Beauchamp, "Paternalism and Bio-Behavioral Control" with Feinberg, *Harm to Self*, pp. 13–14.

[21]   Mill, *On Liberty*, p. 294.

[22]   Judgment and will can come apart. Out of weakness of will, we can do things that we judge we should not do. This presents an interesting case for paternalism. If my will can be voluntary and unimpaired but nonetheless contrary to my judgment, then is it an impaired will, one eligible for soft paternalist interference, or does it instead demand respect as a sovereign will? Soft paternalists can disagree on this issue. Hence, the clear case of hard paternalism involves overriding both a person's judgment and will.

hard paternalism in, what is to stop it from extending too far, ushering in "a Spartan-like regimen requiring rigorous physical exercise and abstention from smoking, drinking and hazardous pastimes?"[23]

While often voiced, slippery-slope worries of this kind should be greeted with caution. Lines can be drawn and distinctions can be made. In considering particular legal paternalism proposals, we can compare the degree to which they would set back our agency interests with the size of the prospective welfare benefits to be secured by them.[24] Requiring people to engage in rigorous physical exercise would very substantially curtail their agency control over their bodies, while requiring them to wear a safety helmet when they drive a motorcycle would do so to a much lesser extent. Further, the welfare gains to people from being required to wear a safety helmet may be sufficient to justify this reduction of agency control, while the welfare gains from being compelled to engage in rigorous physical exercise, while possibly substantial, very likely would not be large enough to justify the dramatic loss of agency control involved.

These balancing judgments are often difficult to make, and we should expect people to disagree over them. But this is true in other areas of the law as well. It is not a special problem for the justification of legal paternalism. Legal paternalism, especially of the hard paternalism variety, does present a special problem of sorts, however. For paternalistic legal measures are purportedly justified on the grounds that they promote the welfare of people by protecting them from self-harming choices. But, as one critic points out, in assessing these measures "we cannot neglect the quantum of disutility, hardship or deprivation needed to reach our paternalistic objective."[25] Take the safety helmets example. If people are imprisoned for failing to wear a safety helmet when driving a motorcycle, then it will be hard to credit the thought that the legal measure has made them better off overall. True, one could reduce the criminal penalty to a mere fine, but then the effectiveness of the measure would be diminished.

In reply, and in defense of legal paternalism, it can be said that for a paternalistic measure to be justified it need not be the case that the measure promotes the welfare of literally everyone who is affected by it. If someone were imprisoned for failing to wear a safety helmet, then they would not, in all likelihood, be benefited by the paternalistic measure. But if the measure induced a sufficient number of others to wear safety helmets, when they would not have done so in its absence, then it would promote their interests. Here some balancing of the interests of the different affected parties is in order, and if the balancing comes out right, then the measure would be justified.[26]

[23] Harris, "Private Consensual Adult Behavior: The Requirement of Harm to Others in the Enforcement of Morality," p. 585n (quoted by Feinberg, *Harm to Self*, p. 24).
[24] This is the approach adopted by de Marneffe in "Self-Sovereignty and Paternalism."
[25] Husak, "Penal Paternalism," p. 51.
[26] See Hurd, "Paternalism on Pain of Punishment."

We should pause and consider the force of this reply. To some ears, it will sound objectionably consequentialist.[27] The person who is sent to prison is sacrificed for the sake of the many who benefit from the paternalistic measure. But proponents of the sovereignty principle standardly reject consequentialist views, and they do so precisely because such views enjoin sacrifices of the kind being contemplated here. The "separateness of persons" blocks the consequentialist aggregation of interests. Further, the people who would lose out if the paternalistic measure were not in place have voluntarily decided to expose themselves to the risk of harm in question. Surely this is relevant to determining how to do the balancing of interests.

Both of these are important points. The first one targets a general feature of consequentialist moral theory. In the example we have been considering, a person goes to prison for a relatively minor offense – to wit, the failure to wear a safety helmet when riding a motorcycle. The punishment here certainly looks to be excessive and undeservedly harsh. But a straightforward summing up of the conflicting interests of all affected parties might well justify the undeserved punishment of this person. Sophisticated consequentialist moral theories, however, can factor considerations of fairness and desert into the formula for aggregating conflicting interests. Doing so may be sufficient to block the intuitively objectionable cases of sacrificing some for the sake of others. Moreover, proponents of the sovereignty principle, as we have already seen, must themselves balance the conflicting interests of persons either in setting the boundaries of personal sovereignty or in determining when personal sovereignty is permissibly infringed upon. We will have more to say about the important issue of balancing conflicting interests in Chapter 5. For now, it will suffice to say that the fact that a defender of legal paternalism may need to balance the conflicting interests of persons to justify their proposals should not be viewed as a decisive problem for their view.

The second point just mentioned also raises complex issues in general moral theory that concern how individual responsibility bears on judgments of fairness. To address these issues, we need first to introduce a key maxim that informs the sovereignty principle on its standard formulations. The maxim will lead us to consider both the normative power and the limits of consent.

4.4 THE VOLENTI MAXIM

Proponents of the sovereignty principle sometimes claim that the harm principle gets the wrong result in cases in which people consent to be harmed. Consider a boxing match where both fighters have freely consented to the risks involved. If one fighter gets seriously injured from the match, then they have been harmed. But, possibly, they have not been wronged.[28] Is this a problem for the harm principle?

---

[27] Husak, "Penal Paternalism," p. 54.
[28] The qualifier "possibly" is inserted here since, as we will see in Section 4.6, there may be limits to the risks that one can validly consent to bear.

Not obviously. Recall the distinction between harms (setbacks of interests) and wrongful harms (wrongful setbacks of interests). The harm principle targets only wrongful harms. But why is it not wrong to seriously injure one's opponent in a boxing match? Different answers can be given to this question, but many have appealed to a very general explanation. If one freely consents to a risk of harm (including a certainty of harm), then one is not wronged when one suffers the harm. The Latin phrase "volenti non fit injuria" expresses the basic idea – a person is not wronged by that to which they consent.

This maxim, which we will refer to as the Volenti Maxim, has a good deal of explanatory power. Consent is morally transformative. Many actions and activities that are morally and legally permissible with the consent of the involved parties would not be permissible in the absence of their consent. For example, the difference between theft and permissible takings of property or between rape and permissible sex is explained by the maxim.

The maxim also illuminates the normative significance of the distinction between soft and hard paternalism. For in cases of soft paternalism, the target of the interference either does not consent to the harm involved or their consent to it is defective. By contrast, in cases of hard paternalism, the consent to the harm involved is not a determining factor. Indeed, hard paternalistic interference can occur even when the target of the interference has validly consented to the risk of harm in question. Thus, the popular liberal position that soft paternalistic interference can be justified, while hard paternalistic interference cannot be, is explained by the harm principle in conjunction with the Volenti Maxim.

The maxim is attractive to proponents of the sovereignty principle as well. For an important part of our sovereign control over our lives is our power to alter our normative relationships with others, as well as our prerogative to assume different kinds and degrees of risks in pursuit of our plans and projects. Still, the Volenti Maxim has some striking consequences that are difficult to accept. Devlin and Hart were in agreement that consent to murder is no defense. But, if the maxim is accepted, then this result is thrown into question.[29] Consider, in this vein, the gruesome but not too far-fetched example proposed by the writer Irving Kristol.[30] Just as the ancient Romans had gladiatorial contests in which the combatants fought to the death, we too could institute such competitions, Kristol pointed out. Imagine a version of the Ultimate Fighting Competition, in which the winner is declared only after the loser has been killed.

Kristol's example troubles proponents of the maxim. Many find it hard to stomach the prospect of such gladiatorial contests, but their permissibility seems to follow from the Volenti Maxim and the rejection of hard paternalism. Perhaps here we have a compelling example of harmless wrongdoing that would justify legal intervention. If so, then a measure of legal moralism would be justified.

---

[29]   As Feinberg concedes (*Harmless Wrongdoing*, pp. 165–166).
[30]   Kristol, "Pornography, Obscenity, and the Case for Censorship," *The New York Times Magazine*, March 28, 1971.

Reflection on Kristol's example – as well as others, such as the cannibalism/murder case described in Chapter 3 – strongly suggests that the Volenti Maxim is an overstatement of an important but more modest claim. Consider now what we might call the Qualified Volenti Maxim: a person is not wronged by that to which they consent, providing that they have a right to consent to that to which they consent. The idea here is a familiar one. X may consent to Y using Z's property, but if X had no right to consent to Y's use of Z's property, then X's consent cannot make it true that Y does not wrong Z by using their property. Consent in the absence of the relevant right has no morally transformative power. The Qualified Volenti Maxim extends this familiar idea to the self-regarding case. I have a right to control how my body is used so long as I do not infringe on other people's corresponding right to do so, but the scope of that right might be circumscribed in various ways. For example, I might not have a right to participate in a gladiatorial contest, even if I very much want to do so.

The Qualified Volenti Maxim can capture the truth in the Volenti Maxim without countenancing its more unappealing implications. To be sure, more needs to be said to justify the proposed qualifications. We will consider two such justificatory strategies in the next two sections. But first we need to return to the issue of how the Volenti Maxim, in either its unqualified or qualified form, bears on the justification of legal paternalism. For, as we noted earlier, whether someone consents to assume a risk of harm seems clearly relevant to whether the person can complain if the harm transpires. And the Volenti Maxim appears to get the right result here. Consent implies no injury, and hence no grounds for complaint. A legal regime that abjures hard paternalism altogether fairly allots the costs between different affected parties, since those whose welfare is set back under such a regime have only themselves to blame.

Appearances, however, may be misleading. In deciding whether it is fair to let the chips fall where they may, we need to consider not only the fact of consent but also the circumstances under which it is given. The circumstances under which consent is given can render it invalid. Forced consent is not valid consent, for example. Call circumstances that invalidate consent *validity-undermining circumstances*. Other circumstances may not undermine valid consent but they may be unfair. They may ground complaints about the fairness of letting the chips fall where they may, even when they do not undermine the validity of the consent that is made under them.

An example from T. M. Scanlon, which I modify here, can help us to appreciate this possibility.[31] Scanlon invites us to imagine a scenario under which a city needs to remove hazardous materials from one site to another safer site. The transport of the materials will impose a substantial risk of harm for those who live nearby, but, so long as they remain indoors during the transport process, they will not suffer any

---

[31] Scanlon, *What We Owe to Each Other*, pp. 256–267. Scanlon uses the example to make a number of points, but his chief concern is to use it to cast doubt on what he terms the "forfeiture view" of responsibility, which has affinities with the Volenti Maxim, as Scanlon points out.

harm. Now suppose that the city informs every resident in the affected area of the dangers of going outdoors during the time when the materials are being transported. Every resident, let us suppose, has been given fair warning of the danger and of the need to stay away from the removal sites and to remain indoors. But one resident, Jane, does not heed the warning. She freely decides to go outdoors near the removal site during the time that the hazardous materials are being transported, and as a result she suffers a serious illness.

Does Jane have a complaint against the city? She consented to the risk of harm, or at least she voluntarily assumed it, when she freely went outdoors after having been duly warned of the dangers of doing so. She cannot claim that the circumstances under which she acted undermined the validity of her consent to the risks. But let us now add some more details to the scenario. Suppose that the city failed to take all of the precautions that it would have been reasonable to expect them to have taken. For example, suppose that city officials failed to wet down the hazardous materials before transporting them, and that this failure significantly increased the risk that the materials would contaminate the surrounding air. Since it would have been reasonable to demand that the city wet down the hazardous materials before transporting them – doing so would not have been prohibitively expensive – the city's failure, it can be said, imposed an unfair risk of harm on people who were disposed to imprudently ignore the warning, such as Jane, even though she consented to it.

Jane's complaint in this scenario is not that the circumstances under which she consented to the risks of harm were validity-undermining, but rather that they were objectionable in another way. The circumstances presented her with an option that was more dangerous than it needed to be, and the fact that she took the option and freely consented to expose herself to the dangers that it imposed on her does not negate this fact. Still, it must be admitted that it is awkward for Jane to raise this complaint herself. After all, she knew the risks. She should not try to shift the blame of her imprudent behavior onto others.

Sometimes when a wrong is done to someone, or a cost is unfairly imposed on them, they do not have standing to complain. If the leader of country A has ordered the torture of prisoners of war from country B, then they lack standing to object when the leader of country B subjects captured soldiers from country A to torture.[32] The torture of prisoners of war is wrong. Both countries should not engage in it, but given that the leader of country A has done so, they are in no position to criticize the practice. The awkwardness of Jane's complaint has a similar explanation. She freely and knowingly helped to bring about her own misfortune. How can she now object to the very thing she contemplated and countenanced? But from the fact that Jane lacks standing to complain, it does not follow that she has no grounds for complaint

---

[32] For discussion, see Cohen, "Casting the First Stone: Who Can, and Who Can't, Condemn the Terrorists?" *Finding Oneself in the Other*, pp. 115–133.

or that no one else has standing to complain.[33] For example, those who care about Jane would have standing to point out that the city did not take all the precautionary measures that it should have taken. They could say: "Jane made a poor decision. That is on her. But you – the city officials – are responsible for putting her in a bad-choice situation. That is on you."

The Volenti Maxim explains why the wrong done to Jane by the city's failure to take adequate precautions is less serious than it would have been had she not freely consented to the risks of harm. But it does not establish what it purports to establish. It does not show that a person is *never* wronged by that to which they consent. It focuses too much attention on the fact of consent and not enough attention on the circumstances of consent.[34] If this is correct, then the Volenti Maxim, whether qualified or not, does not foreclose the justification of hard paternalism. People might be treated unfairly under a no-paternalism regime, even if the harms they suffer are ones to which they have given their free consent. (We will defend a version of this argument in more detail in Chapter 6.)

4.5 AUTONOMY AND PATERNALISM

The qualified version of the Volenti Maxim is more plausible than the unqualified version. Still, as noted earlier, proposed qualifications stand in need of justification. Something should be said to explain their appeal. This section explores an internal conflict within the notion of personal sovereignty. A resolution of this conflict will introduce an important qualification to the Volenti Maxim.

One thing that sovereign persons can do is bind themselves. They can make promises and enter into contracts that restrict their future actions. On Monday Jack can promise Jill that he will have lunch with her on Wednesday. Relatedly, Jack, on Monday, can enter into a contract with Jill that requires him to provide her with a service on Wednesday, such as mowing her lawn. By promising and contracting, Jack's present will can bind his future will. This kind of self-binding is familiar to us all. But it is more puzzling than it first appears. Suppose that on Wednesday Jack no longer wants to provide the service to Jill that he entered into a contract to provide. Now his present will is at odds with his prior will, and we can ask why it should take priority. The injunction "respect a person's sovereign will" does not answer our question, for we are asking why we should respect his past will (his will on Monday) rather than his present will (his will on Wednesday).

There are many reasons why we should hold Jack to his contract. Jill has relied on him. Her interests will be frustrated if we let him ignore his prior commitment. More

---

[33] For a similar point, see Dworkin, "Harm and the Volenti Principle," p. 320.
[34] Proponents of the Volenti Maxim do not ignore the circumstances of consent altogether. They take seriously those circumstances that are validity-undermining. But they do ignore aspects of these circumstances that are unfair or objectionable, even when they do not undermine the validity of consent.

generally, if people were not bound by the contracts that they made, then they would have no reason to enter into them, and we would all be worse off, since much valuable and mutually beneficial cooperation is made possible by contractual agreements. These reasons do not speak to our question, however. They do not explain why the sovereignty principle itself supports the judgment that Jack is bound by his contract.

Sovereign persons are extended across time. The sovereignty principle directs us to respect the will of these persons, but their will can change as time changes. Earlier we spoke of the agency interests of sovereign people. By attending to these agency interests, we may be able to answer our question. Our agency interests are served by having options to bind our future selves. This empowers us to cooperate with others in ways that further our goals and projects. Here is how one influential writer on contract law has explained the situation:

> In order that I be as free as possible, that my will have the greatest possible range consistent with the similar will of others, it is necessary that there be a way in which I may commit myself. It is necessary that I be able to make nonoptional a course of conduct that would otherwise be optional for me. By doing this I can facilitate the projects of others, because I can make it possible for those others to count on my future conduct, and thus those others can pursue more intricate, more far-reaching projects . . . . But, of course, this purely altruistic motive is not the only motive worth facilitating. More central to our concern is the situation where we facilitate each other's projects, where the gain is reciprocal.[35]

The possibility of self-binding creates new options for us, which, in turn, further our agency interests by facilitating our projects. This is clear in simple cases. Suppose that one never changes one's mind. Then options to bind oneself in the future only increase one's ability to get what one wants overall. They unambiguously expand the domain of one's sovereign will.

Nevertheless, even granting this important point, our question remains. People do change their minds, and when they do, how can we be sure that the increase in their options at earlier times is not overbalanced by the loss of their options at later times? Put otherwise, options to self-bind expand the domain of one's sovereign will in the present by contracting that domain in the future, but there is no guarantee that the present expansion will be greater than the future contraction. The issue in question is vividly illustrated by the possibility of voluntary slavery. With voluntary slavery, a person enters into a contract that transfers, and transfers permanently, to another all their rights to govern themself.[36] If people have the sovereign right to enter into such a contract, and if such a contract were valid, would the exercise of this right increase or diminish their agency interests overall?

---

[35] Fried, *Contract As Promise*, p. 13.
[36] For instructive discussion of this kind of contract, and how it relates to the law of contract generally, compare Kronman, "Paternalism and the Law of Contracts" with Alexander, "Voluntary Enslavement."

To be sure, voluntary slavery is an extreme case. But there are other examples of self-binding contracts that raise similar concerns, such as marital arrangements that do not allow for divorce. Or consider a contract to work for one's current employer – eight hours a day for five days a week – for the rest of one's working life. This is not slavery, but it is permanent binding. Beyond self-binding contracts, people can take actions in the present that permanently damage or destroy their capacities for future control over their lives. For example, people could take drugs now that would seriously impair them for the rest of their lives, or they might decide to maim themselves in serious ways or end their lives altogether. By doing so, they arguably would fail to value appropriately their lives and their capacities for autonomous agency.[37]

Proponents of the sovereignty principle disagree as to whether options to enter into self-binding contracts of this kind and/or options to engage in autonomy-undermining actions should be protected by the principle. Mill was clear on the matter. "The principle of freedom cannot require that [a person] should be free not to be free. It is not freedom to be allowed to alienate his freedom."[38] We can add to this a corollary. It is not freedom to be allowed to act in ways that destroy or seriously damage one's capacities to engage in future free action. The issue here is not one about the meaning of the word "freedom." It is rather an issue about how to understand the content of the sovereignty principle, and Mill is suggesting that the justification for that principle provides an answer.

> The reason for not interfering, unless for the sake of others, with a person's voluntary acts is consideration for his liberty . . .. But by selling himself for a slave, he abdicates his liberty; and he foregoes any future use of it beyond that single act. He therefore defeats, in his own case, the very purpose which is the justification of allowing him to dispose of himself.[39]

Mill is assuming that the value of having sovereign control over one's life is grounded in the interest that one has in living a free or autonomous life. The nature of the sovereign control that matters is shaped by that interest. On this understanding, the sovereignty principle reflects our interest in living an autonomous life.

Not every proponent of the sovereignty principle has agreed with Mill on this fundamental point. Feinberg distinguishes an "autonomous life" from an "autonomously chosen life."[40] A life lived as a slave to another cannot be an

---

[37] Sometimes we act rightly, or at least not wrongly, in exposing ourselves to high risks of death and/or damage to our capacities, for we can have good reasons to do so. We volunteer to fight in a just war, for example; or we participate in athletic events that present risks of serious harm to us. By doing so, we do not fail to value our lives and our capacities appropriately. Thus, the distinction between, say, a free solo rock climber who pursues excellence in their achievements and a drug abuser is not to be explained solely, or even principally, in terms of the risks assumed, but by the value of the activities taken to justify the risks. We fail to value our lives and capacities appropriately when we knowingly risk to a high degree damage to them for ends that have little or no value.

[38] Mill, *On Liberty*, p. 300.

[39] Ibid., p. 299.

[40] Feinberg, *Harm to Self*, p. 78.

autonomous life, but it can be a life that is autonomously chosen. And, for
Feinberg, it is our right to dispose of our own lot in life, which the sovereignty
principle most fundamentally secures. Feinberg thus concludes that if one does
not have the freedom not to be free, then one does not enjoy sovereign control
over one's life.[41]

Our conclusions for now must be modest. In this section we have sought to clarify
a problem internal to the sovereignty principle. This problem concerns the temporal
dimension of sovereign control in a temporally extended life. To resolve the problem, it is necessary to appeal to the values that underlie sovereign control. On one
understanding championed by Mill and others, sovereign control is valuable
because it is grounded in our interest in leading an autonomous life. On this
understanding, a certain kind of paternalism – autonomy-protecting paternalism –
is consistent with the sovereignty principle. Thus, on this understanding, we can
explain and justify certain qualifications to the Volenti Maxim; namely, those that
concern our interest – our temporally extended interest – in leading an autonomous
life. By contrast, on an alternative understanding, sovereign control is not grounded
in our interests in living an autonomous life but rather in our basic right to
determine our lot in life, a right that includes the right to alienate our freedom or
permanently destroy our capacities for free action in the future.

To make progress on this issue, we must dig deeper. We need to think about how
we might try to show that one of the rival understandings of the sovereignty
principle is superior to the other. On all its formulations, the sovereignty principle
directs us to respect the will of sovereign persons. It is to this demand of respect that
we now turn.

4.6 SOVEREIGNTY AND SELF-RESPECT

The possibility of voluntary slavery highlights one way to think about a person's
relationship to their body and to their future self. This is the relationship of
ownership. A sovereign person, it can be said, owns their body; and, because of
this fact, they have a right to dispose of it at will. There are limits. If a person has
incurred duties to others, then they do not have the right to dispose of their body in
ways that prevent them from discharging those duties. For example, a parent has
no right to kill themself if they have brought a child into the world and if they must
stay alive to discharge their duties of care to the child. Be this as it may, the main
point stands. On the assumption that no such duties are in effect, then a person, on
the view we are considering, has a sovereign right to dispose of their body at will in
virtue of the fact that they own it.

This idea is open to an immediate objection. Sovereign control over ourselves
cannot be ownership control. We have ownership rights to use and dispose of the

[41] Ibid., p. 77.

things that we own. But things, as opposed to persons, do not demand respect from us. This matters. For we cannot unqualifiedly own that to which we owe respect.[42]

This is a very compressed statement of the objection. It will be helpful to spell it out a little more fully. We can own things to which we owe respect. For example, we can own an artistic masterpiece, such as Picasso's *Les Demoiselles d'Avignon*, even though we have duties to respect it in the sense that we have duties to not destroy it and to preserve it. Relatedly, we can own nonhuman animals, even though we owe them duties of respect, such as the duty not to subject them to gratuitous suffering. These claims are consistent with the objection. For ownership is best thought of not as one undifferentiated right but as a bundle of rights.[43] The bundle of rights includes, *inter alia*, rights to use, sell, rent and dispose of the property in question. Full ownership includes all the rights in the bundle, but less than full ownership of a thing is possible, and actually quite common. Ownership rights, we can now say, are constrained or limited by duties of respect. One can have no ownership right to dispose of a thing at will that one has a duty to respect.

Persons, and their bodies, are owed respect. That is why they cannot be sold and treated as mere things. But, if so, then not only must others treat me and my body with respect but I must do so as well. These self-regarding duties are duties of self-respect, and their recognition is inconsistent with the self-ownership understanding of the sovereignty principle.

The respect argument that we have been describing supports and complements the argument for autonomy-protecting paternalism mentioned earlier. That argument supported restrictions on sovereign choices that alienate our rights to govern ourselves or destroy our capacities to do so. These sovereign choices frustrate the agency interests that, on the argument, ground the principle of sovereignty itself. The present argument appeals not to our interest in exercising our agency but to the demands of respect that the capacities for that agency place on others and ourselves. As such, it potentially supports a range of restrictions on our self-regarding conduct that extends beyond that covered by autonomy-protecting paternalism. For example, some have argued that the wrong involved in rape is partly explained by the "sheer use" of a person that is essential to the act of rape.[44] This sheer use disrespects the victim, and it would remain wrong even if the victim consented to it.[45] To press this argument, one need not think that consenting to sheer use by another must damage

---

[42] The objection is suggested by Kant. See Kant, *Lectures on Ethics*, p. 165. And see the critical discussion of this passage in Cohen, *Self-Ownership, Freedom and Equality*, pp. 211–213.

[43] The notion that ownership is best understood in terms of a bundle of rights has become a familiar one in the legal and philosophical literature on property rights. See Honore, "Ownership," in *Oxford Essays in Jurisprudence*, ed. Guest (Oxford: Oxford University Press, 1961).

[44] Gardner and Shute, "The Wrongness of Rape," in *Offences and Defences* (Oxford: Oxford University Press, 2007), pp. 1–32.

[45] The argument is controversial, since some will think that consent makes all the difference here. Consent makes treatment that would otherwise constitute sheer use into that which does not constitute sheer use. See Tadros, *Wrongs and Crimes*, p. 221.

one's capacities for autonomous self-direction. If such treatment is wrong, and if consent to it does not make it cease to be wrong, then the qualifications to the Volenti Maxim extend beyond those that protect the capacities for autonomous agency.

The self-respect argument can be challenged in the following way. Persons are owed respect in virtue of their capacity to freely and rationally control their lives. We respect them by respecting the exercise of their free and rational consent. No restrictions on the content of what they can consent to can be generated by considerations of self-respect, for the respect in question just is the respect owed to one in virtue of one's capacity to consent.

The issue in dispute concerns how to understand the value of the capacity in question. On the assumption that the capacity to consent is valuable, it plausibly supports duties to refrain from damaging it and to preserve it as well as duties to respect its exercise. The unstable position is to hold that we have duties to respect the exercise of a capacity but no duties whatsoever to preserve it. One possibility is that the duties to respect the exercise of the capacity block interference from others, even when such interference is necessary to prevent people from destroying it themselves. On this possibility, the self-regarding duties of self-respect, while genuine and important, are not enforceable duties.

This, I believe, is the best line for critics of the self-respect argument to adopt. But for it to go through in a way that blocks the enforcement, legal or otherwise, of all self-regarding duties of self-respect, then the duty to respect the exercise of the capacity to consent must be an absolute one. This, on reflection, is hard to accept. Consider a colorful example from Richard Arneson.

> Tom is unreasonably distressed at some disappointment he has suffered. Perhaps he has been bested in competition for a job he coveted. Perhaps his romantic partner has called it quits. Perhaps a particularly charming rabbit he saw at the Humane Society pet adoption center and hoped to choose and make his pet was adopted first by another person. Whatever the cause of his distress, he is unhappy, feels vaguely cheated by the world at large, and wants at the moment nothing more than to express his disappointment by committing suicide. He is not deceived, is aware that if he lives, he will come to forget his disappointment and go on with his life, but right now he has no interest in doing that. He wants above all to die. He is not mentally ill or incompetent, he just has unusual – and unusually self-indulgent and immature – preferences.[46]

Tom's decision is wrong. It violates his self-regarding duty to preserve his life and his rational capacities. Now consider the situation of a bystander – call him Marcos – who is in a position to interfere and prevent Tom from carrying out his suicide. Marcos may have a duty to respect the exercise of Tom's capacity to decide how to live (and end) his life, but this duty is plausibly overridden by the gravity of what is at stake. Marcos is, at least, permitted to interfere to save Tom's life, whether or not Marcos also has a duty to do so.

---

[46] Arneson, "Joel Feinberg and the Justification of Hard Paternalism," pp. 278–279.

It would be wrong for the state to penalize or punish Marcos for intervening to save Tom's life. The duty to respect the self-regarding choices of others is not absolute. Now consider a variant on the example. Suppose Tom enlists Marcos's help in his efforts to end his own life. If Marcos assists in his suicide, then he plausibly acts wrongly. The fact that Tom consented to his assistance does not change the fact that Marcos acts wrongly in assisting him. Whether the law should criminalize assisted suicide in cases like this one is a further question. Many legal systems do. And, if assisting suicide is wrong (not necessarily in all cases, but in cases like Tom's), then there is at least a presumptive case for its criminalization.

Reflection on this example suggests that a similar response is available concerning Kristol's gladiators. Mutual consent to participate in this practice would fail to render it immune to interference by others. The stringency of the duty to refrain from interfering with the exercise of our capacity to consent is not great enough to make interference with mutually consensual activities that harm no one else always impermissible. Some might try to seize on the "harm no one else" clause in this formulation to argue that permitting suicides by young, healthy adults and allowing fight-to-the-death sports would, in actuality, harm all of us. It would do so by contributing to a culture that does not appropriately value human life. Feinberg in his discussion of Kristol's example expressed this concern, claiming that "it is widely improbable that hundreds and thousands of spectators could come to be so bloodthirsty without constituting a threat to at least *some* of the rest of us."[47]

What to make of this purported indirectly harm-causing effect? The best explanation for why the practice of fight-to-the-death contests would be dangerous in this way is that the practice itself is wrongful. If the participants valued their lives and their capacities appropriately, they would not engage in the practice. The disrespectful attitudes that are encouraged by the practice are a function of the disrespect that the participants show toward one another and toward themselves, as well as the celebration of that disrespectful treatment evinced by willing spectators. The indirect harm-causing effect of the practice is a supplementary, not a stand alone, consideration for interfering with it.

Even if the sovereignty principle were limited by considerations of self-respect in the way suggested here, it might still ground significant protected liberties to engage in wrongful behavior. It might support various rights to do wrong. We will revisit this issue in Chapter 8. But the time has come now to turn to the positive case for enforcing morality, one that moves away from the sovereign rights of individuals and looks toward the common good of the societies in which they live and cooperate with others.

---

[47] Feinberg, *Harm to Self*, p. 133.

PART II

Critical Legal Moralism

Critical legal moralism, unlike Devlin-style social legal moralism, holds that it is a proper function of law, including criminal law, to enforce and support sound morality (in the broad sense) as opposed to morality that may or may not be sound but is widely accepted in the society. In partial support of critical legal moralism, the chapters in this part defend the practice of ethical environmentalism. A social environment provides its members with options for choice, patterns of living and examples of how people ought to live and ought not to live, as well as practices that constitute and sustain these options, patterns and examples. Such an environment also includes public discussions and semipublic discussions about how to live, including celebrations, exhortations, condemnations and warnings about the opportunities that are available within it. The practice of ethical environmentalism is the deliberate effort to improve the ethical character of the social environment by political, legal and other means.

The presumptive case for ethical environmentalism, and its connection to the common good of a society, is set out in Chapters 5 and 6. Chapter 7 discusses the value of personal liberty and confronts the objection that ethical environmentalism is insufficiently sensitive to the goods of personal liberty. Chapter 8 next considers the rights of citizens to do wrongful things, and explains how such rights affect the structure of ethical environmentalism.

A particularly challenging issue for ethical environmentalism, one that implicates both the good of personal liberty and the rights of citizens to do wrong, concerns the nature and value of free expression. Chapter 9 discusses the possibility of a right to free expression, distinguishing its justifying grounds from the institutional arrangements that purport to secure it. This chapter also discusses the contribution that a robust regime of free expression can make to the practice of ethical environmentalism. Chapter 10 concludes the discussion by turning from principles and general moral factors to an examination of pragmatic considerations that call for a healthy dose of caution and restraint in enforcing morality either through law or by other means.

5

Ethical Environmentalism I

Legal systems – the laws and directives they contain and the measures that legal officials enforce – substantially impact the social and cultural environment of those who are subject to them. There is no getting around the fact that we live in a social and cultural environment and there is no denying the fact that the laws of our society deeply affect its character. Still, from the fact that law impacts the environment of those who are subject to it, it does not follow that legal officials ought to, or permissibly can, attempt to improve its ethical character. The purpose of this chapter is to present a presumptive case for why legal officials are not only permitted but also have a duty to do so. The nature of this duty will be clarified in this chapter and Chapter 6, and the limits of this duty will be discussed in Chapters 7 to 9.

5.1 THE IDEA OF AN ETHICAL ENVIRONMENT

Ethical environmentalism, as understood in this book, refers to a political project. The sense in which it is a political project will be explained shortly. But to understand this project, we need first to clarify the idea of an ethical environment. The general notion of an environment is perhaps well enough understood. We readily distinguish ourselves from the world that surrounds us. Our surroundings include ubiquitous features of the natural world, such as oxygen or light, as well as aspects of the social world that are culturally distinctive, such as the architecture of the town in which we live. But it is not immediately clear what is meant by the term "ethical environment." This is a term of art, but how is it best understood for the purposes of our inquiry?

An ethical environment consists of features or properties of our surroundings that have moral significance. A bit more precisely, an ethical environment includes options for choice, patterns of living and examples of how people ought to live and ought not to live, as well as social practices that constitute and sustain these options, patterns and examples. Such an environment also includes public discussions and semipublic discussions about how to live, including celebrations, exhortations, condemnations and warnings about the opportunities that are available within it.

Naturally, no one can escape the influence of this kind of environment, and we all have an interest in its shape.

Thus understood, the adjective "ethical" covers a lot of ground, and so it will be helpful to distinguish subdivisions within it. Recall from Chapter 1 the distinction between a narrow and a broad understanding of morality. On the narrow understanding, morality concerns our duties to others, what we owe them and what they owe us. The broad understanding of morality encompasses the narrow understanding but also includes ethics ("the art of living well," to use Mill's apt phrase) and whatever duties we have to respect impersonal goods. In this chapter we will be concerned mainly with narrow morality and ethics. (When we use the term "moral," we will have narrow morality in mind.) We will discuss impersonal goods only insofar as they are integrated with ethical and moral concerns.

Ethics concerns the project of living well, which may include, but is not the same as, the project of living rightly or morally. One lives rightly if one shows appropriate concern and respect for other persons, and possibly other sentient creatures. One can live rightly while failing to live well. One may make a mess of one's own life, even if one faultlessly responds to the claims of others. Can one also live well while failing to live rightly? Some have thought not. They have held that that no one can succeed in living well if they do not live rightly. This imposing thought is a substantive claim. Its assessment is made easier by distinguishing conceptually the ethical from the moral.

The distinction between the ethical and the moral, on this way of contrasting them, is sometimes expressed metaphorically. Here, for example, is a metaphor from Ronald Dworkin: "Morality, broadly understood, defines the lanes that separate swimmers. It stipulates when one must cross lanes to help and what constitutes forbidden lane-crossing harm. Ethics governs how one must swim in one's own lane to have swum well."[1] On this metaphor, the lanes that separate the swimmers are part of the ethical environment, broadly understood; but in speaking of the ethical environment we might want to hold the lanes fixed and focus specifically on the range of influences that affect whether the swimmers swim well or poorly within their lanes.

The swimming metaphor is helpful, but it can also mislead. To some it may suggest that ethics is independent from, and hence has no bearing on the content of, morality. On this view, in thinking about our duties not to harm others and our duties to aid them, we do not need to engage with ethical questions at all. This was not Dworkin's view. Ethics and morality, he insisted, are interlocking parts of a complex whole. We cannot know the content of either without thinking hard about the content of each.[2] On this integrated picture of the relation between ethics and morality, we can still view morality as defining the swimming lanes and ethics as defining the standards of swimming well within those lanes, but we will not think that we can do a good job of defining the lanes while taking no stand on what it means to swim well.

---

[1] Dworkin, *Justice for Hedgehogs*, p. 371.
[2] Dworkin, *Sovereign Virtue*, pp. 278–279.

The integrated picture supports the broad understanding of the idea of an ethical environment with which our discussion began. We may start only with an interest in morality, but eventually we will be led to consider the demands of ethics, and vice versa. The narrow understanding of an ethical environment will lead us naturally to consider the totality of social practices and influences, ethical as well as moral, that make up our surroundings.

To be sure, the integrated picture of ethics and morality can be challenged. I invoked it in order to dispel a possibly misleading interpretation of the swimming metaphor that illustrates the distinction between ethics and morality. One can accept the metaphor while rejecting the interpretation. In the next chapter, I will present an argument for accepting the integrated picture. For now, it can be left as a suggestive proposal, but one whose implications we will be exploring.

The swimming metaphor connotes a couple of further important ideas that are worth marking. First, whether a person swims well in their lane is not a simple matter of how they prefer or desire to swim. To swim well requires skill. To acquire this skill, one must not only practice swimming in the right way, thereby acquiring good habits, but also understand to some degree the art of swimming. By analogy, living well or flourishing requires some degree of understanding of what is worth doing and what should be avoided, as well as habits to engage in worthwhile pursuits and avoid worthless ones. Knowledge and good character are necessary to live well, in short. To be sure, the analogy on this point is controversial. While everyone can agree that swimming well is an objective matter, many reject the thought that living well is similarly objective. A life high in well-being, they contend, is a function of how well one's life conforms to what one desires or cares about.[3] A second idea the swimming metaphor connotes is a certain measure of unique determinateness. There is not a plurality of different and conflicting ways of swimming well.[4] Some techniques may be better for some swimmers than for others, given their body size and type; but, generally speaking, to swim well one must master some common techniques of swimming. If the analogy were to hold, then living well or flourishing would require successful engagement with a common set of valuable patterns of pursuits. But here the analogy surely breaks down. Living well admits of a much wider variety of pursuits than the swimming metaphor suggests. On a deep form of pluralism about the good life, there are different and incompatible ways of living that can be equally (or incommensurably) good.[5]

Our discussion of ethical environmentalism assumes the first connotation – objectivity about living well – and rejects the second – determinate uniqueness. An adequate defense of objectivity about human well-being is not possible here, but the integration picture of ethics and morality provides some support for it, for it is

---

[3]   For a skillful articulation of this subjective view of living well, see Frankfurt, *The Reasons of Love*.

[4]   In competitive swimming there are, of course, different strokes, such as backstroke or the butterfly, that come with their own relatively unique determinate styles of swimming well.

[5]   See Raz, *The Morality of Freedom*, especially chapter 13.

much less plausible to think that morality, as opposed to flourishing or well-being, is a matter of preference-satisfaction. If living well requires attending to how one treats others, then living well is not plausibly a simple matter of living in line with what one cares about. The rejection of determinate uniqueness, in turn, allows us to explain the plausible thought that there is not a single way, or small number of ways, to live well or flourish that is suitable for all people without abandoning the commitment to objectivity. This embrace of pluralism, moreover, is innocent in the present context. For if pluralism about the good life were false, then the project of ethical environmentalism – for reasons to be explained later – would be easier to vindicate.

Leaving the swimming metaphor behind, we can now ask: does an ethical environment include more than that encompassed by the value-based domains of ethics and morality? Some things in our surroundings may have value, even if they are not valuable to us. Objects that are *purely impersonally valuable*, if any such objects exist, would have value even if no persons existed. Some people think that this is true of non-sentient ecosystems, for example. Other objects may be impersonally valuable in an impure way. They contribute to the flourishing of human beings but their value is not exhausted by this contribution. G. E. Moore's characterization of the value of works of art fits this description. For him, the primary value of beautiful works of art is that they can be contemplated and experienced by human beings, but they might have some residual value in the absence of all human beings (and other creatures capable of appreciating them). If so, their value would be a function of both their contribution to good human lives as objects that can be contemplated and appreciated and their intrinsic value that is independent of this contribution.[6]

Our interest in characterizing the idea of an ethical environment is in picking out features or properties of an environment that have moral significance. In the broad sense of the moral, impersonal value, if it exists, clearly qualifies. We have reason to preserve and create objects within our environment that have this value. These objects can be usefully divided into two categories – objects of natural beauty or wonder and objects of perfectionist achievement. A good society, it may be thought, is, among other things, one that preserves and respects natural beauty and creates works of perfectionist achievement, which are then preserved and respected.

Ethical environmentalism, I said earlier, is a project. It is not a personal project but a project that the members of a society must pursue collectively, one that is grounded in the deep and substantial interest that they all have in the character of their ethical environment. Put differently, the proponent of ethical environmentalism claims that we have reasons to care about the quality of our ethical environment, and that these reasons bear on the justification of efforts, including legal efforts, to improve it. With

---

[6] Moore, *Principia Ethica*, pp. 237–238. Moore appears to have been in two minds on the question of whether beautiful objects, in fact, had value independently of their contribution to aesthetic experience. Compare the discussion in *Principia Ethica* with that in *Ethics*. See also Baldwin's discussion of this issue in his introduction to the Cambridge edition of *Principia Ethica*.

this in mind, it might be argued that impersonal value, while relevant to the description of an ethical environment, is not relevant to the project of ethical environmentalism. Concern for objects of impersonal value could not provide reasons to alter the legal rights and obligations of citizens, for example. For this reason, in the present context, it is a distraction. We would do better to work with a pared-down characterization of an ethical environment. But, once again, it may be replied that the domain of the ethical is integrated in a way that frustrates this response. Judgments of ethics and of morality may implicate judgments of impersonal value. As an illustration, consider an example from T. M. Scanlon.

> [P]art of what it means to say that the Grand Canyon is of value is that visiting and enjoying it is worthwhile. From the point of view of those who might engage in these activities in the future, then, there is reason to reject a principle that would allow someone to decide to flood the Grand Canyon without taking these benefits into account. These reasons for rejecting a principle are ... personal reasons, but their force as reasons depends in part on further judgments of impersonal value, namely the judgment that these objects are worth seeing and should be admired.[7]

Personal reasons, as Scanlon characterizes them, concern the well-being, claims or status of individual people. For him, they are the basic currency of the interpersonal morality of right and wrong.[8] But these reasons are not always insulated from impersonal reasons, which are reasons to respond appropriately to objects of impersonal value. In some contexts, such as in the example just quoted, to gauge the force of the personal reasons in play we must attend to the (purported) impersonally valuable properties of the environment in which the interaction takes place. If Scanlon is right, then the integrated picture of the ethical domain mentioned here encompasses impersonal value as well as ethics and morality.

Ethical environmentalism can look vacuous. Does anyone seriously deny that the law should be concerned in some way with the character of a society's social environment? Acceptance of the integration thesis – roughly, the claim that the ethical, the moral and the impersonally valuable interlock in ways that make an exclusive focus on one without attending to the others inapt – makes the project of ethical environmentalism much more contentious. For, given the thesis, if you care about morality and the contribution that the environment of your society makes to its recognition and realization in your society, then you must engage with the full range of considerations that affect the ethical character of the environment that is the object of your concern.

The political and legal implications of accepting the integration thesis, however, are not straightforward and by no means obvious. Engagement with ethics and

---

[7] Scanlon, *What We Owe to Each Other*, p. 220.
[8] This is not quite right, since Scanlon's contractualist account of morality centers on "generic reasons," which are approximations of the relevant personal reasons based on "commonly available information about what people have reason to want" (ibid., p. 204).

impersonal value may reveal distinctive limits to their direct promotion. Dworkin himself claims that "it is implausible to think that someone can lead a better life against the grain of his most profound ethical convictions than at peace with them," and he argues that this claim, which is itself an ethical claim, shows that much that falls under the rubric of legal paternalism is self-defeating.[9] We will consider Dworkin's argument on this issue more carefully, and critically, in Chapter 7. But, for now, it is important to appreciate the larger point that it illustrates. Ethical considerations concerning human flourishing or well-being can themselves ground significant limits on measures that are designed to improve the character of the ethical environment – measures that might well be justified absent these considerations. In a similar vein, Scanlon claims that "impersonal values do not provide, in themselves, reason for rejecting principles of right and wrong."[10] He thinks this because he holds that the principles of right and wrong are concerned with the claims people can make on one another. By destroying an object of beauty, one may wrong no individual, and so the principles of right and wrong do not apply. Accordingly, in some contexts, an appeal to impersonal values will not be able to justify various kinds of interference in people's lives that are deemed necessary to protect them. Whether or not Scanlon is right about this particular judgment, the broader point holds. Attention to the structure of moral justification can reveal limits to measures designed to improve the ethical character of the environment along the dimension of impersonal value.

5.2 THE COMMON GOOD

The ethical environment of a society, I have been claiming, is constituted by a range of different, albeit interlocking, broadly moral features or properties. These properties are common properties of the society. They help to constitute its shared social world. This world is shared in the sense that it affects all, or nearly all, its members.[11]

The political project of ethical environmentalism centers on the common good of a society. It follows from two broad claims. First, in virtue of the fact that the ethical environment of a society deeply and substantially affects the interests of all, or nearly all, of its members, it is an integral part of the common good of their society. And, second, since it is an integral part of the common good of the society, the law of that society has a proper role to play in regulating its character. Plainly, for these two claims to be credible, the notion of the common good that is advanced in them must be defensible.

[9] Dworkin, *Sovereign Virtue*, p. 217. (Dworkin is here rejecting what he terms "critical paternalism," which is distinguished from "volitional paternalism.")
[10] Scanlon, *What We Owe to Each Other*, p. 222.
[11] For a helpful discussion of the collective properties of a society that informs some of what I am saying here, see Christiano, *The Rule of the Many*, pp. 59–62.

How then to understand the complex, and often slippery, notion of the common good, especially for a large modern society? The common good can be understood in terms of the common properties of a society. Not all of these properties are ethically significant, to be sure. The average annual rainfall that occurs in a city is a common property of the city, but it is not aptly characterized as an ethically significant property of the city. Still, it is part of the shared world of the city in the sense that if it affects one member of the city, it affects them all. Now contrast this property with a property of the city's environment that is not common. The interior design of a privately owned home is an important part of the environment of the home, but its character only affects the inhabitants of, and to a much lesser degree visitors to, the home.

These examples suggest several further points. First, some common properties of a society are alterable by deliberate human intervention and others are not. We can decide to change the interior design of our home but the residents of a city cannot, at least given current technology, intervene to change its annual level of rainfall. Second, the sense in which a property is common is always indexed to a group. The interior design of a home is a common property with respect to the inhabitants of the home, but not with respect to the members of the society who never visit the home. Our concern here is with the ethical environment of a society, but one could also speak of the ethical environment of the members of a city within the society, or even the ethical environment of the inhabitants of a home within the city. Third, the common properties that we are interested in here, for the most part, are territorially bounded. They are the common properties of a geographical space. We can speak also of the shared social world of people who are territorially dispersed. The digital age has made it possible for people from all corners of the world to share experiences and, in a sense, occupy a common social world. It will be useful for certain purposes to distinguish these virtual environments from physical environments and to discuss their common properties. However, in discussing the common good in this chapter, the primary focus will be on the common properties of territorially bounded social worlds.

Ethical environmentalism is a justificatory project that encompasses social as well as political action. But let us begin with a narrower concern. How should we use the law to improve, or attempt to improve, the ethical character of the environments of the societies in which we live? This narrowing of focus fixes the boundaries of the ethical environments that are relevant to the project of ethical environmentalism. Roughly, legal systems claim jurisdiction over people in defined territories, and legal efforts to alter the ethical environment concern the territories associated with these jurisdictional claims.[12] The relationship between legal jurisdictions and territories can be complex. For example, in federal systems, such as the United States, states have considerable independence to regulate the law in their respective territories, even as

---

[12] I do not mean to deny that legal systems ever claim jurisdiction over people who reside outside their territories, as when the tax law of the United States applies to Americans who live and work abroad. The point here is only that legal systems principally claim a right to rule over those who reside within a defined territory.

they remain subject to the legal jurisdiction of the national government. Further, within individual states different localities have legal leeway to shape their own ethical environments. The legal project of ethical environmentalism can be pursued at all of these levels. The local environments remain part of the wider environment, and their character is conditioned by it, but they retain a measure of independence from it.

The ethical environment of a society, where a society is identified with the territory over which the highest level of government claims jurisdiction, encompasses all the local ethical environments contained within it. The common properties of this societal environment include properties that reflect the diversity or uniformity of its parts. For example, the ethical environment of a society that prohibits gambling throughout its territory will differ from the ethical environment of a society that prohibits it in some places but not others.

Since the ethical environment of a society affects the interests of all its members, everyone in the society has an interest in its character. But in saying this we now bring into view some complications that infect the idea of the common good of a society. Let p be a common property of a society. Let it also be an ethically significant property, one that helps to constitute the ethical environment of the society. From this it follows that p affects the interests of all the members of the society. But it certainly does not follow from this that it must affect the interests of each member in the same way or to the same degree. Indeed, for all that has been said, the obtaining of p could be good for some members of the society and bad for others. And if p is good for some and bad for others, then how could its obtaining be part of the *common good* of the society?

This is where talk of the common good tends to get slippery. It is often invoked to cover up the fact that tradeoffs need to be made between the interests of different people. The common good of a society, it might be said, is a function not of all of its common properties, or even all of its ethically significant common properties, but rather (only) the subset of those common properties that further the ends or interests of all of its members in some respect (and not necessarily on balance). Peace, or the absence of war, is perhaps one such common property. Every member of a society has an interest in peace, since its absence will set back their concerns. That, at any rate, is the claim; but even if it were true, it would not establish that peace is anything more than a convergent good of the members of the society. Jack has a reason to value peace, and Jill has a reason to value peace, but Jack's reason to value peace may have nothing to do with what is good for Jill and vice versa. A plausible account of the common good presumably should identify properties of the society that are good for its members in a more substantial way than is instantiated by this convergent approach. It should account for the commonness of the common good.[13]

---

[13]   See Murphy, *Natural Law in Jurisprudence and Politics*, p. 62. Note, however, that one could hold that it is for the common good of a society that its institutions and policies be justified to each member, and that convergent goods (like peace) can figure in the requisite justification. Here the property of being justified to all members – call it J – would be a common-good property of the society in a substantial sense, even though the goods that make J possible need not be. Likewise, the interest of each in being

Consider another complication. People not only have ends and interests. They also have conceptions of (or ideas about) what ends are worth adopting and what is in their interests. They also often have conceptions of what furthers the ends and interests of others in their society. With this in mind, the common good of a society could be construed in terms of the set of ethically significant common properties of the society that all agree, or would agree on after appropriate reflection, are good or valuable for its members. For example, Jack and Jill might agree on very little about what is good for their society, but they might agree about the importance of peace, acknowledging that it is good for both of them and every other member of their society, and that it should be valued as such. Accordingly, peace, on this common-agreement understanding, would be in the common good of their society.

There is a kernel of truth to this view. Common agreement about important matters can be a fact about a society that contributes to, and hence is a part of, its common good. But the significance of common agreement can be, and often is, overstated. Describing an ideally just society as well ordered, John Rawls writes: "it is a society in which everyone accepts and knows that the others accept the same principles of justice, and the basic social institutions satisfy and are known to satisfy these principles."[14] Is this a good thing? Imagine a society in which there is common acceptance of the same principles of justice and in which the commonly accepted principles effectively regulate its basic social institutions, but the principles are unsound. This would not be a well-ordered society. Rawls's conception of a well-ordered society is one in which not just any, but the correct, principles of justice are commonly accepted. This no doubt is the right view,[15] but it suggests that while common acceptance of principles of justice in a society can contribute to the good of its members, and thereby contribute to the common good of their society, its contribution depends crucially on the views of its members being sound.

Since this point is important, it merits elaboration. In a well-ordered society the members of the society accept the principles of justice that they accept because they think that the principles are sound. As they understand the situation, common acceptance is common recognition of the soundness of the principles. To underscore this point, suppose that everyone in one's society except for oneself accepted the same principles of justice. Would one have grounds for revising one's views on justice so as to make it true that everyone including oneself in one's society accepted the same principles of justice? Surely not. And this suggests that whatever contribution common acceptance of principles of justice makes to the common good of a society depends on the soundness of the principles in question.

---

treated fairly is common in a substantial, and not merely convergent, sense. The fair treatment of each member of a group requires the fair treatment of the others.

[14] Rawls, *A Theory of Justice*, pp. 453–454.

[15] However, this is not to say that Rawls was right about the content of the principles, or even that there is a single correct set of principles of justice, as opposed to a plurality of sets of principles of justice with an equal claim to acceptance.

Justice is not the only ethically significant common property of a society. But the point here plausibly generalizes to the other common ethically significant properties of a society. Common agreement or acceptance of the property in question would contribute to the common good of the society only if it were a genuinely valuable or worthwhile property. Proponents of the common-agreement understanding of the common good need not deny this point. Their view could be stated as follows. A common property of a society is a component of its common good only if it is (i) ethically significant, (ii) good for all of its members, (iii) commonly accepted and (iv) genuinely valuable. This view is coherent, but now we should wonder why (iv) is a required condition. Common acceptance, as I have allowed, may augment the contribution that a genuinely valuable common property makes to the common good of a society, but if common acceptance is not forthcoming, then the property may still be a component of the common good.

We have reviewed and rejected two understandings of the common good. The first appealed to convergent goods; the second relied on common agreement. The view that has emerged holds that a common property of a society is part of its common good only if it is ethically significant, good for all and genuinely valuable. But a common property could be ethically significant, good for all and genuinely valuable but not something that was on balance beneficial to each of its members. A society might redirect resources away from those in dire need in order to construct beautiful buildings. The buildings might enrich the ethical environment of the society, but their construction would not be for the common good. While contributing to the good of some, the buildings would come at the expense of others. Their construction, while good, would not be part of the common good.

The common properties of a society that constitute its common good in addition to being ethically significant and genuinely valuable must contribute to the good of all its members. This, in turn, raises a complication. To say that something benefits a person, or contributes to their good, one must have some idea of the baseline from which this assessment is made. To return to our example, someone might claim that those in desperate need do benefit from the construction of the buildings. This person might point out that these people, in common with others in their society, have a genuine interest in living in a beautiful cultural environment. If the relevant baseline is simply living in a society without the buildings, then the construction of the buildings benefits everyone, including those in dire need. But this would be a misleading characterization of the baseline. For surely what is relevant includes what has been lost as well as what has been gained. Accordingly, the baseline could be characterized in terms that take account of the resources that those in dire need would have had if they had not been redirected for the construction of the buildings. And by reference to this more adequate characterization of the baseline, the construction of the buildings is decidedly not beneficial to those in dire need.

Notwithstanding this point, it can remain true that the construction of the buildings benefits them in one respect, even if it does not benefit them overall.

They too have an interest in living in a beautiful cultural environment. Their complaint is better expressed in terms of fairness. They have been unfairly burdened by the promotion of this common-good benefit. Should we say then that for something to contribute to the common good of a society, it must benefit all, and not be produced or sustained in a way that unfairly burdens some? This more attractive proposal is still too demanding.

Consider the justice of the basic social institutions of a society. All benefit from living under just institutions when compared with the state of nature. But it also seems true, and likely is true, that the transition from an unjust status quo to the establishment of justice can set back the interests of at least some of those favored by the status quo. So, the transition to just institutions would not benefit them. In response, we might try incorporating justice into the baseline by discounting any claim grounded on unjust entitlements. We might say that those who benefit from an unjust arrangement should forgo those benefits, and if they were to do so, then we can say further that their interests would not be set back from the transition to a more just arrangement. The transition from an unjust state of a society to a just state would be for the common good. For if the costs to those who benefit from the injustice were fully discounted, as required on the proposal, then they at least would not be made worse off by the transition. And the victims of injustice would benefit from the transition, since the injustice to them would be removed or ameliorated. The transition, accordingly, would be for the common good of the society.[16]

Is this response plausible? An initial problem with it is that it cannot explain why transitions from less just states to more just states are mutually beneficial. These transitions may bring the society closer to the state in which it is fully just, but there is no guarantee that this will be beneficial for all. Consider this simple example.

State 1 (A:10; B:30; C:50)
State 2 (A:20; B:25; C:45)
State 3 (A:30; B:30; C:30)

A, B and C are equal-number groups of people and the corresponding numbers represent the resource shares that each member of the respective groups enjoys. Assume that State 3 is the fully just state. (Perhaps the resources have fallen from heaven and each person has an equal claim to them.) Although State 2 is not fully just, it is more just than State 1. So, a transition from State 1 to State 2 is a transition that justice favors, but is it a transition that is for the common good? Not on the present proposal; for while the losses to C will be fully discounted relative to the fair baseline, the losses to B will not be. The members of B are worse off relative to both the status quo (State 1) and the fully just state (State 3) in which they receive their fair share.

---

[16] Each member of the society, as I argue later, has an interest in living under just arrangements. If so, then all would benefit from the transition.

We can say to the members of B that they have reasons of justice to accept their lesser share in State 2, since the alternative would require the members of A to accept an even greater sacrifice. But the issue now is whether the transition from State 1 to State 2 benefits or harms the members of B. On the proposal we have been considering, the answer is clear. The transition harms the members of B. Accordingly, if a transition must be beneficial to all, or at least harmful to none to be for the common good, then the transition here, while a transition toward justice, is not for the common good of the society.

The example is very simple, but the point that it illustrates is endemic to political life. Actual societies fall short of justice in all sorts of ways, and proposals to bring them closer to justice often involve tradeoffs between the interests of different groups of people of the sort illustrated by the example. Beyond justice, the members of a society have different and conflicting interests regarding other kinds of common properties that could obtain in the society. Proponents of reasonable or worthwhile conceptions of the good may compete for societal support in various ways. When some win, and others lose, how can it be said that the common good is furthered?

We have claimed that each member of a society has an interest in living under just institutions. Each member of a society has an interest in being treated fairly. Analyzing the common good in terms of the good of the individual members of a society, John Finnis writes: "The collectivity is of individuals, and the good (or well-being) of each individual and of their community, involves, as an intrinsic aspect, that he or she is treated with fairness."[17] The interest in fairness suggests a response to the problem that has been occupying our attention. If each member of a society has an interest in being treated fairly, then the common good of the society requires that each of its members be treated fairly. This follows on the assumption that the fairness in question is comparative. On this view, if Jack and Jill are members of the same society, then Jack is treated fairly by the law of his society only if Jill is treated fairly and vice versa. For if Jack is wrongly favored at Jill's expense, then neither receives fair treatment under the law.[18] But why exactly should we think that fair treatment between people contributes to their good? If one has received an unfairly large share of some good, then one may not benefit if one's excess share is taken away. Establishing fairness is good for the victims of unfairness, but it is not so clearly good for those who lose what they unfairly had.

Still, on the notion of the common good that we are seeking to clarify, it is not a requirement that all benefit on balance. Each member of a society may have an interest in living with others on terms that are fair to all. The interest is grounded in a distinctive type of good, which we can call a *relational good*. Friendship is

---

[17] Finnis, "Human Rights and Their Enforcement," in his *Human Rights and Common Good*, p. 33.
[18] By contrast, on a noncomparative understanding of fairness, Jack is treated fairly if he is given what he deserves in a noncomparative sense. How Jill is treated compared to Jack is not relevant to this assessment. For discussion of comparative and noncomparative desert, see Feinberg, "Noncomparative Justice," *Philosophical Review* 83 (1974): 297–338.

a paradigmatic token example of such a good. Friendship benefits both parties to the friendship, and its existence presupposes that the friends treat, and are disposed to treat, each other in various ways. In like fashion, a society that treats all its members fairly can make possible a less personal, but still valuable, relational good, one that has been variously called "civic friendship" or "a relation of mutual recognition."[19]

The common good of a society, we can now say, includes this relational good. Any society that fails to realize it will fail to realize fully its common good. Accordingly, the transition from a state of a society in which fair treatment among its members is not realized to one where it is realized is a transition that furthers the good of each member of the society. This claim does not establish, however, that the transition in question will be overall beneficial to each member of the society. For, even if it is true that all members of a society have an interest in fair treatment, one that is grounded in their participation in a society-wide relational good, it may not be true, and likely is not true, that this interest always takes precedence over all their other interests.

For this reason, the common good of a society must in practice be an aspirational ideal. One envisions a state of affairs in which the fair treatment of all does not frustrate the good of any member. Transitions that move a society closer to the realization of this aspirational state further its common good, but not because, or in virtue of the fact that, they thereby further the good of each member. We can ask: what constraints, if any, apply to societal efforts to further the common good? Do those who have benefited from unfair arrangements by past practice have claims now to have their established entitlements honored, at least to some degree? And, if so, what would ground or explain these claims? We will not tackle these difficult questions here.[20] We will say instead that transitions that move a society closer to the state of affairs in which all are treated fairly, and which do not violate any applicable constraints, are for the common good of the society.

The understanding of the common good of a society that has emerged from our discussion can now be summarized. The common good consists of a set of common properties that affect all the members of the society. These properties are ethically

---

[19] The terms are taken from Rawls, *Political Liberalism*, p. li and Scanlon, *What We Owe to Each Other*, p. 162, respectively. In using these terms, and in appealing to the relational good of fair treatment between members of a society, we do not need to accept the substantive views of either of these authors. The relational good in question, it may be said, requires more than fair treatment. It requires, in addition, that the members of the society perceive that they are treated fairly. Fair treatment may be beneficial to people because it makes it possible for them to realize the relational good, even if that good is not in actuality realized.

[20] Nor will I present a detailed account of fair treatment. I have been assuming that a transition that made all the members of the society worse off, even if it removed unfairness between them, would not be for the common good. So, either the connection between fair treatment and the common good must be qualified or the notion of fair treatment must be formulated to exclude leveling down. It is also possible that people have an agent-centered prerogative to oppose some transitions that would impose very substantial losses on them, even when these transitions were favored by fairness. (See my "Rooted Reciprocity," *Journal of Moral Philosophy*.) Accounting for such prerogatives would further complicate the relationship between fair treatment and the common good.

significant, genuinely – as opposed to being merely perceived to be – valuable and beneficial, albeit not necessarily on balance, to all members of the society. A transition from one state of society to another can be for the common good of the society if it, without violating any applicable constraints, advances the good of the members of the society overall and brings the society closer to the realization of a state of society in which all members are treated fairly.

In explicating this notion of the common good of a society, I called attention to the very real possibility that the interests of different members of a society can come into conflict, thereby necessitating some kind of fair accommodation of their claims. This holds true even when the potentially conflicting aims are genuinely worth-while. The common good, on this understanding, is not like a perfectly conducted symphony in which each musician contributes to, and complements, the others, thereby producing a harmonious score. Pluralism and conflict between genuine goods rule this out. But while the potential for this kind of conflict must be borne in mind, it also should not be overstated. In myriad ways, the valuable pursuits of others in one's society contribute to one's own good, and one's valuable pursuits contribute to their good. This is true not only for the basic reason that we need to cooperate with others to achieve most of our ends but also because we can enjoy, and participate in, the diverse achievements and accomplishments of others.[21]

5.3 NEUTRALITY AND ITS SCOPE

The evident fact that people in modern societies pursue different goods and have conflicting interests in shaping the ethical environment of their societies lends support to a principle of political morality that has found favor among many recent writers on politics. This principle – we shall refer to it here as the Neutrality Principle – holds that governments should not attempt to favor some conceptions of the good life over others, providing that the conceptions in question are themselves consistent with fairness or justice.[22] The Neutrality Principle imposes a powerful constraint on ethical environmentalism.[23] Roughly, if a proposal to improve the ethical environment of one's society is informed by a controversial understanding of what is valuable in human life or of intrinsic value more generally, then it should not be undertaken, given the Neutrality Principle.

Sometimes the Neutrality Principle is supported by an appeal to fairness. Suppose a society includes Christians and Muslims. Each religious group is of roughly equal size, but the Christians are in the majority and are in a position to get the

---

[21] This point is emphasized by von Humboldt, *The Limits of State Action* and later by Rawls, *A Theory of Justice*, pp. 523–529.

[22] For a variety of perspectives on the Neutrality Principle, see Wall and Klosko, *Perfectionism and Neutrality: Essays in Liberal Theory*.

[23] There are a number of complexities that inform different formulations of the Neutrality Principle and thus affect the content of the constraint. For present purposes, we need not consider these issues.

government to favor their religious practices. It might be unfair for them to do so, as this would likely impose costs on the Muslim citizens and these costs could not be justified by appeal to the common good of the society. The Neutrality Principle supports this conclusion. Consider a second example. Suppose a society includes speakers of two different languages, English and French. The French speakers constitute a significant minority, but the English speakers are in a position to mandate by legal means the use of English in all public forums. Once again, it might be unfair for them to do so. Fairness might require the society to be even-handed in its support of English and French language use. And, once again, the Neutrality Principle supports this conclusion.

The Neutrality Principle, however, is not a direct implication of the notion of fairness that features in the account of the common good that informs ethical environmentalism. In some contexts, the relevant notion of fairness will support the Neutrality Principle, but in other contexts it will not. To see this, note two important features present in both of the examples just presented. First, although this was not made explicit until now, both religions and both languages in the examples are valuable. So, the neutral treatment that is extended between them involves neutral treatment of goods. Second, as described in the examples, the number of adherents between the rival groupings is roughly equal in size, although the Christians and the English speakers are in the majority. Both of these features come into play when one considers how to fairly balance conflicting interests in a manner that is in line with, or furthers, the common good of the societies under consideration. For recall that the common good of a society consists of genuinely valuable common properties, as opposed to common properties that some believe, perhaps mistakenly, to be genuinely valuable. And recall in addition that fair treatment of people requires some accommodation of their conflicting claims, and while the fair accommodation of these claims is not reducible to a simple aggregative calculus, it must be sensitive to the size of the benefits and costs involved, which in turn is a function in part of the relative size of the groups that have conflicting interests. The plausibility of this last claim is perhaps clearest in the language example. If the English speakers were in the overwhelming majority, and the French speakers constituted a small minority dispersed territorially throughout the society, then the case for governmental neutrality between the two languages would collapse.[24]

Bearing these points in mind, we can restrict the scope of the Neutrality Principle. We can say that fair treatment between those with conflicting conceptions of the good life requires neutral treatment when (i) the conflicting conceptions of the good reflect genuine values and (ii) fair aggregation of the interests of the adherents of the

---

[24]   For a sensitive discussion of government support of language, neutrality and fair treatment, see Patton, *Equal Recognition*, especially chapter 6. Patton characterizes the Neutrality Principle in terms of fair treatment. Better, in my judgment, to view fairness as fundamental and neutrality as sometimes supported by it and other times not. Indeed, as Patton's discussion brings out (although he does not express the point in these terms), sometimes neutral treatment would be unfair treatment.

conflicting conceptions does not support non-neutral treatment. This restricted version of the Neutrality Principle is fully consistent with the fundamental aim of ethical environmentalism, which is to improve (or sustain) the ethical value of the common properties of the social environment of the society. More generally, pluralism about the good makes space for a version of governmental neutrality that is grounded in the very concerns that motivate critical legal moralism.

The restricted Neutrality Principle permits the government to favor valuable over worthless conceptions of the good. But conceptions of the good, and the ways of life that they inform, can be valuable to varying degrees. Does the principle permit the government to favor the excellent over the merely good? Yes, but subject to qualification. Each member of the society can permissibly pursue a valuable but not optimally valuable way of life; but also it seems permissible for a society to favor the excellent over the merely good. Public resources can be spent to support art museums over racetracks, for example; and at least part of the justification for doing so appeals to the superior value of art museums. Still, people who are invested in valuable, but not excellent, pursuits have an interest in continuing to engage in them, and this interest must register in the calculus of fair aggregation. How the societal interest in supporting excellence should weigh against these interests must be determined by the context in question. But this much seems plain. The mere fact that part of the justification for government support of some valuable pursuits over others appeals to their superior value does not establish that the government support contravenes the restricted Neutrality Principle.

Much more could be said about the Neutrality Principle in general, and the restricted Neutrality Principle in particular, but the present discussion has had a modest purpose. No defense of the principle has been ventured here. Instead, we have aimed to show how, if the Neutrality Principle is derived from a concern for fair treatment, there is a version of it that is not only consistent with ethical environmentalism but also grounded in the fair accommodation of conflicting valuable interests that lie at its heart.

5.4 LEGAL MORALISM AND CHARACTER

Each society has an ethical environment that is constituted by a set of common properties. The character or shape of this environment is of concern to all who live within it, and so it is an appropriate object of common-good concern. The project of ethical environmentalism is the project of using the law to preserve or bring about valuable aspects of the ethical environment or to eliminate or discourage disvaluable aspects of it. The central claim of this chapter is that this project, when undertaken successfully, can serve the common good of a society and is, for that reason, presumptively justified.

In the previous two sections we have discussed at some length the issue of the fair treatment of individual members of a society and how this is related to the common good of their society. Let us now put the issue of fair treatment aside (we will return to it in Chapter 6) and discuss some legal measures that fall under the project of ethical environmentalism as we have been conceiving of it. To focus our inquiry, it will be helpful to imagine a society that has established a just framework for social cooperation. Each member of the society has a protected set of basic rights and a fair share of resources. The legal arrangements that constitute this just framework are themselves, as we have emphasized, significant components of the ethical environment of the society. What further legal measures, if any, might be pursued under the aegis of ethical environmentalism?

Consider legal moralism. As we noted in Chapter 3, the legal measures that fall under this category are commonly contrasted with those of legal paternalism. On this common understanding, if a law prohibits someone from doing something for that person's own good, then it is paternalistic; but if it prohibits them from doing something on the grounds that it is simply wrong to do it (and not because it is detrimental to either their good or the good of others), then it is moralistic. The distinction here, as we noted in our discussion of Devlin's view, is not as sharp as is commonly supposed. For if we have an interest in having a good character, and if we do something that is immoral, such as participate in an activity that is corrupting – even if not otherwise harmful – to us, then we may thereby harm ourselves in virtue of damaging our character.

Legal measures that are designed either to restrict or discourage behavior that is damaging to a person's moral character can be characterized as moralistic legal paternalism. These measures then can be distinguished from instances of ordinary legal paternalism. With this distinction, one can claim that laws that require motorists to wear seatbelts, to take one example, are paternalistic but not moralistic. By contrast, laws that restrict gambling on the grounds that participation in gambling is a vice would qualify as moralistically paternalistic.

One might wonder about the significance of this distinction. If a legal measure effectively advances the good of those who are its intended beneficiaries, then why is it important to ask whether it does so by advancing our interest in having a good character as opposed to advancing our other interests? Perhaps it is not important. On subjective views of well-being, whether or not something advances or sets back our interests depends on whether it furthers or frustrates our preferences (or idealized preferences). These accounts of well-being, accordingly, do not give us any deep reason to care about marking the difference between the interests served by moralistic paternalism and those of ordinary paternalism. Whether seatbelt restrictions or gambling restrictions are in the interests of those whose liberty is restricted depends on what these people care about. If they care about their physical safety, then the seatbelt restrictions will be for their own good. Likewise, if they care about having a good character, then the gambling restrictions will be for their own good. However, on more objective views of well-being, the difference between the two kinds of paternalism may assume greater importance. Many writers have argued that moral virtue is a central prudential good, a key element of a flourishing life. But many others have claimed that while a person's well-being is a function of the objective goods that they engage with, these prudential goods do not include moral virtue or good character. For these writers, a life can score high in terms of well-being but manifest poor character; and a life can be excellent in terms of the virtue it manifests while scoring low in well-being.

So, on at least some objective views of well-being, the distinction between moralistic legal paternalism and ordinary legal paternalism will be important to mark. For, on these views, moralistic legal paternalism will look a little suspicious from the start. For if a legal measure that helps a person sustain or acquire a good character does not thereby advance the person's well-being, then it is not aptly described as paternalistic. (To be sure, the measure in question might advance the person's well-being indirectly. Perhaps having a good character would enable the person to more effectively participate in the relevant prudential objective goods, but it would not contribute to their well-being directly.)

The options we have been outlining can be refined further. We can distinguish two standpoints for assessing the quality of human lives. The standpoint of well-being assesses the life in terms of its overall well-being. The standpoint of character assesses the life in terms of the virtues and vices it manifests. Whether or not good character contributes directly to the well-being of people, the two standpoints offer different assessments of the quality of the life under consideration. For even if good character is itself a prudential good (on either objective or subjective accounts of well-being), it is not plausibly the only prudential good.

To appreciate the distinction between these two standpoints, it will be helpful to consider an example. Suppose someone enjoys watching films that depict the torture of animals. Deriving enjoyment from viewing these films is vicious. The enjoyment manifests an inapt response to the suffering of sentient creatures. Accordingly, from the standpoint of character, this person's activity would make their life go less well. However, even if it were granted that having a good character is an element of well-being, the enjoyment that this person derives from watching the films might be substantial. Indeed, it might be so substantial that the prudential value from the enjoyment would outweigh the prudential disvalue they would suffer from its effect on their character. If so, then from the standpoint of well-being, the activity, while vicious, would make their life go better overall.

Legal measures designed to discourage people from viewing films of this kind thus could have a moralistic rather than, or in addition to, a paternalistic rationale. On this moralistic rationale, to justify the measures in question one would not need to show that the measures promoted the (overall) interests of anyone. One would need to show only that the measures were effective in dissuading people from damaging their character.

The two standpoints allow us to distinguish moralistic legal paternalism from *legal moralism proper*. The former is justified from the standpoint of well-being, whereas the latter is justified from the standpoint of character. Still, as we will explain more fully in 5.6, legal moralism encompasses more than what can be justified from the standpoint of character. Character-centered legal moralism, as we might describe it, is just a subcategory of the more general class of legal measures that fall under legal moralism.

5.5 PUBLIC AND PRIVATE

Ethical environmentalism, in principle, includes both moralistic legal paternalism and character-centered legal moralism. For a legal measure of either type to contribute to the project of ethical environmentalism, and hence to be justified by it, the measure must effectively sustain or promote the common good of the society, however. For even on a very expansive understanding of the common good, some activities that are character-damaging to the members of the society will be no part of the common world of their society. The purely mental activity of thinking vicious thoughts is an example. Imagine that someone frequently fantasizes about raping children, but never expresses these thoughts to anyone else. The thoughts may be detrimental both to the person's well-being and to their character, but they are no part of the shared world of their society.[25]

Next consider immoral acts conducted in private. Consensual activities between adults can be immoral, even when no rights are violated. Consider prostitution. Even when the sex is genuinely consensual, it is (or at least can be) corrupting to those who participate in it. However, if arranged discreetly, and carried out in private, the activities of the prostitute and their customer are no part of the common world of their society. There may be reasons for the law to prohibit, or interfere with, their activities, but, if so, these reasons are not reasons that are grounded in the interest that the members of the society have in the ethical character of their common world.[26]

There are limits, then, to the legal moralism that can be justified by ethical environmentalism. In this respect, ethical environmentalism presupposes a public/private distinction. The shared public world, and not the private thoughts and activities of individuals, defines its scope. (Mill showed a sensitivity to this point when he drew a distinction between punishing vice, such as gambling or fornication, and punishing those who operate a business that encourages vice, such as a casino or a brothel. The latter activity, but not the former, is opposed to "the public

---

[25] George Sher has argued forcefully that the mere thinking of such thoughts, or any thoughts whatsoever, is never wrong. The purely mental life of the mind, he claims, is a morality-free zone. See *A Wild West of the Mind*. The point here is considerably weaker. Whether wrong or not, non-expressed thoughts are no part of the common good of a society. Regulation or interference with them could not be justified under the project of ethical environmentalism.

[26] Compare with Finnis's claim that whereas the political common good of a society includes concern for "a social environment conducive to virtue," it does not include concern for "the secret and truly consensual acts of adult vice." See his "Limited Government," pp. 91 and 93.

weal" of a society.[27]) Importantly, the examples we have used to illustrate this point do not involve the violation of anyone's rights. No one has a right that others do not entertain evil thoughts. No one has a right that others do not participate with them consensually in the degradation of their character.

Rights-violating conduct is a matter of common concern. This is true whether or not the rights violation occurs in private. One cannot protest that the law should leave one alone in one's home if what one is doing is violating the rights of one's family members. Can this be explained by ethical environmentalism? It need not be. The justification of rights does not depend, at least not exclusively, on common-good considerations. From the fact that a commitment to respecting the rights of all is a key component of the common good of a society one should not infer that a concern for the common good is the ground for the rights.

Yet, once again, matters are more complicated than they first appear. For one thing, as we will explain (in Chapter 9) in discussing the right to free expression, the specification of many rights depends on common-good considerations. But, for a second reason, and one that is more germane to our present purposes, the public, and legally enshrined, commitment to respecting the rights of the members of a society itself requires the law to concern itself with what goes on in private. The same is not true of the kind of legal moralism that is concerned with cultivating good character or discouraging vice.

5.6 LEGAL MORALISM AND STATUS WRONGS

There is more to legal moralism proper than character-centered legal moralism. Private self-regarding acts and consensual activities between adults may harm no one and may violate no one's rights, but they can remain wrongful nonetheless; and their wrongfulness, moreover, may not be captured fully by attending to the consequences that the acts/activities have for the character or well-being of those who participate in them. The conduct may be wrongful in a more direct and inherent way.

Recall the gruesome example from Chapter 3 concerning the German man who engaged in cannibalism with a willing victim. The example put pressure on the Volenti Maxim (the claim that consensual harms are not harms for the purpose of applying the harm principle). In response to the example, we noted that one could appeal to legal paternalism, either soft if the consent in question were suspect or hard if the consent was sufficiently voluntary, to justify criminalization of the conduct in question. This was how Hart tried to explain why the law properly does not recognize consent to murder as a defense. He thus granted the permissibility of legal paternalism and held the line against legal moralism. Yet with some crimes between consenting adults the wrong that is done is not fully, or even aptly, explained in terms of imprudence. The German cannibal certainly set back the interests of his

---

[27]   Mill, *On Liberty*, pp. 97–98.

victim. He killed him. But he arguably did more than that. He treated his victim in a way that failed to honor the victim's status as a moral being.

Talk of an entity's status as a moral being is admittedly a little obscure. We can understand moral status in terms of proper treatment. Shelly Kagan explains: "We can think of each creature as having a normative profile, consisting in the set of features that govern how it is to be treated. Talk of a given being's moral status is a way of referring to the contents of that profile."[28] The thought here is that human beings or persons have features that make it wrong to treat them in certain ways, even if they consent to such treatment. As we saw in Chapter 4, this thought can be invoked to support qualifications to the Volenti Maxim. Here is one substantive proposal along these lines. You fail to treat a person in accord with their moral status, and thereby wrong them, if you act toward them in a way that substantially sets back their interests for no worthwhile end or purpose. Paternalistic legal restrictions can be defended as a consequence of this proposal. By acting in a way that is seriously imprudent, a person may fail to treat themself in accord with their moral status, and by engaging or participating in their self-harming behavior, others may join them in the wrongful treatment of themself.

This substantive proposal turns some forms of imprudence into wrongful treatment (by self or others). But notice that, even on this proposal, wrongful treatment is not just a matter of setting back a person's interests. It is a matter of failing to honor their moral status. To see the significance of this point more clearly, it will be helpful to consider another example. Consider:

> *Dwarf-tossing*: "This is a 'bar sport' in which dwarfs are fitted out with padding and a helmet, and have a handle attached to their backs. The contest is to see who can throw them the farthest."[29]

Imagine now that all the parties involved in this "sport" decide autonomously to participate in it. Imagine further that those who submit to the humiliating treatment of being thrown for sport are compensated well – so well, in fact, that it is in their interests to participate. Could an appeal to their moral status as a person justify a policy that penalizes or discourages this activity?

Perhaps. The proper treatment of people may require not treating them in degrading ways and not assisting them in their own efforts to treat themselves in degrading ways, even when their doing so is in their interests. Legal measures that prohibit or penalize those who participate in activities that degrade themselves or degrade others with their consent, such as activities like dwarf-tossing, would not then be aptly characterized as paternalistic. The measures would be better characterized as instances of legal moralism proper, instances that we now can refer to as *status-centered legal moralism*.

---

[28] Kagan, *How to Count Animals: More or Less*, p. 8.
[29] The example is introduced and discussed by Dworkin in "Harm and the Volenti Principle."

The dwarf-tossing example is a bit recherche, but one does not have to search for long to find more common examples. Feminist critics of violent pornography often claim that its production is not consistent with respecting the moral status of the women who participate in it. Participation in its production, they claim, is dehumanizing and "self-betraying."[30] Even if this view were accepted, it is a further question, of course, whether the law ought to criminalize these activities, or adopt measures to dissuade people from participating in them. But the critics may want to insist only that there is a presumptive case for interfering with these activities. Our point is that the contemplated interference can be defended as a form of status-centered legal moralism.[31]

We have not yet said anything about how legal moralism of this sort relates to the common properties of a society and thus does or does not fall under the rubric of ethical environmentalism. Among the common properties of a society are laws, or their absence, that honor and uphold the moral status of their members. Is there a significant distinction here, as we claimed there is with character-centered legal moralism, between the public and private domains? Presumably not. For status-centered considerations resemble rights-based considerations in this respect. The public, and legally enshrined, commitment to honoring the moral status of the members of a society, which itself is plausibly a part of its common good, requires the law to not be indifferent as to what goes on in private.

---

[30]   Gardner, "The Wrongness of Rape," pp. 19–21.
[31]   Proponents of status-centered legal moralism, accordingly, need not claim that sex workers, or certain classes of such workers (and/or their customers), have false views about what is in their interests. They need only claim that these people have false views about moral status if they deny, which they may not, that they are doing anything wrong.

6

Ethical Environmentalism II

The project of ethical environmentalism, as I have expounded it, encompasses a wide range of legal measures from legal paternalism and moralistic legal paternalism to legal moralism proper. The presumptive case for the project is strengthened considerably by the truth of the integration thesis. Recall that the integration thesis is the claim that the ethical, the moral and the impersonally valuable interlock in ways that make an exclusive focus on one without attending to the others inapt.

In the previous chapter I briefly reviewed some preliminary reasons to accept the integration thesis, but no sustained argument was given for it. This chapter presents a series of arguments that support it. Each argument builds on the integral connection between fairness and the common good of a society. The first argument centers on legal paternalism, but the argument applies to moralistic legal paternalism as well on the plausible assumption that some significant number of the members of a society have an interest in having a good character. The key to the argument is to appreciate that legal paternalism and its absence have distributive consequences.[1] For this reason, legal regimes that either enact or forgo paternalistic measures can be assessed from the standpoint of distributive fairness. The second argument centers on our duties with regard to impersonal goods, encompassing both the goods of the natural world and the goods of human achievement. Here, once again, an issue of fairness is implicated in the enforcement of these duties. The third argument extends the second argument and applies considerations of fairness to the goods of tradition.

6.1 ETHICS AND FAIRNESS

Debates over distributive fairness have loomed large in contemporary political philosophy. Two main issues of contention in these debates need to be addressed before we consider the distributive argument for legal paternalism. The first

---

[1] The argument I present here owes much to Richard Arneson's critical discussion of anti-paternalism in two papers: "Mill, Utility and Fairness" and "Joel Feinberg and the Justification of Hard Paternalism." I develop the argument in fuller detail in my "Egalitarian Justice and the Distributive Argument for Paternalism."

concerns the content of principles of distributive fairness. Do they require equal shares, sufficiently good shares or deserved shares, for example? The second site of contention concerns the nature of the shares in question. Do they consist of money, opportunities, freedoms, resources more generally, welfare or some combination of all of these?

We will not take a stand on the first of these issues. The argument to be presented here should go through on any of the main principles of distributive fairness.[2] We will assume a modest egalitarian principle solely for illustrative purposes. On the second issue we will take a stand, however. We will assume that welfare is a significant part, not necessarily the whole, of the *distribuendum* to which principles of distributive fairness apply.

The significance of welfare to paternalism is straightforward. Legal paternalism is justified, if it is justified at all, because of its effects on the welfare of those who are subject to it. Paternalism comes in different varieties. We have already distinguished soft from hard paternalism. A second divide between types of paternalism is also worth noting. Dworkin distinguishes "critical paternalism" from "volitional paternalism."[3] (As we shall see in Chapter 7, it is only critical paternalism that is problematic on his view.) Critical paternalism is ethically laden. It reflects judgments about the worth or value of various forms of acting that are not accepted by those, or at least some of those, whose liberty is restricted. By contrast, volitional paternalism is not ethically laden in the same way. The liberty it restricts does not run counter to the ethical convictions of those who are its targets. The justification for seatbelt requirements, for instance, does not rest on any controversial judgment about human welfare.

For the purposes of the argument to be presented here, we will work with a paternalistic restriction that is plausibly both hard and critical. Consider a dangerous recreational drug, such as heroin.[4] People can voluntarily choose to consume this drug. Their decision to do so can reflect their genuine will. Laws that criminalize the consumption of heroin, accordingly, involve a measure of hard paternalism. Likewise, some people have a conception of the good life that involves the recreational use of hard drugs. They believe, rightly or wrongly, that the benefits they derive from the drugs outweigh any risks the drugs present to them.[5] Laws that

---

[2] The argument might seem to be inapplicable on entitlement conceptions of distributive justice of the sort championed by Nozick in *Anarchy, State and Utopia*. These conceptions mandate respect for the distributions that result from the free and voluntary choice of individuals using the resources to which they are entitled. Possibly the argument could support, or at least be consistent with, soft legal paternalism on such conceptions, however. Much here would turn on how free or voluntary transfers were understood.

[3] Dworkin, *Sovereign Virtue*, pp. 216–218.

[4] Some have argued that heroin is much less dangerous than commonly supposed. But this is a decidedly minority position. Most pharmacologists and drug experts, especially in light of the recent opioid crisis, believe it to be a very harmful recreational drug. See Wallace-Wells, "Is There a Case for Legalizing Heroin?" *The New Yorker*, April 29, 2021.

[5] The positive case for responsible heroin use is pressed by Hart, *Drug Use for Grown Ups: Chasing Liberty in the Land of Fear*.

criminalize the consumption of recreational drugs, accordingly, involve a measure of critical paternalism.[6]

Critics of legal paternalism will object to laws that criminalize the sale and possession of dangerous drugs such as heroin, especially if, as we have stipulated, these laws involve paternalism that is hard and critical. Invoking Dworkin's metaphor mentioned in Chapter 5, they could say that the law should define the swimming lanes fairly, not tell the swimmers how to swim within their lanes. The distributive argument for legal paternalism challenges this picture. It seeks to show that the fair definition of the swimming lanes requires us to take a stand on how swimmers should swim within their lanes. In short, fairness and ethics are fused.

Some will be surprised by the thought that there is a distributive argument for paternalism. Discussions of distributive justice tend to assume a narrow focus. Attention is fixed on the tax and transfer system; or, a bit more imaginatively, on regimes of property ownership. This narrow focus is understandable, of course. Taxes and property rights play a major role in determining the distribution of wealth, a distribution that indirectly affects the distribution of welfare. But it is important to bear in mind a point that is often not borne in mind by writers on distributive justice. This is the fact that the distribution of welfare in a society is a function not only of the economic resources and power that its members possess but also of the ethical environment in which they live, and the types and range of options that it provides to them.

To be sure, the character of the ethical environment of a society is determined by a bewilderingly large number of factors. Simplifying greatly, we can distinguish the effects of the legal framework on the shape of the ethical environment from the effects of the decisions that people make within this framework. We can assess different possible legal arrangements by considering their framework effects on the ethical environment, asking whether these effects are salutary and asking whether they confer benefits and impose costs on people that, when compared to other eligible alternative frameworks, are fair or just. Such an assessment will be complex, for alterations in the legal framework will have consequences for the decisions that people make within the framework. Proposals with good intentions are ripe for frustration, given the ever-present possibility of counterproductive and unforeseen decision effects. But, for the moment, let us abstract from these practical difficulties. (We will return to them in Chapter 10.) Let us imagine that we know what will happen if different legal frameworks are put in place.

Simplifying even further, imagine we are considering only two frameworks. Framework 1 is a framework that is ideal with respect to anti-paternalist ideology. It is the framework, let us suppose, that sophisticated and informed critics of paternalism would adopt, if given a free hand to do so. Framework 2 is a framework that is ideal

[6] Realistically, the justification of such laws will involve soft as well as hard and volitional as well as critical paternalism. The targets of such laws will differ in terms of the voluntariness of their choices and the extent to which their choices reflect their critical judgments about living well.

with respect to pro-paternalist ideology. It is the framework that sophisticated and informed proponents of paternalism would adopt, if given a free hand to do so. Both frameworks are otherwise identical to each other and both are otherwise ideal with respect to distributive justice (on whatever conception is deemed correct). The distributive argument invites us to assess the two frameworks at the bar of distributive fairness.

Let us imagine, finally, that Framework 2 is the established framework and we are contemplating a switch to Framework 1, as the anti-paternalist writers would urge us to do. The two frameworks almost certainly will have different effects on the decisions that different people make about how to lead their lives, and these decisions, to varying degrees, will have an impact on their welfare. The choice to move from Framework 2 to Framework 1, accordingly, will engender winners and losers. Different people will fare better and worse under the different frameworks.

There is accordingly a question, a *prima facie* question at least, of distributive fairness presented by the choice between the two frameworks. Which framework, we can ask, is favored by considerations of fairness? Utilitarians will urge us to adopt the framework that produces the greater sum of welfare aggregated across persons. If Framework 2 leads to more aggregate welfare than Framework 1, then we should stay put. If it is Framework 1 that yields more aggregate welfare, then we should make the switch, assuming the transition costs are not too great. But egalitarians, and distributive-sensitive theorists of distributive justice more generally, will see that our choice presents an issue of distributive fairness.

Now, possibly, those who would be generally better off under Framework 2 – the pro-paternalism framework – would lose the most from the switch to Framework 1. But this possibility would be unlikely. The reason why is that there is a positive correlation between people's welfare and their skill at making decisions about their own good. Call this the *welfare–prudence link*.[7] If it obtains, then there will be a rough correlation between prudence and welfare, and this will mean that better-off people will, with necessary caveats and qualifications, tend to avoid taking up bad options that are made available to them by their ethical environment. Or, more cautiously, they will tend to do better on this score than those who are less well off and less prudent. For this reason, these people would benefit less from the pro-paternalism framework than those who would be more likely to take up the bad options that the framework effectively forecloses. Consequently, the biggest losers from a shift from Framework 2 to Framework 1 would most likely be those who are less prudent, and hence expectably less well off under both frameworks. The shift to the anti-paternalism framework would thus increase the inequality that obtains between the prudent and imprudent by opening up new opportunities for poor welfare-reducing choice.

---

[7] The welfare–prudence link is best conceived as a tendency claim. See Arneson, "Egalitarian Perspectives on Paternalism."

The welfare–prudence link is coarse-grained. It asserts a general tendency and does not draw distinctions that a more fine-grained analysis would reveal. Prudence or imprudence can be situational. Those who are generally well off and generally make good decisions can make poor decisions with respect to some particular activity. To take an example: advanced skiers, on the whole, are a relatively affluent group. Options to ski on dangerous, off-trial slopes present enticing opportunities for imprudent choice, but the "victims" of such choice are likely well off overall relative to the general population. The distributive argument for paternalism may not apply, or have less force, in this type of context. Its force is most apparent in contexts where the "victims" of imprudent choice tend to be those who are already worse off than others.

The potential benefits from a shift from Framework 2 to Framework 1 would also need to be considered. Might they counterbalance the welfare costs engendered by the shift? Some people think that more liberty is always a benefit for people, even if having the liberty is not on balance beneficial to them. I doubt that that is true. But plausibly, there are considerations of autonomy in play here (this issue will be considered more fully in Chapter 7), and these are more compelling. Paternalistic restrictions, such as the restriction on heroin use that we are now imagining, plausibly set back our autonomy, and hence our welfare, other things equal. To appreciate the thought, consider the situation of two people, let us call them Jack and Jill, who will be affected by the shift to the anti-paternalism framework. Being prudent, Jack will not take up the heroin option, but he may benefit nonetheless from its availability. For in not choosing it, and choosing instead to engage in other options, his choices may be more autonomous than they would have been had he not had access to the heroin option.[8] The autonomy welfare boost is likely to be small for someone like Jack, but if it registers on the scale at all, then Jack will able to point out correctly that his interests are advanced by the shift to the anti-paternalism framework. Furthermore, Jack may be able to press a further complaint. He may know that he can use heroin for recreational purposes in a prudent way. Unlike most people, Jack may be able to use the drug without succumbing to its harmful effects. If so, then Jack will benefit in a more direct way from the shift to the anti-paternalism framework, for the shift will open up an option that gives him enjoyment without self-injury.

Turn now to Jill. Sadly, she is the kind of person who when given access to bad options tends to take them up. Presented with the heroin option, she will likely go for it; and she will likely suffer the kind of welfare-diminishing effects from the use of the drug that most heroin abusers suffer. I trust that we need not dwell on whatever possible benefits Jill may get from the shift to the anti-paternalist framework. These benefits will be swamped by the costs in welfare that Jill will experience as a result of the shift.

Jack and Jill are stand-ins for classes of people. The Jacks in our imagined example can join ranks and press for the shift, pointing to the benefits that they will receive

---

[8] Hurka, "Why Value Autonomy?"

from it. The Jills can join ranks and oppose the shift. (If they are too imprudent to do so, we can press their case for them.) Confronted with this conflict of interests, what does fairness demand that we do?

Now suppose that one is a modest egalitarian. A modest egalitarian, I hereby stipulate, is one who has special concern for those who are least well off.[9] They may have this special concern because they think that distributive fairness requires that all have a sufficient level of welfare and those who are least well off are most at risk of falling below the sufficient level, or they may accept some general principle of distributive justice that always gives priority to those who have less. Whatever the grounds for their special concern, they will think that there is a substantial reason of fairness to favor the Jills in our example over the Jacks. This reason, they will think, militates against moving from the pro-paternalism framework to the anti-paternalism framework.

The distributive argument for legal paternalism, as presented here, is grounded in modest egalitarian concern. This understanding of distributive fairness can be challenged, and I have not argued for it. The appeal to modest equality has been invoked mainly for illustrative purposes. This fact about the grounding of the argument, however, has important implications for how the paternalism it justifies should be viewed.

Someone who endorses modest equality as a requirement of distributive fairness can hold that a state of affairs in which it obtains has impersonal value. This is a value over and above the value the state of affairs has for the individual people in it. To see this vividly, consider a version of distributive fairness that countenances leveling down. This view could favor a legal framework with restrictions on behavior that make both the prudent and the imprudent worse off relative to the eligible alternative. Such a framework might reduce the gap in welfare between the relevant parties, as it reduces the welfare of all parties. In this case it is transparent that the distributive argument for the restrictions would need to be grounded in a concern for impersonal value. A proponent of equality of welfare could hold that while it is not good for any individual that the restrictions are in place, the restrictions contribute to a state of affairs that is nonetheless impersonally good.

A view of distributive fairness that permits or requires leveling down is not an attractive view.[10] And I do not wish to tie the distributive argument to it. Still, the view is instructive. It helps us to see that the force of an objection to a paternalistic restriction can depend on the kind of argument that has been offered in its support. For example, suppose that Jill protests the legal restriction that forecloses her access to heroin. She complains that this restriction treats her, an adult woman, as if she were a child. This complaint has force if the argument for the restriction is grounded in simple beneficent concern for Jill. But the distributive argument for the

---

[9]   Not the absolute priority that Rawls's difference principle requires, but at least some priority or extra weight on the scales.

[10] But see Temkin, "Equality, Priority and the Leveling Down Objection."

restriction, when it comes from the lips of the egalitarian concerned with distributive fairness, need not evince any such concern. (Indeed, in the leveling-down scenario, the argument could not be grounded in such a concern, since the restriction would make her worse off!) Suppose next that Jill tries a different tack. The restriction, she says, expresses an insulting message to her. The restriction expresses the view that she, Jill, cannot make responsible decisions about her life. Once again, the distributive argument for the restriction does not support this charge. For the point of the restriction, on this argument, is to establish a fair distribution of welfare among the affected parties. It really has nothing to do with Jill in particular. To be sure, if everyone were always prudent, there would be no need for the restriction. So, the argument expresses the message that not everyone is always prudent or that people in general are not equally prudent. But these messages are not insulting to Jill. In fact, they are messages that scarcely anyone would be inclined to contradict.

Some familiar objections to paternalism, then, do not get traction if the distributive argument is the argument that is doing the justifying work. The appeal to the impersonal value of a fair distribution of welfare across persons, and not any type of busybody mentality, stands behind the paternalistic restrictions. In addition to impersonal value, the distributive argument for paternalism can also appeal to the fact, if it is a fact, that members of a society have an interest in fair treatment. Fair treatment is good for them in one respect, even if it is bad for them in others. If so, there is a common-good argument for the restrictions. Once again, no disrespectful message need be expressed.

I have been suggesting that the distributive argument can support legal paternalism. The application of the argument to any policy context, however, must be sensitive to possible confounding factors. Jack and Jill represent classes of people, but discriminations within each class almost certainly will need to be made. Heroin restrictions may benefit the imprudent overall but harm those who are most imprudent. The most imprudent in this context would be those who would continue to seek out heroin and successfully obtain it, despite the legal restrictions imposed on its use, thereby exposing themselves to additional risks of harm and risks of punishment/penalty that they would not experience under an anti-paternalism framework. The net effect of the framework shift on their interests may be negative, even if it is positive with respect to the larger class of poor choosers with respect to the drug. The regulatory framework supported by the distributive argument, accordingly, in practice will be more complex than the simple framework choice represented in our example.

Return now to the integration thesis. Those who insist that it is fitting and proper for the law to concern itself with distributive fairness, but that it is impermissible for the law to impose paternalistic restrictions on its members, now must explain why the concern for the former does not extend to the latter. The called-for explanation may be forthcoming. The issue of distributive fairness that is presented by the case of legal paternalism is, as I intimated earlier, merely *prima facie*. Further reflection may reveal that the inequalities of welfare engendered by a shift from a pro-paternalism legal framework to an anti-paternalism framework would not, in actuality, be unfair. I now want to argue that this kind of explanation, assuming that it was forthcoming, itself would need to be an argument from within distributive fairness. If successful, it too would provide support for the integration thesis.

6.2 THE RESPONSIBILITY OBJECTION

The distributive argument for legal paternalism made no mention of the responsibility of the parties affected by the envisioned legal paternalism. But, intuitively, considerations of responsibility matter in this context, and matter in a deep way. It is not just for pragmatic reasons that responsibility matters. True, people need some space to make mistakes if they are to develop their capacities for responsible choice. True, if legal measures ignore responsibility altogether, then they may end up creating perverse incentives, encouraging more rather than less imprudent behavior. And these realities must be taken seriously by anyone who proposes a paternalistic measure. But the responsibility thought cuts deeper. If someone is responsible for their own welfare-reducing behavior, then how can it be fair to impose costs on others to rectify it? Forget about paternalism. Consider compensation. If Jack and Jill start off with a fair share of resources, and Jill makes foolish decisions about her own life, how could it be fair to ask Jack to compensate her for the effects of her own imprudence?

These rhetorical questions motivate an important objection to the distributive argument for legal paternalism. The responsibility objection holds that welfare inequalities due to imprudent behavior are not unfair. Accordingly, if the shift from Framework 2 to Framework 1 in our stylized example would engender welfare inequalities in virtue of the fact that people would make better and worse choices with respect to the options opened up to them, then these engendered inequalities would introduce no distributive unfairness into the picture.

To be sure, one could resist the objection by denying the intuitions about responsibility that undergird it. Responsibility skepticism is a live option.[11] But the intuitions are firm. The distributive argument for legal paternalism would be much less compelling if it had to be conjoined with responsibility skepticism. One might also respond to the objection by pointing out that not all imprudent behavior is the product of irresponsible choice. Sometimes people choose poorly because they lack good information or their decision-making is impaired in a way that undermines their responsibility for what they do. But while this response is a good one as far as it goes, it does not go far enough. For some of the paternalism that the distributive argument is meant to justify is hard paternalism and hard paternalism targets choices and behavior for which people are responsible.

The responsibility objection, then, is a formidable objection to the distributive argument for legal paternalism, one that is not easily rebutted. Let us start our consideration of it by distinguishing two versions of the objection.

[11] Pereboom, *Living without Free Will*.

Strong view: Responsibility negates the unfairness of inequalities of welfare that otherwise would be unfair.

Modest view: Responsibility diminishes the unfairness of inequalities of welfare that otherwise would be unfair.

The strong view defeats the distributive argument for legal paternalism. It renders fair (or at least not unfair) the presumptively unfair inequalities in welfare that are engendered by the shift from the pro-paternalism to the anti-paternalism framework. By contrast, the modest view does not defeat the argument but complicates it. It requires proponents of the argument to attend to and take into account the unfairness-diminishing power of responsibility considerations.

Which version of the responsibility objection is more plausible? This question itself is a question about distributive fairness. The strong view has been criticized as unjustly harsh. In an influential critique of responsibility-centered accounts of egalitarian justice, Elizabeth Anderson argued that these views objectionably abandon the imprudent to their dire fates. For example, on these views, if someone who meets the conditions of responsible choice were to decide against purchasing medical insurance, taking a deliberate gamble, as it were, with their health, then the misfortune they suffered when the gamble went south would not engage egalitarian concern, no matter how dire their misfortune. The force of this objection is blunted if we move from the strong view to the moderate view of the responsibility objection. For doing so allows us to say that even if one's misfortune were of one's own making, and even if justice were sensitive to responsibility considerations, it does not follow that one must altogether lack a claim in justice that others alleviate one's misfortune.

A trace of Anderson's objection remains intact on the moderate view of the responsibility objection, however. For, on the moderate as well as the strong view of the objection, one's responsibility or lack of it for one's fate affects the strength of one's claim to receive assistance. If others have competing claims to the assistance, then one's responsibility for one's fate could effectively undermine one's claim to it. But this consequence of the view is easy to accept. Intuitively, if two people in equally bad predicaments desperately need one's help and one can help only one of them, and if one person is responsible for their predicament and the other is not, then the one who is not responsible for their predicament has the stronger claim to your assistance, absent some other relevant factor.[12]

The moderate view of the responsibility objection, accordingly, can avoid some of the more unsettling consequences of responsibility-centered justice to which Anderson called attention, while retaining the attractive thought that responsibility is relevant to justice. However, since on this version of the objection responsibility does not negate but merely diminishes the unfairness of otherwise unfair inequalities,

---

[12] Arneson, "Luck Egalitarianism and Prioritarianism," *Ethics* 110/2 (2000): 339–349.

it may leave the distributive argument for legal paternalism largely intact. Much will depend on how small or large the diminishing factor of responsibility is taken to be. I have not ventured a view on that question. But this much can be said. The larger the diminishing factor is taken to be, the less clear it will be that the moderate version of the responsibility objection avoids the types of worries pressed by Anderson. If one is impressed by those worries, one should not set the diminishing factor very high.

A first response to the responsibility objection, then, holds that the moderate view is more plausible than the strong view of the objection and that the moderate view, when it is plausibly construed, does not give us reason to reject the distributive argument for legal paternalism. A second response to the objection is also available. To appreciate it, it will be helpful to distinguish two types of responsibility judgments. One type, let us call it *framework responsibility*, concerns the decisions that a society makes about changes to its legal framework when these changes or failure to make them have effects on the character of its ethical environment. The second type, call it *personal choice responsibility*, concerns the choices that people make given the legal framework to which they are subject. Imagine for a moment that a society had for some reason an unalterable legal framework. In this imagined society, there would be no framework responsibility, but there would be personal choice responsibility. If Jill were worse off than Jack in this society because of her poor decisions, then she might have only herself to blame.

Now drop the assumption about the unalterable legal framework and assume that the society has made a deliberate transition from a pro-paternalism to an anti-paternalism legal framework, thereby making available new options to its members. Under the anti-paternalism framework Jill could be responsible for the consequences of her bad decisions. But Jill, or those who care about her, could still raise a question about framework responsibility. Who is responsible for the character of the ethical environment that has been brought into being by the shift in frameworks?

The answer to this question is not "Jill"; or if Jill is responsible here, then she is no more responsible than other citizens who supported the change. (And, for all that has been said here, Jill may have opposed the change.) In short, Jill is responsible for her personal choices, but she is not responsible for the menu of options from which she chooses. The distributive argument targets inequalities in welfare that are engendered by framework shifts. The responsibility for these inequalities rests both on those who make or support the shifts and on those who make imprudent decisions once the shift has been made. The unfairness of the resulting inequalities is perhaps mitigated by the fact that they are the consequence of imprudent personal choice, but they are not eliminated by this fact since it can be unfair to people to place them in choice environments where they are likely to fare poorly.[13]

---

[13]   It would be odd to say "yes, we treated Jill unfairly by placing her in that environment, knowing full well how she would likely fare in it, but since Jill made responsible choices in that environment, the resulting loss in welfare that she suffered is not at all unfair."

Unfair inequalities in welfare can be assessed from the standpoint of framework responsibility as well as personal choice responsibility. For this reason, it is an error to focus on the latter to the exclusion of the former. An analogy from the economic realm may be helpful here. Suppose that Jack has a very idiosyncratic set of talents. Under his current legal framework, the talents command little return. But, fortunately for Jack, his society switches to a legal framework that subsidizes his talents and handsomely rewards those who have them. To get the rewards he will need to make responsible choices to exercise his talents. Suppose he does. Then should we say that he is entitled to the full increase in welfare that accrues to him in virtue of his responsible choices? If we believe in economic desert, then we should say that he deserves some reward for his responsible choices, but we should not conclude that there is no unfairness in him having as much as he does under the new framework. For, to know that, we would need to address the fairness of the shift in framework that so greatly improved Jack's circumstances of choice.

Taken together, these two responses do much to defang the responsibility objection. Or so I think. But whether or not I am right about this, the appeal to responsibility reinforces the case for the integration thesis. The responsibility objection brings out clearly that legal paternalism raises the distributive question of when it is fair and when it is not fair to make people bear the consequences of their imprudent choices. Those who advance the distributive argument in support of legal paternalism disagree with those who oppose it not on the issue of how people should swim in their fairly defined lanes but rather on the issue of how the lanes should be defined in the first place.

6.3 IMPERSONAL GOODS

The common good of a society is furthered by the fair treatment of its members. Fair treatment is partly a matter of distributive fairness, where distributive fairness concerns the distribution of the benefits and costs of social interaction. But fair treatment also implicates matters that concern the public culture of the society. Here the issue is not primarily one of securing fair shares of advantage or opportunity but rather one of giving each member of the society a fair say in deciding on matters that affect the shape of its public culture.

One way to ensure that all have a fair say on such matters is to respect the free decisions of all the members of a society, as they interact with one another in the cultural marketplace. On this view, the public culture of a society should not be directed by the law in any significant way. It should just emerge organically from the uncoordinated decisions of its members. An organic process of this kind could have economic consequences that engage distributive fairness, but this is not our present concern. We are focusing instead on the idea that each member of a society should have a fair say in deciding on the shape of its cultural environment. To think about this issue, let us return to the impersonal goods that were mentioned in the previous chapter. These goods are impersonal in the sense that their value is not exhausted by the contributions that they make to the good of people.

In the previous chapter we saw that impersonal goods can be usefully divided into two categories – objects of natural beauty or wonder and objects of perfectionist achievement. A good society, we suggested, is, among other things, one that preserves and respects natural beauty and creates works of perfectionist achievement, which are then preserved and respected. But what, it is fair to ask, does this have to do with the enforcement of morality?

Recall our earlier discussion of Scanlon's view. Scanlon claimed that our duties to other people are sensitive to the reasons we have to respect and engage with impersonal goods. To use one of his examples, we have a duty to others not to flood, or otherwise ruin, the Grand Canyon because doing so would deprive them of opportunities to enjoy its beauty. The fact that the Grand Canyon has impersonal value is important here, for it helps to explain why it would be wrong to destroy it.[14] Facts about impersonal value can feed into and support judgments of personal wrongdoing. These facts, however, are only part of the explanation of the wrongfulness of destroying impersonal goods, since it also must be true that other people have sufficient reason to engage with them. Now suppose that no one was particularly interested in viewing the Grand Canyon, and that there existed plenty of other objects of natural beauty for people to appreciate and enjoy, as there surely seem to be. Would it still be wrong for someone to destroy the Grand Canyon? If so, would it be appropriate for the law to prevent them from doing so?[15]

It might indeed be wrong to destroy the Grand Canyon in this type of scenario. But the wrongness of doing so would not involve wronging any person. In Scanlon's terms, we do not owe it to others not to destroy the Grand Canyon (at least in the scenario we are now imagining). It might be objected that even if no one now cares about the Grand Canyon, it should be preserved so that future generations have the option to engage with its beauty. It is doubtful, however, that we have a duty to preserve it for this reason. Our duty to future generations on this matter is imperfect. We have a duty to ensure that they live in an environment that is sufficiently rich in natural beauty, but it is doubtful that we have a duty to preserve particular objects – even very grand ones – of natural beauty.

Forget about the future generations issue. Suppose no one now or in the future will care about the Grand Canyon. No one will appreciate its beauty. We could still claim that we and future people ought to care about it, and that this fact can ground

---

[14]   Scanlon, *What We Owe to Each Other*, pp. 221–222.

[15]   Scanlon is not clear on these matters. He allows that morality (in the sense of what we owe to each other) could conflict with the reasons we have to protect or preserve impersonal goods. In such situations, he claims "we may have to choose between impersonal values and what we owe to each other" (ibid., p. 223). But what does it mean to choose between these two? Does it mean that there are cases, or there might be cases, where we can rightly interfere with people on grounds that have nothing to do with what we owe to others?

an enforceable duty on us all not to destroy it. Victor Tadros provides an instructive example:

> Consider a beautiful country inhabited by people who do not care at all for natural beauty. They cover the whole land with hideous buildings and road systems, leaving no natural beauty at all. No one cares that this has been done, because no one values natural beauty, and no one would have valued natural beauty had they not done this.[16]

Tadros plausibly claims that these people should care more about natural beauty than they do. He claims further that it could be appropriate for them to criminalize its destruction, doubtful as it may be that they would be motivated to do so.

The persuasive force of the example depends in part on the supposition that the people in the example destroy all the natural beauty in their country. If they destroyed only some of its natural beauty in pursuit of worthwhile ends, it is much less clear that they would be making a mistake. Generally speaking, in cultivating and preserving the beauty of their public environments, societies will confront tradeoffs between different types of goods. Some natural beauty may need to be sacrificed for the sake of housing and transportation needs, for example. While mistakes no doubt can be made, there is plausibly much legitimate variation in how societies manage these tradeoffs.

Tadros's example is fanciful. No one in the country cares one whit about preserving natural beauty. We can make the example more fanciful. Imagine the natural beauty is not replaced with ugly buildings and roads but with awe-inspiring architecture. The inhabitants of the country greatly value beauty. They think that it is vitally important that the public space in which they live remain beautiful. They just prefer artifactual to natural beauty. Do they make a mistake?

Likely, they do. An appropriately rich public environment may need to include both kinds of beauty. To sacrifice all the natural beauty in one's country for the sake of other kinds of beauty would be an error. Both natural beauty and artifactual beauty may be necessary for a rich public environment, but the tradeoff rate between them may not be constant. Possibly, the less natural beauty one has, the more important each remaining unit becomes, and the more artifactual beauty one has, the less important each additional unit becomes. Whether or not this is the case, it is very plausible to think that different mixes of the different kinds of beauty can be appropriate, and that different societies can make different tradeoffs without making mistakes. If so, what matters may be that societies create or sustain an appropriately rich public environment (assuming they have the resources to do so), and that their members – who, in all likelihood, have different preferences or views about what kind of public environment is best – should have a fair say in the process that determines its shape.

We will come back to this point in a moment. But, first, we need to pause and consider an important issue that our discussion has passed over. I have asserted that

---

[16] Tadros, *Wrongs and Crimes*, pp. 295–296.

impersonal goods, whether they be objects of natural beauty or great works of architecture, have a value that is not exhausted by the contribution that they make to the good of people. Yet our discussion of natural beauty centered on the contribution that it makes to a rich public environment, which presumably matters only because of its contribution to the good of those who live within it. A rich public environment is part of the common good of a society, but the common good of a society is a good for its members. It is not good *tout court*.

Part of what is troubling about the people in Tadros's example is that they show such disregard for natural beauty itself. Many will think that natural beauty commands respect. The people in the example have a duty to respect natural beauty in their country, or at least some of its more excellent instantiations. And this duty is not a matter of securing an appropriately rich public environment for themselves and for future members of their country. It is a matter of respecting the natural beauty itself. On the more fanciful variant of Tadros's example, the people care about beauty but they do not respect it. They are too eager to replace one kind of beauty – natural beauty – with another kind – architectural beauty. But what might it mean to respect an impersonal good like natural beauty?

Here is one answer. To respect an impersonal good, one must value it appropriately. What it means to value it appropriately requires analysis, but it demands that one not treat it as dispensable or as a mere means to the creation of value. For example, one does not value a great work of art appropriately if one is ready to destroy it in order to bring about a work of art that is equally great, or even a little greater.[17] In our variant of Tadros's example, the people do not value natural beauty appropriately because they are too willing to sacrifice it for the sake of other impersonal goods. Even if the new environment that they ushered in were stipulated to have greater beauty than the environment that they destroyed, they still could have made the mistake of not valuing the natural beauty appropriately.

Respecting impersonal goods in ways that go beyond any consideration of how they contribute to our flourishing raises difficult issues that cannot be pursued here. We can say that *if* we have duties to respect impersonal goods in these ways, then these duties could be enforceable, and enforceable by law. The enforcement of duties of this kind would then be part of the enforcement of morality, but it would not be a part that was explained by the project of ethical environmentalism.

Having noted this possibility, we can return to the notion of fairness that is implicated by concern for impersonal goods. I have suggested that there is wide variation in how societies can appropriately respond to impersonal goods. Goods such as natural beauty and the goods of perfectionist achievement enrich a society's public environment, but so long as the society discharges its duty to create or sustain a rich public environment for its members, and so long as it honors any duties that its

[17] For insightful and stimulating discussion of this conservative idea, see Cohen, "Rescuing Conservatism: A Defense of Existing Value."

members may (or may not) have to respect impersonal goods as such, then it has wide latitude to determine the shape of its public environment. This latitude permits it to pick and choose among particular impersonal goods it wants to support and sustain, and to decide on the tradeoffs it makes between these goods and other (non) impersonal goods.

These societal decisions about the shape of the public environment obviously have important effects on the lives of those who live in the society. So, it matters how the decisions get made. Since there is only one public environment, it is not possible to let each member decide for themself what its shape should be.[18] For this reason, it is plausible to think that each member of the society has a fairness-based claim to have a say in the decisions that affect the shape of its public environment. It is not immediately clear, however, what is meant by having a fair say in decisions of this kind. Why not say instead – and more simply – that each person has a claim to have their interests and concerns on these matters fairly taken into account?

Decisions about the shape of the public environment are to some extent preference-sensitive decisions. A preference-sensitive decision is a political decision whose correct solution depends on the distribution of preferences in the society.[19] We need, accordingly, some method or process for identifying the distribution of the relevant preferences in the society. The cultural marketplace is one such process, as I intimated earlier. Let people freely express their preferences in the cultural marketplace and the public environment that emerges will fairly reflect their interests and concerns.

This is an important part of the answer to our question. But it is not the full answer. For, as is well known, in a variety of circumstances markets can fail. The good of securing an appropriately rich public environment for one's society is a public good; and political action may be necessary to secure it. When political action is necessary for this task, it becomes incumbent on us to address how the political decision-making process can be made to treat each member of the society fairly with respect to the decisions that need to be made. And here, in resolving these political preference-sensitive issues, some have found an argument for democracy.[20] For only by allowing each member of the society to express their preferences and then granting those preferences equal weight with the preferences of others in the political decision-making process, it is held, can the society reach correct solutions to these issues.

This argument for democracy is modest. If sound, it justifies only a minimal form of democratic rule. In principle, an aristocratic body itself could decide all the political issues that were not preference-sensitive and then use polling methods to

---

[18] I am assuming here that each member of the society does not prefer the very same public environment as every other member.

[19] Here I follow Dworkin (*Sovereign Virtue*, pp. 204–205). He uses the term "choice-sensitive" but I prefer the term "preference-sensitive" for reasons that will become apparent.

[20] See Dworkin and Raz, "Liberalism, Skepticism and Democracy."

acquire the necessary information about the distribution of preferences in the society in order to make sound decisions about the preference-sensitive issues. Many would not find this form of political rule to be very democratic. But our concern in this chapter is not with the justification of democracy. We are trying to explain what is required for the members of a society to have a fair say in the preference-sensitive issues that concern the shape of their public environment. The details of the process that would do this best are not our concern. Whether this would be best achieved by allowing each member of the society to vote their preferences, or whether it could be done better by some alternative means, is no doubt an important issue but one that is not fundamental to our purposes.

Each member of a society's claim to a fair say with respect to the resolution of preference-sensitive issues within it can explain why some conduct that is not wrongful prior to or independent of law can be appropriately subject to penalty or punishment. (Such offenses in legal jargon are referred to as *mal prohibita*.[21]) Imagine that a society has fairly decided to preserve and protect a number of picturesque dunes on its coastal territory. The legal protection of these objects of natural beauty is part of its plan to ensure a sufficiently rich public environment for its members. Prior to the legal decision to protect the dunes it is not wrong for anyone to climb on them, or ride dune buggies over them, but after the decision has been made to protect them, it becomes wrong to do so. Further, the society can rightly enforce the legal requirements needed to protect the dunes. This remains the case even when it is true that the society legitimately could have decided not to protect the dunes at all, preferring instead to protect some other objects of natural beauty, for example.

The upshot of our discussion can now be summarized. The members of a society have duties with regard to impersonal goods, such as natural beauty and perfectionist achievement. The duties are, first, to ensure that the public environment of their society is sufficiently rich, given the circumstances of the society and the resources available to it; and, second, to show appropriate respect for these goods, if it is held (and we have left this open) that at least some goods of this kind command respect as such, and are not to be valued merely as means for advancing the interests and concerns of human beings. These duties can be satisfied in myriad ways, but fairness requires that they be discharged in a manner that gives all a fair say in how they are discharged. Having done this, a society can with justification legally enforce the duties that have been made determinate by the fair decision-making process.

---

[21] *Mal prohibita* offenses contrast with *mala in se* offenses. The latter are taken to be wrong in themselves, whereas the former are taken to be wrong in virtue of being legally proscribed. Efforts to sort offenses into these two categories become problematic in various ways, but the idea behind the distinction is clear enough. See Green, "Why It's a Crime to Tear the Tag Off a Mattress: Overcriminalization and the Moral Content of Regulatory Offenses," *Emory Law Journal* 46/4 (1997): 1553–1616.

6.4 DEVLIN'S THESIS REVISITED

This account of impersonal goods and the duties that they ground can be extended to cover other kinds of goods. The goods that I want to discuss in this section can be referred to as goods of tradition. These goods make an appearance in Devlin's defense of legal moralism. This will require some explanation, however. Recall that, for Devlin, a "society may legislate to preserve itself."[22] And since, on his view, a society is held together "by the invisible bonds of thought,"[23] it may use the law to enforce the shared ideas that constitute these invisible bonds. From these two claims, Devlin concluded that societies are justified in legally enforcing their positive morality.

Let us refer to this conclusion as Devlin's Thesis. Virtually no legal theorist has found his argument for it to be persuasive. The claim that a society may legislate to preserve itself is not true without qualification if by "may legislate" is meant "has a (moral) right to legislate" (what Devlin clearly meant by it). For some societies are not worth preserving. A society run on slave labor, to take one example, has no right to exist and hence no right to take steps to preserve itself. In response, it may be said that societies that are not worth preserving retain the right to exist, but only if they are committed to reforming their ways. This bring us to the second claim that societies are held together by invisible bonds of thought. This claim, as Hart and others were quick to point out, seems to imply that when the positive morality of a society changes, it ceases to exist. But surely societies can and do survive changes in their positive moralities. So, for this claim to be at all defensible, it too must be qualified. The claim must be that certain kinds of changes to a society's positive morality could threaten its survival as a valued good. The members of a society may know that if their positive morality were to change in certain anticipated ways, then it would cease to be a society that they thought was worth preserving.

The claims that support Devlin's Thesis, accordingly, need to be adjusted; and when they are adjusted, they do not support his thesis but a revised version of his thesis. The revised version of the thesis can be stated as follows:

> Societies that are worth preserving have a right to preserve the traditions that constitute their identity as a valued good.

The term "tradition" is here understood to encompass the established practices and patterns of behavior that reflect and express the positive morality of a society. The positive morality of a society is not simply a set of believed propositions but a set of practices and patterns of behavior that are widely valued in the society. To the extent that the law aims to enforce this positive morality, its focus is on sustaining these practices and patterns of behavior.[24]

---

[22] Devlin, *The Enforcement of Morals*, p. 89.
[23] Ibid., p. 10.
[24] Some might think that the law should enforce the positive morality of a society by preventing its members from changing their minds on the issues it addresses. Mind control and the suppression of the free discussion of moral ideas would be appropriate instruments for such enforcement. This totalitarian view was not Devlin's view, however.

The "goods of tradition" is my phrase for these valued social practices and patterns of behavior. They form part of a society's ethical environment and legal efforts to preserve them are part of the political project of ethical environmentalism. To be sure, the fact that certain practices are widely valued in a society does not establish that the practices are valuable and worth preserving. It establishes only that the members of a society believe the practices are valuable.[25] If the members of a society change their mind and come to view the once-valued practices with suspicion or indifference, then they will cease to value them. They value them on the condition that they are in fact valuable. The reference to "a valued good" in the statement of the revised version of Devlin's Thesis, accordingly, contains an implicit presupposition. The good in question is not only valued but worth valuing.

A puzzle now presents itself. If the goods of tradition must be genuinely valuable in order for a society to have a right to preserve them, then why is it necessary to appeal to tradition at all? Why not say more simply that a society has a right to establish and preserve social practices that are genuinely valuable? The answer to the puzzle is that with social practices, just as with political decisions about impersonal goods, there is scope for legitimate variation.[26] Traditions are contingent and parochial, differing from place to place, but they can be genuinely valuable and consistent with a sound universal political morality. Indeed, one important function of tradition is to make more abstract universal principles concrete and determinate for those who are subject to them. But they serve another function as well, one that relates them to the identity of a society. We can identify a society by its structural features alone. Does it, for example, have the same legal system from one time to the next? This is a helpful way to explain the continuity of societies, even as they undergo substantial changes in the attitudes of their members. But a society can also be characterized by its character as well as by its structure.[27] Many societies strive to preserve a national language and view the preservation of their national language to be an important component of their identity as a society, for example.

Hart's critique of Devlin's argument succeeds when a society is understood to be a function of its structural features. For, on this understanding, societies persist as they undergo radical changes in the beliefs and values of their members, as the positive morality of the society is transformed into a very different system or set of beliefs and values. But if societies are individuated by their character, as well as by their structure, then this critique does not go through so smoothly. For now, it

[25]   Here I follow Scheffler in holding that to value something, one must believe that it is valuable; see Scheffler, "Valuing."

[26]   Conservative writers often appeal to epistemic limits in defending traditions. Paraphrasing Burke, they claim that while individual thinkers are often foolish, the species is wise. Rather than aiming to perfect our arrangements, we do better, they argue, to conserve the good in them. This epistemic defense of traditionalism is distinct from the idea advanced in the text. If traditions represent legitimate variations on sound practices, they can be defended without any appeal to epistemic limits.

[27]   The distinction between cultural structure and the character of a culture is highlighted in Kymlicka's influential account of multicultural rights. See Kymlicka, *Liberalism, Community and Culture.*

becomes important to distinguish those changes to a society's practices and patterns of behavior that are continuous with what has gone before from those changes that mark radical breaks with the past. For the latter sensibly can be viewed as a threat to the society's continued existence as a valued good.

All societies that persist for a significant period of time preserve established practices and undergo changes to their character. Everything here is a matter of degree. But, on the assumption that there is scope for legitimate variation, societies have a right to preserve their character or to transform it dramatically. Within limits, they have a right to determine the character of their society.

A society's positive morality is reflected in established social practices and established patterns of behavior, constituting what I have been calling goods of tradition. But talk of a society's positive morality can mislead. It may suggest a greater degree of consensus on moral matters than is found in modern societies. Questions about the character of the society, and the goods of tradition that merit support, are often contested questions. Since the members of the society have a stake in its self-definition, and since there is often no consensus on how it should define itself, these matters also engage fair treatment. The common good of the society is served when all have a fair say in the decisions that determine the society's character, as this is reflected in its traditions.

Goods of tradition, like other goods, can be supported by legal means. Legal support for established social forms, such as the institution of monogamous marriage or the preservation of a cherished language, raises issues of justice. Societies are not (morally) free to do as they please with respect to supporting these goods. That is why it is crucial to the defense of the traditionalism that I have been discussing that sound morality on such matters admits of legitimate variation. Assuming that the goods of tradition in question fall within the scope of this legitimate variation, and assuming that the decisions to support them have been made fairly, the force of law legitimately can be used to help to sustain them.

6.5 AN ENCOMPASSING COMMON GOOD

Our discussion in this chapter has ranged widely over different kinds of issues. I have sought to show how paternalism, respect for impersonal goods and support for the goods of tradition all fall within the ambit of the legal enforcement of morality. Moreover, I have tried to show how each of these issues implicates the fair treatment of individual persons, since the resolution of each issue helps to define the ethical environment that is part of a society's common good, and political decisions that are intended to shape the character of this environment plausibly engage issues of fairness.

Reflection on and critical discussion of these issues provides support for the integration thesis, which is the denial of the claim that there is a deep distinction between different departments or domains of morality that explains why some are appropriately enforced by law and others are not. Morality in a broad and

encompassing sense includes the just and fair treatment of persons, "ethical"
questions about living well and matters involving the proper regard for objects of
impersonal value. This encompassing morality is, I have argued, presumptively
a proper object of legal enforcement. It is a proper object of legal enforcement in
a society because, and to the extent that, the resolution of the issues to which it
applies is part of the common good of that society. Properly understood, ethical
environmentalism is the political project of attending to and advancing this
encompassing common good.

7

The Good of Personal Liberty

Many distinguished writers on criminal law aim to articulate principled limits on the kinds of considerations that properly can be appealed to in justifying the legal enforcement of morality. Such an approach is often identified with liberalism. The liberal, we are told, asks not whether the law "can pass judgment at all in matters of morals, but rather which matters of morals are its proper business."[1] And the liberal, we are further told, is tightfisted when it comes to which matters of morals can be properly enforced, limiting these to harm or offense, for example, or insisting that the law must not be justified by ideals of the good that are the subject of reasonable disagreement in the society. In this respect, the approach articulated in the preceding two chapters has a decidedly non-liberal structure. Ethical environmentalism, as our discussion has made plain, is generous in the kinds of considerations that it allows are the proper business of the law, including the criminal law. From the fact that the approach taken here is non-liberal in its structure, it does not follow that it is non-liberal in content, however. As I have stressed, the project of ethical environmentalism, at least as it has been articulated thus far, establishes just a presumptive case for the legal enforcement of morality. When countervailing considerations are given their due, the content of our approach may move much closer in content to the liberal position.[2]

Notwithstanding this point, it is a mistake to focus much attention on the question of whether an approach to the legal enforcement of morality is liberal or not, whether in structure or content. Over the past two centuries, liberalism has been associated with a variety of political movements, and its content has shifted across time and place. Theoretical efforts to identify the core or essence of liberalism as a political theory invariably end up presenting it in a way that is false to its history, playing up certain currents of thought and downplaying or excluding others.[3]

---

[1] Postema, "Public Faces and Private Places: Liberalism and the Enforcement of Morality," in *Morality, Harm and the Law*, ed. Dworkin (Boulder, CO: Westview Press, 1994), p. 77 (quoting Joel Feinberg).
[2] For example, Moore describes his own position on the legal enforcement of morality as "quite liberal in its content, even if not in its form." *Placing Blame*, p. 756.
[3] See my introduction to Wall, *The Cambridge Companion to Liberalism*.

For this reason, it is better to talk simply of sound or justified limits on the criminal law, leaving the political or ideological label "liberal" aside.[4] The considerations canvassed and analyzed in this chapter all concern liberty and notions closely associated with it. Since liberalism is often associated with doctrines of personal liberty,[5] perhaps little mischief will result in referring to the limits supported by these considerations as liberal limits on the enforcement of morality. Still, the focus here is on the soundness of the limits, not on their political characterization.

Personal liberty, as I have mentioned before, can be viewed through the lens of the good or through the lens of the right. Do we value liberty because it is part of our good, or a means to our good, or do we value it because it is our right to have it? To be sure, we can value it under both descriptions. But it is useful to distinguish the two standpoints for valuing personal liberty nonetheless, for doing so can help us to appreciate the range of arguments that can be marshaled in support of it. In this chapter, our concern is with liberty as a personal good; in the next chapter we will consider the claim that we have a right to it even when it does not serve our good or the good of others.

7.1 THE PRESUMPTION IN FAVOR OF LIBERTY

Start with an important question. Is there a general presumption in favor of personal liberty? Our discussion of ethical environmentalism highlighted the common properties of the environment in which people make choices about how to lead their lives. Much of the discussion centered on the character of this environment, but not too much was said about the *range* of choice it provides to those who live within it. This lacuna needs to be addressed. For the range of choice that an ethical environment provides to those within it is one of its common properties, and one that profoundly affects its character. The law of a society is not the only variable that affects the range of choice that its ethical environment provides to its members, but it is an important variable, and it is the variable that is most germane to our present purposes.

How might the law impact the range of choice that a society's ethical environment provides to its members? An inquiry into this question can usefully be divided into two parts. On the one hand, we can investigate how the law enables choice by sustaining or bringing into existence options that otherwise would not exist. On the other hand, we can ask how the law constrains choice by eliminating, or making it more difficult to pursue, options that otherwise would exist. Most writers on criminal law focus attention on the latter. It is coercive law and its impact on our option sets

---

[4] Here I follow and am in substantial agreement with Finnis, "Limited Government," p. 94 note 38: "The only sensible way to deal with philosophical claims framed in terms of liberalism, liberal political institutions, etc. is to treat them as rhetorical code for 'sound', 'true', 'warranted', 'just', or the like; one translates accordingly and carries on with the consideration of the arguments or claims on their merits."

[5] As one writer puts it, "liberalism is a doctrine of political morality which revolves round the importance of personal liberty." Raz, *The Morality of Freedom*, p. 17.

that occupies their minds. We will follow their lead here, but the former inquiry is not irrelevant to our concerns. If there is a presumption in favor of liberty, as many have contended, then it is not straightforward how it applies to laws that simultaneously enable and restrict options.

The presumption in favor of liberty, at any rate, is a popular idea. Many people feel instinctively that restrictions on choice are always bad, and many philosophers have defended the idea of such a presumption in favor of liberty in one form or another.[6] Let us start by unpacking the notion. Two senses of "a presumption in favor of" need to be distinguished here.[7] First, a presumption in favor of something can mean that the burden of proof is on the would-be denier of it. Applied to the presumption in favor of liberty as it relates to law, this understanding holds that the burden of proof is always on those who propose to restrict the liberty of people for the sake of some political goal. Second, a presumption in favor of something can mean that there is a standing reason in favor of it. Applied to the presumption in favor of liberty as it relates to law, this understanding implies that there is a standing reason for the law to respect the liberty of people. This reason can be overridden but it is always present and it always takes something to override it.

The first sense of the presumption, when it is clearly distinguished from the second sense, applies to certain institutional contexts, such as the presumption of innocence in a criminal trial. There are a variety of reasons why the presumption makes sense in these contexts. But it is hard to see how or why a presumption of this kind would apply to an inquiry like the one we are presently engaging in – a theoretical inquiry about the moral limits of the law. On fundamental questions about the nature of morality, and its application to law, neither the liberty-lover nor the liberty-hater enjoys an argumentative advantage.[8] The interesting sense for our purposes, then, is the second one. Indeed, this sense of the presumption in favor of liberty can explain why the first sense seems initially plausible. It is because there is always a standing reason in favor of respecting liberty that the argumentative burden seems to tilt against the would-be interferer with liberty. The would-be interferer starts with a hurdle that they must overcome if they are to succeed in making their case.[9]

---

[6] Philosophers who explicitly endorse the presumption include J. S. Mill, J. Rawls, J. Feinberg, S. Benn and G. Gaus.

[7] Raz distinguishes these two senses and a third evidential sense, which we can pass over. See Raz, *The Morality of Freedom*, pp. 8–12. See also Husak, "The Presumption of Freedom," *Nous* (1983).

[8] Raz, *The Morality of Freedom*, pp. 9–10.

[9] Interference disrupts the status quo. Might the presumption against interference be explained by a presumption against disrupting the status quo? Here is one reason to think so. Consider two cases.

   Fence 1: There is a beautiful canyon that people visit. Occasionally, a visitor gets perilously close to the edge of the canyon's cliff to get the best view of the canyon. A proposal is made to erect a fence to keep visitors at least 3 feet from the canyon's edge. Such a fence will restrict liberty, and so there is a presumption against erecting it.

   Fence 2: Same canyon, but the restrictive fence has been erected. A proposal is made to remove the fence. The removal of the fence will expose visitors to the risk of harm of getting too close to the canyon's edge. So, there is a presumption against removing it.

The presumption of liberty, accordingly, is best understood as a claim about the purportedly ever-present reason to respect the liberty of individual people. One way to challenge the presumption is to deny that it applies to all liberties. Granted, it may be said, there is a reason to respect important or significant liberties, but no reason to respect liberty as such. In reply, some have claimed that there is always a cost to restricting liberty, even if the liberty restricted concerns an option of no value. The restriction of liberty, on this view, while not necessarily intrinsically bad, is always instrumentally bad. Michael Moore provides a good summary of the considerations that can be marshaled in support of this claim.[10] Restriction of a person's liberty always involves:

(1) A reduction in the person's opportunities for choice.
(2) A reduction in the likelihood that the person will make choices for the right reasons.
(3) A frustration of the person's preference to make their own decisions.
(4) An expenditure of scarce resources.

Each of these considerations often bears on decisions about whether to restrict this or that liberty, but none of them, I now will argue, can establish the truth of the presumption in favor of liberty. That presumption, to stress again, is the claim that there is *always* a standing reason in favor of liberty (and against interference with liberty).

Very often a reduction in our opportunities for choice is bad for us. We may not be able to get what we most want if some of our options are restricted, or we may lose opportunities for discovering what we would desire. And very often the frustration of our wants and desires is bad for us. But the reduction in our opportunities for choice is sometimes good for us. It can make our decision-making easier or less anxiety-producing, or it can take options off the table that we know would be bad for us and would tempt us to act against our better judgment, for example.[11] Sorting out when and why a reduction in our opportunities for choice is good or bad for us is not straightforward, and the claim that a reduction in opportunities for choice is bad for us is, if true, at most an empirical generalization, subject to all sorts of exceptions and qualifications. It thus cannot vindicate the presumption in favor of liberty.

The second consideration is even less plausible than the first if it is taken to state an exceptionless claim. Sometimes when the law restricts opportunities for choice, people are induced to make choices for the wrong reasons. But other times the restrictions the law imposes on people have no effect on their decision-making. For

Now suppose that the liberty interests and the safety interests in both variants of the case appear to be balanced. Neither the liberty interest nor the safety interest clearly outweighs the other. Given this supposition, a plausible presumption favors rejecting the proposal to erect a fence in *Fence 1* and the proposal to remove it in *Fence 2*, thereby favoring the status quo in both scenarios.

[10] Moore, *Placing Blame*, pp. 746–750.
[11] For further examples, see the classic discussion of this issue by Dworkin, "Is More Choice Better Than Less?" *Midwest Studies in Philosophy* 47 (1982).

example, the law prohibits murder, but most of us have no inclination to murder. We are motivated by the moral reason to abstain from unjustified killings. This example might seem to prove the point, however. For presumably there would be no law prohibiting murder unless some people were inclined to murder and would be motivated to abstain from doing so for the wrong reason, namely to avoid legal punishment. When legal restrictions on murder are effective, they work by inducing people to do the right thing for the wrong reasons. But this does not imply that the restrictions decrease the likelihood that people will not murder for the right reasons. It implies only that the restrictions decrease the likelihood that people will murder. It would be very odd if someone were motivated not to commit murder because they appreciated the moral reasons not to do so, but then, when a legal restriction against murder was imposed, they ceased to be moved by the moral reasons and were motivated not to murder by the fear of legal penalty.

The third consideration may seem to be on firmer ground. Legal restrictions on personal conduct perhaps always frustrate the preferences of at least some people to whom they apply. Still, even if this is granted, it is not true that the frustration of preferences is always bad for them or has disvalue. For a variety of reasons, it is often good for people to have their preferences frustrated. To take an easy example, their preferences may be based on false beliefs about their objects. (Thinking that the glass in front of me contains gin, I have a preference to drink it, but unbeknownst to me, it contains petroleum.[12]) More controversially, but still plausibly, the frustration of my preferences to engage in wrongdoing can be good for me in virtue of the fact that it is bad for me to engage in wrongdoing.[13] These points are compatible with a more modest claim. Pervasive frustration of our preferences might be bad for us because it prevents us from leading our own lives. But this modest claim, while plausible, does not support the presumption in favor of liberty.

The final consideration applies to all legal action. No legal measure is costless. It takes time to draft and pass a measure and then resources to enforce it. But we should not infer too much from this commonplace observation. Legal measures can have benefits as well as costs. Suppose the passage and enforcement of a proposed traffic law will save a society $1 million over a one-year period, but it will cost the society $250,000 to pass and enforce it over that period. It would be infelicitous to say that there is a presumption against the traffic law because it will cost the society $250,000. It would be more natural to say that there is a presumption in its favor because it will provide an economic benefit to the society.

None of the considerations here canvassed on their own can support the presumption in favor liberty. Each admits of exceptions and qualifications that reveal that the presumption in favor of liberty that they purportedly support would not be fully general. Might they be more successful in combination?

[12] The example is from Williams, "Internal and External Reasons."
[13] For good discussion of this point, see Tadros, *Wrongs and Crimes*, pp. 1–3.

This is unlikely, for the considerations do not sum up in ways that overcome their limits. Moreover, in a range of cases, the considerations militate against one another. Some legal restrictions that reduce opportunities for choice (consideration 1) may increase, rather than decrease, the likelihood that people will make choices for the right reasons (consideration 2). Example: I might be inclined to donate my blood out of beneficent concern for others, but if I have the option to sell my blood for profit, then I will be induced to do the latter. Here the removal of the option to sell my blood for profit can make it more likely that I will do the right thing for the right reasons.[14] Similarly, some legal restrictions frustrate preferences (consideration 3) in ways that increase, not limit, opportunities for choice (consideration 1). Example: I might now prefer to sell myself into slavery. The frustration of this preference when compared with its satisfaction would greatly increase my opportunities for choice.[15]

The presumption in favor of liberty, accordingly, is better viewed as an umbrella phrase that encompasses a set of valid considerations, which, while important, do not add up to a standing reason to oppose legal restrictions. But there is another reason to be wary of this notion. We have been focusing on the *scope* of the presumption. It purports to apply to all legal restrictions on liberty, but the considerations that lie behind it do not establish this. We also need to ask about the *strength* of the presumption. The presumption could be very strong in that it requires a very weighty reason on the other side to be overridden, or it could be very weak and easily overridden, or somewhere in between. The presumption could also be either uniform or variable in strength. Reflecting on these possibilities, it seems very likely that the presumption is variable, being strong for some liberties and weak for others. On this view, the presumption in favor of the liberty to do something significant, such as to attend the church of one's choosing, is strong, whereas the presumption in favor of doing something trivial, such as splitting pebbles on a beach, is weak. But now it seems plain that it is the significance of particular liberties that should be the focus of our concern rather than any presumption in favor of liberty as such. For, even if it were true that the presumption were uniform (which we have denied), in all likelihood it would not be strong enough when applied to trivial liberties to support a significant bulwark against the enforcement of morality.

Talk of a presumption in favor of liberty, accordingly, directs us to consider qualitative differences in liberties rather than the value of liberty as such. This inquiry, some writers have argued, invites us to consider values other than liberty that can explain why some liberties are more valuable than others. Referring to this as the "revisionist challenge," Raz puts the point in these terms: "any assessment of degrees of liberty depends on the importance of various actions for the protection and promotion of values other than freedom. If so then the value of freedom depends on the other

---

[14] Titmus, *The Gift Relationship*. For Dworkin's discussion of this example, see "Is More Choice Better Than Less?" (pp. 53–54).
[15] Mill, *On Liberty*, pp. 101–102.

values which the freedom to perform some action serves."[16] This is a challenge to liberty's value insofar as it implies that it is values other than liberty that account for the value that liberty has. Let us call these *grounding values*. If liberty has value only in virtue of the grounding values that support it, then liberty itself would seem to have no value. Any value it had would be derivative from the (non-liberty-implicating) grounding values. But many have thought that there is a value that implicates liberty and explains its value.[17] This value is a deeper ideal of human freedom. It implicates liberty because it is an ideal of liberty itself, not the liberty to do this or that action, but the liberty that is realized when one becomes a self-determining person. It is by appeal to this deeper ideal of liberty that the revisionist challenge can be overcome.

7.2 AUTONOMY

A presumption in favor of self-determination, or autonomy as I will refer to it, is a promising candidate to supersede the presumption in favor of liberty. For autonomy can explain why some liberties are more significant than others. Further, it is an ideal that many consider to be of great importance.

Autonomy is sometimes understood as the *right* to lead one's own life on one's own terms free from the interference of others. On this understanding, autonomy is a principle of self-sovereignty.[18] As I have already discussed this principle in Chapter 4, we do not need to consider it again here. Presently, we will understand autonomy not as a sovereign right but as an ideal, the realization of which tends to make a life go better for the person who realizes it than it would have gone had they not realized it.[19] If this ideal contributes substantially to people's flourishing, then it can ground rights that make its realization possible. But the rights do not come first, as it were. They are derivations from the ideal.

Mill understood autonomy in these terms. His term for it was "individuality." His characterization of this notion has some idiosyncratic features that are not essential to the ideal of autonomy. But the important point for present purposes is that Mill presented this notion as a central element of well-being.[20] He thought that this ideal

---

[16] Raz, *The Morality of Freedom*, p. 16. (Note that one can affirm the second claim in this passage – the claim about the value of freedom – while rejecting the first claim – the claim about the degree of freedom. One might think, that is, that the value of freedom, and hence the strength of any presumption in favor of it, depends on values other than freedom, while thinking that degrees of freedom itself can be determined independently of its value. For an extended defense of the idea that evaluative considerations must be invoked to ascertain degrees of freedom, see Kramer, *The Quality of Freedom*, chapter v.)

[17] This is the route that Raz takes. See also the position that Moore comes round to in *Placing Blame*, pp. 763–777.

[18] See Feinberg's account of autonomy as personal sovereignty in his *Harm to Self*.

[19] For skepticism about the idea that autonomy has this kind of value, see Valdman, "Outsourcing Self-Government," and for a response to this skepticism, see my "Autonomy As a Perfection."

[20] Its achievement, he claims, is "one of the principal ingredients of human happiness." *On Liberty*, p. 54.

explains why a person's "own mode of laying out his existence is the best, not because it is the best in itself, but because it is his own mode."[21] Call this the *Autonomy Claim*. As we will see, it requires qualification, but it is one that has much to recommend. Each of us has a strong interest in self-determination, in making ourselves the part-authors of our lives,[22] but this interest will be frustrated if too many of our options for choice are foreclosed by others. Even if others succeed in forcing us down better paths, our lives will be marred by the fact that we are not leading our lives on our own terms. In this way, the ideal of autonomy, and its contribution to our flourishing, can ground freedom-centered limits to the ethical environmentalism that we discussed in the previous two chapters.

The interesting question is how extensive and robust these limits are. Traffic restrictions remove options, but not in a way that is damaging to anyone's autonomy. But now suppose some people have adopted a traffic-related project that has become central to their idea of how they want to lead their lives. Imagine that it is important to them to minimize the number of times that they bring their automobiles to a complete stop when traveling on the roads, as this, they believe, increases the fuel efficiency of their automobiles and thereby contributes to reducing fuel emissions. This project makes traffic restrictions, such as the requirement to come to a complete stop at a stop sign, significant to them. Given this, do the restrictions set back their autonomy?

Mill's own discussion of the value of liberty suggested two qualifications to the Autonomy Claim. The first qualification is expressed in the second clause of the following statement: "If a person possesses any tolerable amount of common sense and experience, the only freedom which deserves the name is that of pursuing our own good in our own way, *so long as we do not attempt to deprive others of theirs or impede their efforts to obtain it.*"[23] Freedom is set back by traffic restrictions, but this freedom is not the kind of freedom that is valuable under the Autonomy Claim. The project that the people in our example have taken up is the kind of project that impedes the efforts of others to pursue their own projects, for presumably all people, or most of us, have a substantial interest in the orderly travel on the roads that the restrictions make possible.

A more dramatic example illustrates the same idea. If you adopt a plan to enslave others and make it central to your conception of living a good life, then the frustration of this plan is not a setback to your autonomy. For your autonomy is bounded by the autonomy of others. What might explain this qualification to the Autonomy Claim? We may not like the content of your slavery plan, but it is your plan, part of your idea of what it means for you to lead your life on your own terms. Why not say instead that the frustration of your plan, while justified, does indeed set back your autonomy?

---

[21] Ibid., p. 64.
[22] Raz, *The Morality of Freedom*, pp. 369–371.
[23] Mill, *On Liberty*, p. 12 (italics added).

One answer is that in appealing to the Autonomy Claim we are trying to distinguish significant from trivial liberties. We want to say that the restriction of some liberties is of little or no moment from the standpoint of freedom's value. But judgments of significance are not purely subjective. They are made against a background view that some plans and activities are genuinely worth pursuing and others are not. We can say of another that while they thought their plan was significant, it was, in fact, a total waste of time. And when we say this, we are not saying merely that we are not attracted by it. By the same token, the slavery plan, we think, is not a worthwhile plan. A person's interest in living a good life is not furthered by it.

Consider next Mill's second qualification to the Autonomy Claim. The statement previously quoted is prefaced by the following words: "if a person possesses any tolerable amount of common sense and experience." The clear implication is that at least for some people, the pursuing of their own good in their own way is not the kind of freedom that deserves the name. If I have no sense and no experience about how to live, then my projects may not contribute to the value of my life. Their pursuit may set back rather than contribute to my flourishing. Put differently, the realization of autonomy is an essential element of a good life, but its realization is not something that is always on balance good for people. When the negative difference in the quality of the path that I go down when I pursue my own good in my own way when compared to the quality of the path I would go down were I to be guided by another becomes great enough, the greater value of the latter can outweigh the value of autonomy that comes with the former. To take an artificially precise example, suppose that if Jane were to let someone else choose her projects for her and that, bracketing the value of autonomy, she would realize 50 units of value in her life, but if she were to pursue her own good in her own way, then, bracketing autonomy, she would realize only 20 units of this value. If autonomy adds 10 units of value to a life, and the absence of autonomy subtracts 10 units of value from a life, then Jane would be better off overall letting someone else choose her projects for her (40 units) rather than choosing them herself (30 units). In short, on this view, we have an autonomy-based reason to make our own decisions and to not outsource our self-governance to others who would make better decisions for us. But this autonomy-based reason is not always decisive, and if a person is sufficiently lacking in good sense and experience, and if the prospects for improving their decision-making capacities are dim, then their good may lie with the life that is not of their own making.

I have drawn the contrast between the autonomous and the non-autonomous life in rather stark terms to make a point about autonomy's non-absolute value. But, in actuality, the realization of autonomy plausibly comes in degrees. Often the relevant issue concerns the removal of this or that option. Here the question that is pertinent is whether the removal of the option would increase the overall value of the option set that formerly included it, where the overall value of an option set is a function of its expected value for the person or persons who have access to it. Imagine an option of little or no value that entices many against their better judgment to take it up when they have access to it, thereby diverting them from pursuing the much more valuable options in their option sets. The removal of this option from the option set that contains it would improve its overall value for these people, even if its removal reduced their autonomy to some degree.

This claim is consistent with another claim, which we can refer to as the *Adequacy Claim*. If too many options are removed from our option sets, then we will not be able to achieve autonomy in our lives. To achieve autonomy to any substantial extent, we must have access to a sufficiently wide range of options.[24] It is a hard task to specify with precision what is required for an option set to be adequate, and we will not undertake this task here. But we can say this much. An adequate range of options does not require that the option set be maximally large in either the number or variety of options that it contains. This implies that the removal of some options from an option set need not run afoul of the Adequacy Claim.

Does the Adequacy Claim sit well with the claim that autonomy comes in degrees? Possibly every time an option is removed from a person's option set it diminishes their autonomy to at least some extent. More plausibly, it might be held that every time an option that is valued by some people is removed from their option sets it sets back their autonomy to at least some extent. On either of these claims, there will always be an autonomy-based reason to oppose the removal of options, if at least one person values the option that is being removed from their option set. This would establish an autonomy-based presumption against any legal measure designed to remove an option that was valued by some who were subject to it. And this, it now might be thought, is enough to establish the kind of general freedom-based presumption against the restriction of personal liberty.

To test this idea, it will be helpful to consider some examples. Consider first the crime of rape. Few will think that people have an autonomy-based interest in having the option to commit this offense. If they have no such interest, then the removal of this option from the option set of a person who valued it would not set back their autonomy. Next consider the possibility that some consensual acts between persons are wrong. These acts, while consensual, might share some of the wrong-making properties of rape. Recall the claim (mentioned in Chapter 4) that certain consented-to actions amount to "the sheer use of another" for one's own pleasure, which is wrongful.[25] Since these acts are consented to by all the involved parties, let us assume that they do not set back the autonomy of any of them.[26] Accordingly, the fact, if it is a fact, that autonomy is bounded by the autonomy of others does not apply to these acts.

It is a good question whether there can be consensual acts of sheer use between people. If both parties consent to the use of each other, then their treatment of each other may fall short of sheer use. But if we have self-regarding duties not to

24   Raz, *The Morality of Freedom*, pp. 373–377.
25   Gardner and Shute, "The Wrongness of Rape," reprinted in Gardner, *Offenses and Defences*.
26   We can assume that the acts do not cause any lasting harm to those who engage in them.

treat ourselves in certain ways, as I have suggested we do, then we can understand sheer use in terms of using others in ways that they are not entitled to license with their consent. We then can apply this analysis to certain purportedly immoral options. Discussing prostitution and certain kinds of pornography, some writers have claimed that:

> [The use of prostitutes and the consumption of pornography can be wrong] because it objectifies the prostitute or model even when her consent is genuine. But when her consent is genuine such resort or use is not a violation of the prostitute's or model's right to sexual autonomy, and so not a wrong against the prostitute or model. Or at any rate it is not a wrong against the prostitute or model under the same heading as that under which rape is a wrong against its victim. For a person's consent is capable of licensing, in the name of sexual autonomy itself, some suboptimal sexual relationships, which in this case means depressingly dehumanizing relationships, relationships of objectification.[27]

Here our concern is not with these particular examples but with the point that is made with them. Autonomy – more precisely, the autonomy regarding sexual relations that is exercised through consent – is taken here to "license" certain sexual relationships that are judged to be wrongful and dehumanizing. The licensing of these relationships rules out permissible interference with them.

Is this compelling? People may have a sexual autonomy right to engage in prostitution, and they may have a free speech right to produce and consume pornography. They may have rights to do these things even when it is granted that doing them is wrongful. More generally, people may have rights to do wrongs. We will consider this important issue in the next chapter. Our present concern is whether people have an interest in being free to engage in these activities, an interest that is grounded in their interest in being autonomous. Keeping this concern in mind, consider the following two contrasting claims about autonomy's value.[28]

(1) Autonomy adds value to a life whether or not it is exercised in the service of good ends.
(2) Autonomy adds value to a life only when it is exercised in the service of good ends.

If the first claim were true, then we would have an autonomy-based interest in having access to options of the sort we have been discussing; that is, options to participate in dehumanizing relationships. By contrast, if the second claim were true, then we might have no such interest. As one defender of Claim (2) explains, "since autonomy is valuable only if it is directed at the good it supplies no reason to provide, nor any reason to protect, worthless let alone bad options."[29]

---

[27] Gardner and Shute, "The Wrongness of Rape," pp. 20–21.
[28] The value in question here is prudential; that is, the value involved in living a life that is good for one. The issue of whether autonomy adds some other kind of value, such as aesthetic value, to a life is not germane.
[29] Raz, *The Morality of Freedom*, p. 411.

Claim (1) is hard to accept.[30] It implies that a person who engages in very wicked pursuits lives a better life if they autonomously engage with them than if they were forced by circumstance to do so. But the reverse is closer to the truth. Autonomy seems to make such a life go worse for the person leading it.[31]

Claim (1) also stands in tension with the idea that our autonomy is bounded by the autonomy of others. If X autonomously enslaves Y, then the fact that this project is autonomously pursued by X does not add value to X's life. Enslaving another violates their autonomy. Further, it is the wrongness of violating another's autonomy that explains why the successful pursuit of a project that involves such enslavement does not add value to one's life. But if this is so, then it would seem to follow that the successful pursuit of projects that involve wrongdoing generally do not add value to a life, whether or not the wrongdoing involves specifically the violation of the autonomy of others. And this conclusion brings us close to the claim expressed in Claim (2).[32]

There is an ambiguity in the idea of successfully pursing, or engaging with, a project or activity that involves wrongdoing, however. One can do wrong to others in the pursuit of bad ends, or can one do wrong to others in the pursuit of good ends. For example, one might steal money from a bank so as to contribute to the funding of some valuable project like the construction of a much-needed new library in one's town. Assuming that the wrongdoing of the means one took did not negate the value of the end one pursued, then this activity could add value to one's life, even under Claim (2). We should accept, then, that sometimes wrongful pursuits add value to one's life.[33] Granting this possibility, Claim (2) would still apply to projects and activities that are in the service of bad ends. If the autonomous pursuit of bad ends would not add value to a life, and if autonomy is valuable as an ideal that contributes to one's flourishing, then does it follow that one could have no autonomy-based interest in having access to bad options?

Maybe not. For, as we saw in the previous chapter, while it may not be good for one to autonomously pursue bad options, it may be good for one to have access to bad options, if one would not take them up. The value of pursuing good options might be enhanced by the fact that one had access to bad options and chose against them.[34] The extra value here is an increase in one's autonomy. Example: two people

---

[30]   Moore claims that the power to choose in ways that affect our character has value "because it is the means by which we bring greater integrity and coherence into our character," and he thinks that this value remains great whether or not we choose well, changing for the better or for the worse. But this, it seems to me, makes a fetish of coherence. Why is it good to become more coherently bad? (Moore, *Placing Blame*, p. 777.)

[31]   Ibid., p. 380.

[32]   It does not get us all the way there since good ends are contrasted not only with immoral ends but also with pointless or valueless ends.

[33]   The thought here is that from the standpoint of personal flourishing or living a good life, morality, while important, is not a concern that always overrides other concerns. For discussion, see Scheffler, *Human Morality*.

[34]   Hurka, "Why Value Autonomy?" *Journal of Social Philosophy*.

both successfully and autonomously pursue the same worthwhile ends, but the first does so in an environment in which certain bad options have been screened off, while the second does so in an environment that makes them readily available. The second person's valuable autonomous life is more autonomous than the first person's in virtue of their larger option set. This adds value to their life. If this is right, then people can have an autonomy-based interest in having access to bad options.

This line of argument has the potential to vindicate the thought we have been examining in this section. This is the thought that there is a standing autonomy-based presumption in favor of personal liberty and against foreclosing bad options. This presumption, in turn, could put in doubt some of the measures that would otherwise be justified by the project of ethical environmentalism. (Granted: if one accepts the Adequacy Claim, then one can rebut this line of argument. For, if autonomy requires only access to an adequate range of options, then the removal of some options, and in particular the removal of some bad options, need not set back anyone's interest in being autonomous. Still, we have suggested that autonomy comes in degrees, and this suggestion lends support to the claim that, other things being equal and from the standpoint of autonomy, it is better to have access to more options rather than less at least up to some point, which is likely to be a point above the threshold of adequacy.)

It will be helpful, at this juncture, to distinguish an autonomy-based interest from an autonomy-based claim. One can have an autonomy-based interest in having an option to do something without having a corresponding claim to have access to that option. Suppose that it were true that it is in my interests to have the option to enslave another person, even it would not be in my interests to take up this option. Accepting this supposition would require a reformulation of the claim that our autonomy is bounded by the autonomy of others. The reformulation would hold that our autonomy-based claims – not interests – are bounded by the autonomy-based claims – not interests – of others. On this reformulation, people might have autonomy-based interests in having access to bad options while having no autonomy-based claims to have access to them. Having the option to enslave others, or to participate in dehumanizing relationships with them, predictably would impose costs on others; and these costs plausibly block elevating to the status of claims whatever autonomy-based interests are implicated by having access to the options.

Focusing on autonomy-based claims to have access to various options, rather than merely autonomy-based interests in having them, brings us back to the dimension of fairness that is integral to the project of ethical environmentalism. Those who would argue that some bad option should be made available to all on the grounds that efforts to foreclose it would set back the autonomy of people must, if the fairness argument presented in Chapter 6 is sound, advance a more complicated argument. They would need to, first, distinguish those that would benefit from having access to the option (those who would not take it up) from those who would take it up and thereby suffer the costs of doing so. And they would need, second, to establish that it is fair to let the benefits that accrue to the former group take precedence over the costs imposed on the latter.

Sometimes this more complicated line of argument will succeed. Other times it will not. What seems plain is that, once the discussion is couched in these terms, the appeal to autonomy no longer is perspicuously understood in terms of establishing a presumption in favor of personal liberty. Generally speaking, that some legal measure, or the refusal to undertake some legal measure, would further the interests of at least some people is not a basis for claiming that there is a presumption in its favor.

7.3 AUTHENTICITY

We turned our attention to autonomy because we were seeking to identify a background ideal that was related to freedom and could establish a substantial presumption in favor of personal liberty. Autonomy seemed to fit the bill. But our critical discussion of it in the previous section provides some reason to think that we were looking in the wrong place. Perhaps a different freedom-related ideal of the good can ground the presumption in favor of personal liberty.

Describing an ideal that he terms "authenticity," Ronald Dworkin takes care to distinguish it from autonomy. He claims that this ideal, but not autonomy, has the resources to explain why various legal restrictions on liberty that improve, or are intended to improve, the ethical environment of a society are illegitimate.

> [A]uthenticity is not autonomy, at least as some philosophers understand that protean concept. They suppose that autonomy requires only that some range of choices be left open by the sum of circumstance, whether these be natural or political. A person's autonomy is not threatened, on this view, when government manipulates its community's culture so as to remove or make less eligible certain disapproved ways of living, if an adequate number of choices remain so that he can still exercise the power of choice. Authenticity, on the other hand … is very much concerned with the character as well as the fact of obstacles to choice. Living well means not just designing a life, as if any design would do, but designing it in response to a judgment of ethical value. Authenticity is damaged when a person is made to accept someone else's judgment in place of his own about the values or goals his life should display.[35]

Now, it might be thought with some justice that authenticity, so understood, is a just component of autonomy, one that we did not address in the previous section.[36] This terminological issue should not distract us. Whether authenticity is viewed as an ideal distinct from or as a component integral to the ideal of autonomy, the

---

[35] Dworkin, *Justice for Hedgehogs*, p. 212.
[36] Raz includes "independence" as a condition of personal autonomy. Independence is a relational condition, one that is intended to capture the significance of the character as well as the fact of obstacles to choice. See *The Morality of Freedom*, pp. 377–378.

substantive question remains the same. Can an appeal to it ground a presumption in favor of personal liberty?

Living authentically requires us to conduct our lives in the light of our own ethical judgments. Not every restriction of liberty offends authenticity, for some restrictions do not rest on ethical judgments that are rejected by those whose liberty is restricted. Dworkin gives the example of seatbelt requirements.

> Making people wear seat belts to prevent or mitigate injury is not ethical paternalism .... True, many people claim (perhaps a few of them sincerely) that a life that courts danger is attractive and that seat-belt legislation restricts people's opportunity to lead such a life. But seat-belt convictions are not foundational, and government need not assume that courting danger is a bad way to live in order to justify measures that reduce the costs of accidents to the community.[37]

Note that this passage gestures toward two distinct limits to the power of authenticity to ground a presumption in favor of liberty. First, if the ethical justification for a restriction is accepted by those whose liberty is restricted, then it does not offend authenticity. Second, if a restriction can be adequately justified by appeal to considerations that do not express or reflect ethical convictions about living well or poorly, then it does not offend authenticity.

No general presumption in favor of liberty, accordingly, follows from a commitment to authenticity, at least if Dworkin is right about its character. But the presumption that is established by a commitment to authenticity might still be substantial, and it might be substantial enough to put into doubt the general project of ethical environmentalism. For that project, as I have outlined it, is infused with ethical judgment.

The final sentence in the first of the two passages just quoted merits scrutiny. "Authenticity is damaged when a person is made to accept someone else's judgment in place of his own about the values or goals his life should display." Read strictly, this sentence implies that the life of the person who values kidnapping others is damaged when they are made to accept the judgment from others that they ought not do so. But this is not what Dworkin has in mind. Presumably, he does not think that we damage the kidnapper's authenticity when we restrict their liberty whenever they reject our judgment about the value of their project of kidnapping others. Read charitably, Dworkin's claim is less sweeping. As his remarks elsewhere make pellucid, it is ethical, not moral, judgment that engages authenticity.[38] If I am made to pay taxes because others judge that justice requires that I pay them, then the fact that I reject this judgment would not show that my life has been damaged. After all, I may be wrong in my judgments about justice and taxation, and, if so, I cannot complain that my life is damaged insofar as my liberty is restricted on the basis of judgments that I do not accept.

37 Dworkin, *Justice for Hedgehogs*, p. 370.
38 Ibid., p. 369.

So, authenticity applies only to a subset of evaluative judgments about how people should live. In Dworkin's terminology, our lives are damaged only when we are made to comply with ethical – not moral – judgments concerning the values and goals that our lives should display. The sustainability of this position looks to be in tension with what I have termed the "integration thesis." For if what Dworkin calls morality is bound up with what he terms ethics, then the claim that authenticity is damaged when ethical, but not moral, judgments are impressed upon us will be difficult to sustain. Political and legal efforts to improve or preserve valuable aspects of a society's public culture can be viewed in terms of what is owed to others, including especially the young. Fairness to them requires that we give them a fair shot at a good life, at least insofar as our efforts can have an impact on this opportunity. This perspective makes what Dworkin terms "cultural paternalism" as much a matter of morality as of ethics.

This response to Dworkin's argument can accept his claim that a person will not lead a good life if they are made to live in a manner that goes against the grain of their ethical convictions. Such a life would indeed lack authenticity. But there are a couple of important caveats – caveats that Dworkin does not properly attend to – that condition this claim. The first one is that a person's ethical convictions are not fixed, but responsive to evidence and argument. When sound policies of "cultural paternalism" are adopted, those who are subject to them, and initially oppose them, can come to recognize their value. In coming to appreciate the value of the policies, they eliminate the conflict between them and their ethical convictions. Even if the prospects for this kind of transformation are quite low, the fact that it is possible means that those who fail to live authentic lives under the policies bear at least some responsibility for their fate. This points us to the second caveat. A person's claim to live under conditions that make it more likely that they will lead an authentic life must be responsive to the claims of others, claims that go beyond the value of authenticity and encompass the full range of conditions relevant to their flourishing. Even if authenticity is a component of a good life, it is not the only component, and it would be a mistake to privilege it over all the other components.

Once these caveats are properly attended to, the force of authenticity comes to resemble that of autonomy, as it was outlined in the previous section. We can see this by reflecting, once again, on the value of option sets for agents. For some agents, having access to a certain option, such as the option to consume a dangerous drug, will decrease the value of their option set overall, even if its presence enhances their authenticity. They lead a better life without the option, even though its foreclosure by legal or other means brings with it a cost. For other agents, having access to the same option will improve their lives by making their lives a little more authentic without any downside. They will not engage with the option, or will not engage with it in a way that is detrimental to their well-being. For some, access to the option decreases the value of their option set; for others, it enhances the value of their option set. And since legal measures that would foreclose the option either cannot, or should not,[39] be tailored to different agents, the question of whether the measures should be undertaken is, among other things, a matter of treating them fairly.

Dworkin would resist this line of analysis. For him, authenticity is a trumping value. You cannot, he claims, improve someone's life by shielding them from bad options. The reason why you cannot do so is because living a good life is a skillful performance. To live well, one must respond well to the challenges that one's circumstances present. The details of this challenge conception of welfare are not important here. The relevant point for present purposes is that if Dworkin is right, then political and legal interventions that foreclose bad options will harm their intended beneficiaries. They will harm them by spoiling the performance value of their lives. And this is exactly what happens, he thinks, when we use legal force to screen out bad options out of paternalistic or moralistic concern. "[A] challenge cannot be more interesting, or in any other way a more valuable challenge to face, when it has been narrowed, simplified, and bowdlerized by others in advance."[40]

This appeal to a particular and idiosyncratic conception of a good life is only as good as the conception itself. And Dworkin's challenge conception of well-being is very problematic.[41] People can respond skillfully to the challenges that their lives present and still fare very poorly. Bad fortune can ruin a life just as much as bad performance. Parents who love their children, and whose concern is rightly fixed on their well-being, may hope that they will live well in the sense of responding well to the challenges their lives present and that they will fare well in the sense that they will realize, and participate in, important goods. But if they were forced to choose between their child living well or faring well, they would not give the former absolute priority over the latter. Indeed, they would likely care more about their child's faring well than their child's skillful performance, even if they cared about both.[42]

Parents have responsibilities to their children that governments do not have to their subjects. The notion that governments should assume parental-like responsibility for the fate of their subjects gives legal paternalism a bad name. But governments do bear some responsibility for the legal framework they put in place and sustain; and this framework, as we have argued, conditions the prospects for living good lives of those who are subject to it. The value of authenticity, at most, is one factor that bears on the justification of this framework.

---

[39] For reasons pointed out in Chapter 6.
[40] Dworkin, *Sovereign Virtue*, p. 273.
[41] For a battery of telling objections to the challenge conception of well-being, see Arneson, "Cracked Foundations of Liberal Equality."
[42] Arneson suggests that living skillfully is an idea that applies more fittingly to an admirable or praiseworthy life than to a life of well-being or flourishing. That seems broadly correct. But on a general notion of flourishing, living skillfully might find a place. If so, it would be one – but only one – component of a flourishing life, and not a component with the kind of priority that Dworkin assigns to it.

7.4 CONVENTIONALISM

Our search for an ideal of freedom that is both plausible and robust enough to establish a substantial presumption in favor of personal liberty has turned up empty. That does not mean that the claims of these ideals have no force. Far from it. But, if our discussion is correct, then they do not provide a standing reason to oppose paternalistic or moralistic measures. Suspicions will persist. Have we not overlooked the special significance that people attach to deliberate interference with their personal liberty? Dworkin put his finger on a concern that most of us share. We care very much about the character as well as the fact of an obstacle to our choices. Consider, for instance, the difference between a warning and a threat.[43] You may credibly threaten to harm me if I leave my house, or you may credibly warn me of an approaching storm that poses the same risk of harm to me if I leave my house. The two situations result in an equal limitation of my options, but there is all the difference in the world between them. In the threat situation, you compromise my independence by coercing me; in the warning situation, you do not.[44]

Several of the reasons why we respond differently to the two situations are plain enough. I can appropriately resent your action in the first situation, but not in the second. I can appropriately hold you to account for the reduction in my options in the first situation, but not in the second. And the character of my relationship with you, to the extent that I have one with you, will be affected in dramatically different ways depending on which of the two situations obtains. All of this is plain enough, as I said. But the less clear issue is why, if at all, it matters from the standpoint of one's freedom or autonomy whether one's options are foreclosed by deliberate interference (being subjected to a credible threat from another person) or by knowledge of natural circumstance (learning of an approaching storm).

A popular approach to this issue directs us to attend to the social meaning of deliberate interference. Expressive or symbolic considerations might explain why coercion and manipulation reduce freedom to a greater degree than can be accounted for by the ensuing reduction of options. Raz observes: "The natural fact that coercion and manipulation reduce options or distort normal processes of decision and the formation of preferences has become the basis of a social convention loading them with meaning regardless of their consequences. They have acquired a symbolic meaning expressing disregard or even contempt for the coerced or manipulated people."[45] Grant that such a social convention is in place in our society. This fact could then explain why coercion and manipulation are perceived by us to be more objectionable than other factors that reduce people's liberty in our society. But the perception, being a perception, looks past itself. It is a perception of some purported reality. And what exactly might that be? When we reflect on this

43   The example is taken from Pettit, *A Theory of Freedom*, p. 131.
44   I am assuming that you are not lying to me about the approaching storm.
45   Raz, *The Morality of Freedom*, p. 378.

question, we should not be content with the thought that the brute existence of the meaning-conferring convention is the end of the story. For that convention itself can be interrogated. We can say, "Yes, it is an established social fact that people in our society attach special meaning to deliberate interpersonal interference. But are we right to do so?"

This question is far from idle. For the social convention, and the meaning that it imposes on deliberate interference, could distort judgments about the good of personal liberty. Raz argues that political coercion is necessary to establish social conditions that enable all members of the society to have access to an adequate range of options, and he cautions us not to object to this coercion in the name of freedom.[46] But the meaning-conferring social convention in our society, when not properly interrogated, may lead us to do exactly that. Likewise, the same convention may lead us to mistakenly condemn sound political measures to improve the quality of the ethical environment in which we exercise our freedom.

One suspects that behind the social convention that deliberate interference has a special importance from the standpoint of freedom lies the thought that we have rights to be free from interference from others, and that the infringement of these rights impedes our personal liberty to a greater extent than do non-rights-infringing obstacles to choice. If this suspicion is correct, then to understand the relevant social convention, we must turn our attention from the good of personal liberty to the rights that protect it.

---

[46] Ibid., pp. 156–157.

8

Rights to Do Wrongs

The preceding chapter surveyed the case for thinking that liberty is a significant personal good, one that is weighty enough to establish a general presumption against legal interference into people's lives. We saw that while ideals of freedom such as autonomy and authenticity can ground significant limits to the legal enforcement of morality, they do not establish a general presumption against interference. Further, the case for personal liberty that is supported by these ideals leaves ample room for the project of ethical environmentalism. Be this as it may, many will think that the case for personal liberty, and against legal interference, does not rest on any appeal to the good. They will contend that personal liberty is best understood as a right, or a set of rights, and that these rights, in turn, rule out, or at least conflict with, legal measures designed to improve the ethical environment of a society by foreclosing, or making it more difficult to take up, some options that are considered to be bad or wrongful. In its starkest form, such a view cleaves to a general formula: the liberty of persons can only be legitimately restricted for the sake of securing the equal liberty of others.[1] We will examine this formula in Section 8.2, challenging both its determinacy and cogency. But even if the formula is rejected, a more moderate position remains in the field and merits careful attention. This position holds that persons are entitled to equal rights, and among these are rights to do various kinds of wrongs. And rights to do wrongs, once they are given their due, place substantial limits on the range of legal measures that can be undertaken to improve the ethical environment of a society.

8.1 THE IDEA

The idea of a right to do wrong can look paradoxical.[2] If a right to do wrong includes a permission to do wrong, then a right to do wrong appears to be a permission to do what is impermissible. This would indeed be paradoxical. But rights come in

---

[1] The formula is standardly taken to apply only to adults of sound mind who are not subject to incapacities of various kinds.

[2] There is no apparent paradox present when it is claimed that one has a right to do something that is merely prima facie, or pro tanto, wrong. Indeed, one can be morally required to do something that is pro

different kinds, and can be understood in different ways. Attending to these complexities can dissipate the perception of paradox in a right to do wrong.

We cannot here present a complete analysis of rights.[3] We limit our analysis to a few key distinctions that are helpful for understanding the arguments of this chapter. For starters, it is necessary to distinguish legal from moral rights. The notion of a legal right to do moral wrong does not court paradox, since plainly one can have a legal permission to do something that is morally impermissible. For example, the law may leave one free to kick a stray dog for no good reason, but in doing so one is doing something that one morally ought not do. The appearance of paradox here results from the failure to see the switch from the legal to the moral sense of rights. In addition, and holding the sense of rights constant, rights need not be understood to include permissions, as just suggested. The claim "I have a right to do X" need not imply "I am permitted to do X." Plausibly, we have a right to free speech that includes the right to say certain things that should not be said. A right that protects free speech, then, need not imply that all of the protected speech is rightful.

Introducing some terminology, we can distinguish choice-protecting rights from permission-protecting rights.[4] The former protect choices, whether permitted or not, while the latter protect only permitted choices. To see the difference, suppose that I am required to give 10 percent of my income to charity. Since I am required to do so, I am not permitted to not give this amount to charity. But I might have a right to decide for myself how much money, if any, I give to charity. If this right is choice-protecting, then it protects my choice to do something wrong, namely to choose not to give to charity.

The protection that a right provides to the rights-holder is protection from the interference of others. This protection can be analyzed in terms of claims and duties. To illustrate:

> "X has a right (with regard to Y) to Z" where X and Y are persons and Z is an action can be analyzed as "X has a claim against Y that Y not interfere with X's Zing and Y is under a duty not to interfere with X's Zing."

Claims and duties are logically connected. The existence of the claim implies the existence of the corresponding duty. But what kind of protection, it may be asked, do claims and duties provide to the holder of a right? Typically, the duties in question are enforceable. This means that those who do not honor the claims of the rights-holder, thereby violating the duties they are under with respect to them, are liable to sanction.

Notice that the right that X has in this simple example is held against one person, Y. But standardly rights are held against classes of people, and at the

tanto wrong. The apparent paradox arises when it is claimed that one has an undefeated right to do something that is all-things-considered wrong. See Enoch, "A Right to Violate One's Duty," pp. 360–361.

[3] The classic analysis of the nature of legal rights is Newcomb Hohfeld, *Fundamental Legal Conceptions As Applied in Judicial Reasoning*. Subsequent discussions commonly extend Hohfeld's analysis to moral rights.

[4] Edmundson, *An Introduction to Rights*, 2nd ed., pp. 108–113.

limit against all people. Lawyers speak of a right held against a specific person as a personal right – right *in personam* – and a right held against all others as a right against the world – right *in rem*.

The idea of a right to do wrong can now be stated with more precision. As it will be understood here, the right to do wrong is a choice-protecting right held against the world (or against all the members of a society) to perform some action that it is wrong to do. This formulation avoids paradox, allowing the rights-holder to claim coherently, "Whether my action is right or wrong, I have a right to do it." And this kind of right, if it can be vindicated, is obviously important for understanding the limits of the legal enforcement of morality.

A final matter needs to be cleared up. Is the right to do wrong, as understood here, a moral or a legal right, and is the wrong that the right purports to protect a moral or a legal wrong? There are a number of possibilities to consider:

(1) Legal rights to do legal wrongs
(2) Legal rights to do moral wrongs
(3) Moral rights to do legal wrongs
(4) Moral rights to do moral wrongs

(1), (2) and (3) are not our concern. The reason is simple. Whether there is a legal right to do legal wrongs, a legal right to do moral wrongs and/or a moral right to do legal wrongs are questions that apply to particular legal systems. There is no uniform answer to the question of whether these rights exist, since it all depends on what the law in this or that jurisdiction happens to contain. There could be legal rights to do legal wrongs (rights granted under diplomatic immunity provisions, for example) in one legal system but no such rights under another.[5] There could a legal right to do something wrong (kick a stray dog, for example) in one legal system but not in another. And there could be moral rights to do legal wrongs (help a fugitive slave escape, for example) under one legal system but no such right under another legal system, which either does not have the institution of slavery or does not have the legal prohibition against assisting fugitive slaves.[6]

If (1), (2) and (3) are put to one side, then only (4) remains. But it too does not accurately identify our concern. For our concern is with law, and the legal enforcement of morality, not simply with morality as such. Consider next:

(5) Morally justified legal rights to do moral wrongs

---

[5] The possibility of legal rights to do legal wrongs is defended in Hernstein, "A Legal Right to Do Legal Wrong," *Oxford Journal of Legal Studies* 34/1 (2014): 21–45. The diplomatic immunity example comes from him.

[6] I am not here taking a stand on the natural law/legal positivism debate. A natural law theorist who holds that an unjust law is not a law in one sense ("law is something that there is reason to have") can accept that it is a law in another sense (it is valid under the legal system in question). See Finnis, "Describing Law Normatively," in volume IV of his collected essays *Philosophy of Law*. Accordingly, such a theorist could agree that a law that prohibits assisting fugitive slaves, while gravely unjust, remains law in the thin descriptive sense here contemplated.

The truth or falsity of (5) is a moral question, but it is a moral question about law. It has the right form of the proposition we are seeking here to investigate.

It might be thought that (5) mirrors (4). After all, if there are moral rights to do moral wrongs, then would not justice require that these rights be recognized in law? Further, as Hart observed, "men speak of their moral rights mainly when advocating their incorporation in a legal system."[7] But matters are not so simple. There are a variety of ways by which (4) and (5) can come apart, two of which can be mentioned here.

First, the moral rights we are considering in this chapter are individual rights.[8] They protect domains of personal choice or safeguard important individual interests, depending on the theory of rights that is adopted. But legal rights, which are assigned to individual persons, can be justified by the contribution they make to the good of others in the society in which the person lives. One can think coherently that an individual has no moral right to do something, but that others should be legally constrained from interfering with them if they decide to do it. The legal right protects their choice to do the moral wrong, but its justification does not lie in the moral claim that they have not to be interfered with.

Second, as we have explained, the rights in question protect choice and this protection, typically at least, is backed up by law's enforcement power. Sanctions can be imposed on those who do not comply with the duties of noninterference that are the logical correlates of the legal rights to do moral wrong. But the officials of a just legal system might not provide this protection, judging correctly that the resources necessary for it are more equitably allocated to other, more pressing tasks.[9] Further, some moral rights to do moral wrongs may extend beyond the reach of the law. For example, people might have, as Mill believed they do have, a moral right to lead unconventional lifestyles that others find offensive, so long as their ways of living do not cause harm to others. But for this right to serve its function in protecting choice, it needs more than the force of law behind it. It must be backed up by "a strong barrier of moral conviction" that is firm enough to dissuade others from imposing crippling social penalties on those who exercise the right.[10]

These possibilities illustrate how (4) and (5) can come apart, but they also disclose some important interrelations that exist between them. The protection that choice-protecting rights provide to the rights-holders is, in part, a function of the sanctioning power that stands behind them. But sanctions, while typical of effective choice-protecting rights, are not necessary for the existence of these rights. The more that the members of a society are motivated to comply with

---

[7] Hart, "Are There Any Natural Rights?" *The Philosophical Review* 64/2 (1955): 175–191, at 177.

[8] This is not to deny the possibility of collective rights. They are not our concern in this chapter, however.

[9] The unprotected legal rights in this scenario still exist, but they might fail to serve their function of protecting choice.

[10] Mill, *On Liberty*, p. 227.

their legal duties because they accept that they have reason to do so, the less important sanctions become.[11] Drawing on Hart, we can express this idea in terms of validity and efficacy. Choice-protecting rights are valid if they are included within the relevant normative system, whether legal or moral, but they are efficacious only if the duties correlated with them are generally honored. The function of choice-protecting rights, including choice-protecting rights to do things that are morally wrong, is to provide protection to the rights-holders against interference from others. But this function can only be served if the rights in question are efficacious, and the efficacy of these rights (typically) is a function in part of the enforcement power behind them.[12]

Enforcement can consist of legal or social sanctions, or both. This means that the kind of protection provided by legal choice-protecting rights need not be the same as the protection afforded by the corresponding moral choice-protecting rights, for the latter right might correlate with enforceable duties against the imposition of social penalties that is absent from the former. To return to Mill's example, the legal choice-protecting rights that protect a person's ability to adopt an unconventional lifestyle may correlate with duties of noninterference that do not protect the rights-holder from certain kinds of social penalty. The rights-holder, while legally protected from a range of interferences, may remain liable to having social costs of various kinds, such as those that result from social ostracism, deliberately imposed on them. This presumably was Mill's concern in cautioning against a too blinkered focus on the law and the sanctions it imposes.

These Millian concerns about social penalties, and the need for rights-holders to be protected from them, will come to center-stage in our discussion of the right of free expression in Chapter 9. For now, we need to tie up one loose end in our discussion of the idea of a right to do wrong. We have analyzed this idea in terms of a morally justified legal right to do moral wrong. We have attributed a point or function to such a right; namely, to provide protection against interference from others. And we have claimed that rights of this kind (typically) can only serve their function if they are backed up by appropriate sanctioning power. In pressing these points, we have focused on the kind of protection that choice-protecting rights provide to those who have them, highlighting the efficacy of the rights as well as

---

[11]   Since Hart, analytic jurisprudence has tended to downplay the significance of sanctions for the existence of law, emphasizing instead the reasons and obligations that law creates. But, as Hart recognized, it is an important fact about actual legal systems that they typically rely on enforcement mechanisms to ensure adequate compliance with the law. For a recent discussion that plays up the role of sanctions and enforcement for understanding law, see Schauer, *The Force of Law*.

[12]   In discussing the "elements of rights," Kagan distinguishes an "injunction" one holds against interference from others from "an enforcement privilege," which gives the rights-holder, or their representatives, the right to enforce the injunction. He stipulates that a full right contains both an injunction and an enforcement privilege (Kagan, *The Limits of Morality*, p. 219). A little differently, I am suggesting that the efficacy of a right – that is, its effectiveness in realizing its function – may in some, perhaps most, circumstances require an enforcement privilege. But there is no necessary connection between the existence and the full efficacy of a right and this privilege.

their validity. But the notion of a legal right to do moral wrong can be looked at from a different perspective, namely the perspective of a conscientious lawmaker or judicial official. From this perspective, the efficacy of the choice-protecting right shades into the background. What matters fundamentally from this perspective is whether legislation or judicial decision honors the rights in question. If there is a legal right to do moral wrong, then its existence constitutes a legal limit on the law's pursuit of its other aims, including its aims regarding the enforcement of morality in a society. Likewise, and more germane to our purposes, if there is no legal right to do moral wrong in a legal system, but there would be such a right if the legal system were fully justified, then the right ought to be established and honored. Here the right constitutes a moral limit on the law's pursuit of its other aims, including its efforts to enforce morality.

Nothing we have said so far supports the claim that rights to do wrong of this kind exist or can be justified. Our preliminary goal has been to clarify the idea of a right to do wrong and to make it clearer how we are construing it here. With this preliminary task completed, we can now turn to the substantive question of whether any such rights exist, and what considerations might be thought to underwrite them.

8.2 THE EQUAL RIGHT OF ALL TO BE FREE

Specific rights to do wrongs might be thought to follow from a more basic and more general right that all persons have in virtue of their personhood. The possibility of such a general right might be thought to be suggested by the language and characteristic use of the notion of rights – specifically choice-protecting rights – when they are defensively asserted. People say, "you have no right to stop me from doing as I please" to express the thought that there is no compelling justification for your interference. But this thought, or so it may be argued, presupposes another thought, to wit that one has a right to be free from interference in the absence of such a justification.

We are here close to the thought, discussed in Chapter 7, that there is a general presumption in favor of liberty, a presumption that ought to be honored by law. We move closer to that thought by narrowing the grounds of compelling justification to those that advert to special relationships between people ("you waived your right that I not interfere with you regarding the matter at hand") or to the fact that such interference is necessary to hinder one person from coercing or injuring another ("I interfered with you to stop you from interfering with them").

Hart claims that the general equal right to be free that emerges from this line of thought can be viewed as a natural right, one that should be incorporated into and regulate the law in a just legal system.[13] Such a right would license legal rights to do

---

[13] Hart commits himself only to the conditional existence of this natural right: "if there are any moral rights at all, it follows that there is at least one natural right, the equal right of all men to be free." Hart, "Are There Any Natural Rights?" p. 175.

moral wrongs whenever the moral wrongs did not violate either a special obligation
or the equal right of others to be free from coercion and injury. The right (or set of
rights) to corrupt oneself or others, for example, would be a particular instantiation
of the more general equal right to be free.

The general equal right to be free, as sketched by Hart and others, has clear affinities
with the sovereignty principle that we considered in Chapter 4. Writers working
within the Kantian tradition often construe an equal right to be free in terms of the
equal right of each person to be independent from the will of others, a sovereign
master over themselves. This appeal to mutual independence and self-sovereignty
severely constrains the kinds of reasons that can be invoked to justify interference.[14]
Since we have already discussed some of the limitations to this idea of self-sovereignty
in that earlier chapter, we need not repeat them here. Instead, and focusing on Hart's
discussion of the idea, we can bring into view some further potential limitations that
bear more directly on the legal enforcement of morality and the project of ethical
environmentalism.

Let us start with Hart's articulation of the Kantian claim that the justification of
coercion engages a special part of morality:

> [W]e must distinguish from the rest of morality those principles regulating the
> proper distribution of human freedom which alone make it morally legitimate for
> one human being to determine by his choice how another should act; and a certain
> specific moral value is secured (to be distinguished from moral virtue in which the
> good will is manifested) if human relationships are conducted in accordance with
> these principles even though coercion has to be used to secure this, for only if these
> principles are regarded will freedom be distributed among human beings as it
> should be.[15]

Although Hart approvingly cites this Kantian view, his own position is considerably
weaker in that it allows that the equal right to be free may not be absolute.[16] Thus, in
principle, on Hart's view other considerations can override this right; and this
means, although Hart does not attend to this implication, the range of considerations that can justify the coercion of others in practice may extend well beyond
those implicated by the right.

Perhaps for this reason Hart acknowledges that some will think that his concession
here may "reduce the importance of [his] contention" about this right. Yet rights,
including the equal right to be free, could be stringent without being absolute. Let us
proceed, then, on the assumption that the right in question is stringent, even if not
absolute, as Kant held it was. On the right, coercion can be justified to hinder or
restrain the coercion of others. Each person can be coerced to secure the equal right

---

"Any real or claimed entitlement of a person or group of persons to tell another what to do, or force
      him to do as he is told, is potentially in tension with the latter person's entitlement to be his own
      master." Ripstein, *Force and Freedom*, pp. 4–5.
Hart, "Are There Any Natural Rights?" p. 178.
Ibid., p. 176.

of others. Call this condition (1). Other forms of independence-compromising interference, such as manipulation or fraudulent dealing, presumably also can be forcibly limited to secure the equal right of all under this condition. So far, so good. But we must also attend to the special rights and special obligations that arise between persons who participate in certain relations of interaction with one another. These special normative relations, as we might call them, can also provide grounds for the justified use of force. Call this condition (2). If I contract with you to provide you with some good or service, but then renege on the deal, I am liable to coercive interference. The law may require me to live up to the contract or to compensate you for the damages you incurred for your reliance on it.

Contractual relations are one kind of special normative relation. Hart mentions several others, including, and most relevant for our purposes, those that arise from various joint enterprises. Participation in these enterprises can give rise to special rights and special obligations. Hart explains: "when a number of persons conduct any joint enterprise according to rules and thus restrict their liberty, those who have submitted to these restrictions when required have a right to a similar submission from those who have benefited by their submission."[17] The core idea expressed in this passage has come to be called the "principle of fairness," and it has been invoked in efforts to justify the obligation to obey the law in reasonably just societies. For political society itself can be viewed as a joint enterprise, as Hart emphasized. As such, it consists of rules that confer authority on some members to make and enforce further rules on others. These rules – or some of them, to be more precise – impose obligations on those who are subject to them. The normative relations that result from the exercise of this authority, in turn, provide new grounds for the justification of coercion.

The principle of fairness has figured prominently in contemporary discussions of the obligation to obey the law, and Hart's discussion of it has been subjected to effective criticism. But before attending to some of this criticism, we can note that the principle of fairness enables proponents of the equal right of all to be free to provide an account of distributive justice and the provision of public goods for a political society, a task that has exercised contemporary Kantians (or neo-Kantians), but did not exercise Kant.[18] Without the principle of fairness, or some cognate notion, the equal right of all to be free looks to be in tension with the rights and obligations, and the justifications for coercion that come with them, that are engendered by participation in a fair scheme of social cooperation.

I believe that the principle of fairness, when properly formulated, is sound. But I will not here try to show that the principle of fairness is sound. Instead, I will argue that *if* the principle of fairness is sound and *if* it succeeds in grounding the

---

[17] Ibid., p. 185.
[18] "Most striking of all from the perspective of contemporary readers, he [Kant] denies that justice [in a political society] is concerned with the fair distribution of benefits and burdens. None of the principles he formulates are in terms of them." Ripstein, *Force and Freedom*, p. 3.

obligations it was introduced to explain, then it and the equal right of all to be free that
coheres with it are broadly consistent with the project of ethical environmentalism
that was outlined in Chapters 5 and 6.

A common and influential objection to the principle of fairness holds that the
mere receipt of a benefit in a joint enterprise does not generate a reciprocal obligation to do one's part in providing it. Thrusting just any good on another partner in
a joint enterprise does not generate any obligation on their part to contribute to its
provision.[19] A natural response to the objection holds that the benefits in question
must be freely accepted. If I freely and willingly accept the benefit that is thrust on
me, then I may have an obligation to contribute to its provision.[20] But, as critics have
been quick to point out, many of the goods provided by political authorities are not
freely accepted by all. Even a paradigmatic public good, such as national defense or
clean air, will be rejected by some as unnecessary or not worth the costs of its
provision.

The principle of fairness was intended by Hart to provide a justification for the
collective provision of various public goods. If it is construed to require the free
acceptance of the relevant goods, then it will fail to ground the obligations it was
intended to ground. This point can be taken to support a non-voluntaristic
understanding of the principle. With many goods, one cannot obligate another
by providing them with goods that they do not freely accept; but with public goods
matters may be different. Public goods are public in the sense that (i) they are
presumed to be beneficial to all members of society and (ii) it is not feasible to exclude
some from receiving them while providing them to others. With respect to public
goods, it has been argued, the principle of fairness grounds an obligation to contribute
one's fair share to their provision, even when the good provided is not freely and
willingly accepted.[21]

We should pause to clarify the notion that public goods are presumed to be
beneficial to all the members of the society. This notion had better not imply that
each member judges the goods to be a benefit to themself, or a net benefit, given the
costs of contributing to them; for then we will be saddled with the problems of the
principle on the understanding that the goods must be freely accepted. Those who
do not freely accept the goods, judging them to be worth the costs of fair provision,
will not be obligated to contribute to them. True, someone might judge that the
receipt of the good was worth the cost of fairly contributing to its provision but
nonetheless refuse to accept it. But, generally speaking, the refusal to freely accept
the good will be based on the assessment that it is not worth the costs of fair
contribution. The non-voluntaristic understanding of the principle of fairness,
then, must presume that the goods in question benefit all, even if all do not accept
that they do.

---

[19]   Nozick, *Anarchy, State and Utopia*, pp. 93–94.
[20]   Simmons, "The Principle of Fair Play," *Philosophy and Public Affairs* 8/4 (1979): 307–337.
[21]   Arneson, "Fairness and Free Rider Problems," *Ethics* 92 (1982): 616–633.

Working with the principle of fairness on the non-voluntaristic understanding, we can now ask, is it consistent with the equal right of all to be free? If the answer is no, then acceptance of the equal right to be free leaves us with the problem of justifying the provision of public goods in political society. If the answer is yes, the equal right to be free permits fairness-based interferences that are not covered by conditions (1) and (2). The equal right of all to be free will now be subject to a third condition, one that accounts for fairness-based grounds for interference that are necessary to secure important goods in nonvoluntary joint enterprises. Such goods will include traditional public goods, such as national defense and clean air, but also, I now contend, other goods that constitute the common good of the political society. Securing and sustaining an environment, ethical as well as physical, that is conducive to the well-being of the members of the society will fall under this heading, bringing the equal right of all to be free into harmony with the project of ethical environmentalism.[22]

I have been discussing the Kantian idea of a natural right of all to be equally free – a right that, if accepted, could provide a general justification for various rights to do wrongs. These rights would protect choices to engage in wrongful activities, provided that the activities did not infringe on the equal rights of others. I have argued that if this purported right is appropriately qualified to take account of the non-voluntaristic fairness-based obligations that arise from participation in a joint enterprise of the kind instantiated by a political association, then it will not ground rights to do wrongs that militate against the project of ethical environmentalism. For people will not have in general rights to corrupt the ethical environment of their society. Just as a government can impose restrictions on its subjects to preserve the quality of the air in their physical environment, it can impose restrictions on them to preserve the quality of their ethical environment. The equal right of all to be free, when qualified by the principle of fairness, accordingly, will ground rights to do wrongs only when those wrongs do not bear significantly on the collective properties of the society that constitute its common good.[23]

Granting this point leaves open an important question. Might not the common good of a society be furthered by the recognition and securement of at least some rights to do wrongs? To this question we now turn.

---

[22] In Rawlsian terms, the idea here could be put as follows. The equal right of all to be free is consistent with the exercise of coercion necessary to establish and sustain a basic structure of society that fairly advances the fundamental interests of its members. Proponents of ethical environmentalism can accept this formal statement, even as they disagree with Rawls over the content of fairness and the characterization of the fundamental interests.

[23] A caveat: the principle of fairness, as Hart understood it, grounds enforceable obligations to contribute to the provision of public goods in a joint enterprise. However, in certain cases, the costs of enforcement would be disproportionate given the significance of the public good in question. Here, in a certain sense, participants in the joint enterprise would have a choice-protecting right to do wrong. They would be obligated to contribute, but if they failed to do so, they should not be penalized. See the discussion in Section 8.4 on the purported right to loot.

8.3 MORALITY-FREE ZONES AND THE PRACTICE OF ACCOMMODATION

In some minds our discussion of ethical environmentalism will conjure up an excessively moralistic picture of society, one that leaves insufficient space for what Mill called the self-regarding sphere of human activity. The common good, they will object, looms too large in this picture. It turns too many seemingly self-regarding acts into matters of public concern.

Perhaps they are right. People may need some freedom *from* morality in order to lead satisfying lives.[24] Too much focus on the common good of a society and too much emphasis on how our decisions and actions affect its ethical character obscure this important point. Rights to do wrong, accordingly, may be vindicated as devices for securing the requisite freedom from morality.

Seana Shiffrin approaches this idea in an instructive discussion of what she terms "accommodation" in a liberal society. Accommodation is needed to secure certain goods, the goods made possible by "less-encumbered free choice."[25] These goods, although Shiffrin does not express the point in these terms, may provide a grounding for rights to do wrongs.

> Where the environment is permeated by cost-exaction and public-spirited reminders that even many seemingly self-regarding acts have other-regarding effects, agents may feel constrained by the sense that everything they do has an impact on others and is subject to accounting. *Even if this accounting is fair*, the ubiquity of the message may nonetheless constrain or chill choice . . .. Some of the goods of less-encumbered free choice may thus be sacrificed.[26]

Accordingly, to secure these goods for its members a society needs to carve out space in which individuals are free to lead their lives, unburdened, or at least less burdened, by the demands of public morality. Crucially, this accommodating space will give them options to impose burdens and costs on others, even when doing so is unfair.

To add some concreteness to this discussion, consider a simple example, which is a variant on one provided by Shiffrin. A society might decide to allocate scarce resources, such as livers for transplant, in a way that is insensitive to the responsibilities of those who are in need of them. On this responsibility-blind policy, Jack who needs a liver transplant because he culpably[27] abused alcohol in the past will have the same

---

[24] The idea here is related to, but distinct from, a point pressed by Nagel. It is "a desirable feature of a social order that within it, people should not be too constrained in the pursuit of their own lives by constant demands for impartial attention to the welfare of others" (Nagel, *Equality and Partiality*, p. 83). Nagel's point is better understood as a call for morality to recognize the importance of the personal point of view than as a call for a measure of freedom from the demands of morality.

[25] "Less-encumbered," not simply "unencumbered," free choice, since the kind of freedom envisioned here is not the freedom to disregard all moral considerations.

[26] Shiffrin, "Paternalism, Unconscionability Doctrine, and Accommodation," p. 239 (italics added).

[27] Those who insist that all alcohol abuse is a disease for which no responsibility falls on the abuser will resist this description. I assume here, as I think most readers will agree, that there are at least some cases of alcohol abuse for which the abusers bear some responsibility.

opportunities to receive a scarce liver as Jill who needs a liver transplant because of a disease for which she bears no responsibility.[28] This policy can be criticized as unfair to Jill. A fairer policy would give at least some weight to responsibility considerations. Under the policy, Jack's seemingly self-regarding decision to drink irresponsibly imposes costs on Jill, since her chances for receiving the needed organ are reduced by his imprudence. Jack might respond to criticism of his drinking behavior by claiming that he has a right to abuse alcohol, even if doing so is wrong in virtue of the costs it could impose on others. He has a right to do wrong.

On Shiffrin's view of accommodation, Jack may have a case. In making decisions about whether or not to drink, he should not have to worry about how his drinking down the line might affect others. Here accommodation "promotes a certain sort of freedom" that "allows an agent to respond to a certain range of reasons that might otherwise be dominated by considerations relating to others, by morality."[29]

The claim here is intriguing and puzzling. Suppose we accept the value of accommodation and believe with Shiffrin that it applies to the liver transplant example. Does this provide a compelling example of a right to do wrong? On the one hand, the answer seems to be "yes," since we are assuming that people like Jack in this example impose unfair costs on others when their choices are protected by accommodation. But, on the other hand, accommodation is itself a good, or, better put, it is a practice that protects certain goods, the goods associated with "less-encumbered free choice." Denying these goods to Jack may be unfair to him. If so, then fairness, far from militating against Jack's claim, provides support for it. The claim here is puzzling in a second, deeper way. The demands of morality are pervasive and categorical. Can Jack, or anyone, insulate himself from them? Can Jack really say that while it is true that it was wrong for him to do as he did, he is not appropriately subject to reproach since his wrongful decision fell within a morality-free zone carved out by the practice of accommodation?

An adequate response to this second puzzle will also resolve the first one. We are assuming that the goods of less-encumbered free choice are genuine goods. The fact that these goods can be secured only by a non-attentiveness to the full range of moral considerations that bear on the choices involved provides a justification for the requisite non-attentiveness. Morality here is complex. The moral value of the goods in prospect provides reasons to exclude certain other moral reasons from consideration in making choices, even though these choices may impose costs on others.[30] While complex, this point about morality is not unfamiliar. We can distinguish the moral assessment about the process by which a person makes

---

[28] For the sake of the example, let us assume that the liver transplant would be just as beneficial to Jack as it would be to Jill. Jack has effectively forsworn his alcohol abuse and would not continue to drink irresponsibly if given the transplanted organ.

[29] Shiffrin, "Paternalism, Unconscionability Doctrine, and Accommodation," p. 247.

[30] Adopting terminology from Raz, the goods of less-encumbered free choice ground an "exclusionary reason" for barring certain moral considerations from deliberation. See Raz, *Practical Reason and Norms.*

a given choice from the moral assessment of the choice that they make. Sometimes people make the right choice but do so for the wrong reasons, or do so because they attended to reasons that they should not have attended to in the situation.[31] Other times people make the wrong choice but do so after deliberating properly. The fact that they deliberated well before acting may excuse their action, but it would not, at least not always, make it the case that they did not act wrongly.

Distinguishing the moral value of a deliberative process from the moral value of the choice made after deliberation brings into view a number of interesting possibilities. Applying them to the example of Jack's choice to drink, consider the following:

(1) Jack chooses well after deliberating well.
(2) Jack chooses poorly after deliberating well.
(3) Jack chooses well after deliberating poorly.
(4) Jack chooses poorly after deliberating poorly.

The first possibility is the best one. The last possibility is the worst one. But how should we rank (2) and (3)? Often it will be better to choose well after poor deliberation than to choose poorly after good deliberation. Often, but not always. In situations where poor deliberation will defeat or impede valuable goods, and where the poor choice will not impose excessive costs on oneself or others, it will be better to deliberate well than to deliberate poorly while making the right choice. The claim that the good of less-encumbered free choice in Jack's situation justifies inattention to certain moral considerations in deliberation thus amounts to the claim that (2) is better than (3) in this situation from the standpoint of morality.

Note that, on this analysis, it remains the case that (1) is superior to (2). For in (1) the goods of less-encumbered free choice are not sacrificed, and the good of distributive fairness is secured, as it is not in (2). We saw in Chapter 6 that paternalistic interference can be justified by appeal to distributive fairness. Jack's imprudent behavior can impose unfair costs on others, thereby providing a fairness-based reason to interfere with his, and others', behavior. But if this interference, or the threat of such interference, defeats or damages the good of unencumbered free choice by causing those who are subject to it to attend to considerations that when attended to damage the good, then there is a reason not to undertake the paternalistic interference in question. And if, in this situation, securing the good of less-encumbered free choice is morally more significant than securing the fair distribution of costs at which the paternalistic interference aims, then this counter-reason defeats the fairness-based reason.

---

[31]   Consider Bernard Williams's well-known example of the man who has "one thought too many" when rescuing his wife from peril. The man does the right thing (rescues his wife) but does so after apparently inappropriate deliberation (giving undue attention to the fact that morality permits him to save his wife in the situation).

In this way, accommodation and the goods that it protects provide a ground for a right to do wrong, a right to impose unfair costs on others. But is this not unfair to these others, and in our example to Jill? This is the first puzzle alluded to earlier. Notice, however, that the goods of less-encumbered free choice are beneficial to all. Jill as well as Jack has an interest in them. In situations in which it is better for people to deliberate well than to choose well, the cost of unfairness in the distribution of costs is compensated by the benefit of the goods of less-encumbered free choice that are secured. And, so, Jill is not treated unfairly by the practice of accommodation, although the distribution of the costs from poor choice that result from it may not be optimal from the standpoint of fairness.[32] In these situations, the practice of accommodation is not opposed to, but part of, the common good of the society.

Shiffrin argues that a good society must be responsive both to our need for interconnection with others and to our need for insulation from them. Practices of accommodation secure the needed insulation. Building on this idea, we have argued that if practices of accommodation secure genuine goods, then these practices further the common good of the society. They do so by facilitating the realization of the goods in question to all members of the society. Doing so has a price, however. The resulting distribution of costs that result from poor choice may not be borne in a way that is optimally fair.

Our discussion has not attempted to define the domain of legitimate accommodation. I have claimed, weakly and vaguely, that where the goods of less-encumbered free choice are significant and where the costs of distributive unfairness are not excessive, then accommodation is appropriate. A limited right to do wrong operates in this space of appropriate accommodation. But this limited right to do wrong does not set back the common good of the society that recognizes it, for the practices of accommodation themselves serve that common good.

8.4 NESTED RIGHTS

Thus far, the argument of this chapter has supported only a modest place for a right to do wrong. Rights that secure the good of less-encumbered free choice do so by shielding choice from certain moral considerations that potentially justify interference with it. Can this modest ground be extended further?

Rather than looking for some general foundation for rights to do wrongs, the proponent of these rights can argue that they emerge from a range of more specific rights. Attention to these rights can help us to understand how rights to do wrongs can be justified. In an insightful discussion of the issue, Jeremy

---

[32] Optimal fairness is achieved only when all deliberate well and all choose well. Our point here can be expressed as follows. In the circumstances we are envisaging, where (2) rightly ranks above (3), then situations that result from either (1) or (2) are fair to all parties, but (1) is the best fair situation.

Waldron lists a number of examples of specific rights that embed rights to do wrongs:[33]

- the rights of ownership
- the rights of freedom of association
- the rights of free political speech
- the right to vote in a democratic society.

Let us assume that all of these rights are justified legal rights. A well-ordered legal system would recognize and enforce them. However, as Waldron points out, recognizing these rights requires us to acknowledge that they can be misused. One can exercise one's right to free political speech or one's right to vote in a democratic election for bad purposes. One might aim to further injustice or to deliberately mislead one's fellow citizens on important political matters, for example. The right to do these particular wrongs is protected by what we might call the *covering rights* under which they are subsumed. Put otherwise, the covering right, the right to free political speech or the right to vote, cannot be fully realized unless the subsumed rights to do wrong are protected.

Waldron claims that the covering rights are moral rights. Nested within them are more particular moral rights to do moral wrongs. The covering rights have a function. Their function is to protect choice among alternatives with regard to "certain key areas of decision-making, which have a special importance for individual integrity and self-constitution."[34] But this invites a natural objection. Why must the protected alternatives extend to wrongful actions? One might think that the alternatives that merit protection are worthwhile options. We have an interest in valuable integrity and self-constitution, not an interest in integrity and self-constitution as such.

Waldron's response to this objection is not persuasive. He contends that if we were to limit the alternatives to morally acceptable options, then we would "impoverish the content of our theory of rights," leaving only "the banalities and trivia of human life" to be protected.[35] But this contention is sound only if the sphere of morally acceptable options does not extend to important choices that are central to our integrity and self-constitution. On a pluralistic account of the good, however, many significant and incompatible, but morally acceptable, options for self-constitution are available. We have wide scope to fashion ourselves into one kind of person rather than another and to become the part-author of our own lives with integrity, all without contravening any of the requirements of morality. Accordingly, Waldron's contention is plausible only if one rejects this kind of pluralistic account of the good and adopts instead a more determinate account that leaves little room for reasonable choice among important ends.[36]

---

[33] Waldron, "A Right to Do Wrong," in his *Liberal Rights* (Cambridge: Cambridge University Press, 1993).
[34] Ibid., p. 81.
[35] Ibid., p. 83.
[36] This line of objection is pressed effectively by George, *Making Men Moral*, pp. 126–127.

Working with this alternative and more determinate account of the good, the value of free choice and the value of the self-constitution that it makes possible are called into question, however. For it is far from clear why it is good for a person to constitute themself in a manner that is practically unreasonable.

This rebuttal proceeds too swiftly. Possibly, while we have no interest in constituting ourselves in unreasonable ways, we have an important interest in having access to options to do so. This possibility was noted in our discussion of the value of option sets in the previous chapter. Valuable self-constitution may be enhanced by the decision to forgo certain disvaluable alternatives for choice. This possibility, however, likely does not take us very far in vindicating the rights to do wrong that Waldron had in mind. Are there other promising possibilities for vindicating these rights? Consider an example provided by William Galston. If, he writes, "an outbreak of looting can only be quelled by a draconian shoot-to-kill policy, it is by no means clear that it is proper to employ such a policy. But our qualms about permissibility obviously do not stem from any suspicion that the looters had a right to do what they did."[37] This example merits closer scrutiny. Let us grant that it would indeed be wrong to adopt the shoot-to-kill policy. This policy would be a disproportionate response to the wrongdoing of looting. Further, let us grant that the government in this example should not only abstain from the shoot-to-kill policy itself but also forbid private parties from employing it. Nevertheless, Galston claims, the looters depicted in the example do not have a right to engage in looting.

Galston is right, but only partially right. Nothing about the activity of looting helps to ground a right to do so in the example. If the looters have a moral right, it is not the moral right to loot but rather a moral right not to be subjected to disproportionate force. However, this right is itself a covering right. As such, it plainly extends to the right not to be subjected to disproportionate force while looting.[38] If a looter is shot, then they have been wronged. Their rights have been violated.[39] (Note that matters would be different if the shoot-to-kill policy were a proportionate response to the wrongness of looting, even though it remained wrong to undertake it for other reasons, such as the possibility that innocent bystanders could be killed. Here the choice to loot is protected, but the justification for the protection has nothing to do with the interests of the looters.)

---

[37] Galston, "On the Alleged Right to Do Moral Wrong," p. 321.

[38] Disproportionate force is force in excess of what is permissibly imposed. The right to loot in the example is nested under the right not to be subjected to disproportionate force, but an agent's interest in looting or claim to have a jurisdiction in which to loot play no role in its justification.

[39] The claim that the looters in Galston's example have a moral right to loot is conversationally odd in the way recently analyzed by Schauer. Generally speaking, it is misleading to single out a particular member of a larger set unless there is some point to doing so ("Free Speech on Tuesdays," *Law and Philosophy* [2015]: 119–140). The right to loot in these circumstances is a particular member of the more general set of rights to not be subjected to unjustified force. To single it out and refer to it as a moral right to loot, when there is nothing about the activity of looting that warrants doing so, misleads.

The question, then, is whether the nested rights that Waldron calls attention to can be analyzed in terms comparable to those of the looting example. Consider Waldron's first candidate for a such a right: "Someone uses all the money that he has won fairly in a lottery to buy racehorses and champagne, refusing to donate any of it to a desperately deserving charity."[40] Note, to begin with, that this example is not ideal for Waldron's purposes. For starters, the example may exhibit ungenerous behavior rather than wrongful behavior. Perhaps it would be morally better for him to donate at least some of the winnings to the charity (or some other worthy cause) rather than keep all of it for himself. Still, morality plausibly allows us to do morally suboptimal actions. We may have a prerogative, as it were, to do less than what would be morally best.[41] If so, then it is not morally wrong for us to act within its scope. In short, "I have a prerogative to do what is morally suboptimal" does not imply that "I have a right to do wrong."

For Waldron's example to be effective, then, it must be assumed that if the person in the example refuses to donate any of the winnings to the charity, then he not only acts suboptimally from the standpoint of morality but also fails to do what he is required to do. Let us grant this claim for argumentative purposes. Now it can be said with plausibility that the person in question has a right that others not take his money without his consent and transfer it to the charity. These others have a duty to respect his property. This duty protects his choice to do what is wrong, namely to keep all the money for himself.

This example differs importantly from the looting example. To see why, suppose that this person's government were to tax his lottery winnings with the aim of distributing some of the money to the deserving charity. If he had a moral right to keep all of the lottery money, then the government would violate this right in taxing him. But he has no such right, given the assumption that he is morally required to give the money to the charity. Since he has no right to keep all of the money, the government does not violate his rights when it taxes him. Accordingly, he does not have a right to wrongfully keep his property in the example.

We have seen that one can have a justified legal right to do wrong even when one has no moral right to do the wrong in question. Attention to this point can help to explain the example. The person has a justified legal right, held against other private persons, that they respect his property, including his windfall gains from the lottery. But he has neither a moral right nor a justified legal right that his government not tax his lottery winnings.

A question remains. What explains or grounds the duties of other private citizens to respect his property rights when he acts wrongly in refusing to donate to the charity? The answer must be the value of the institution of private property. This institution serves the common good of the society. All the members of the society

[40] Waldron, "A Right to Do Wrong," p. 63.
[41] For discussion of this prerogative, see Scheffler, *The Rejection of Consequentialism*.

have an interest in the security of legally recognized property. If private persons were free to seize the property of others whenever they judged that the property was being used wrongfully, then the institution of private property would collapse. But the institution of private property is not threatened by taxation (as such).[42]

The analysis of the purported right to do wrong in the lottery example, accordingly, has a complex structure. There is no moral right to wrongfully hoard one's property. There is, however, a justified legal right to security of one's legally recognized property, a right that is grounded in the fact that institution of private property serves the common good of the society and the fact that this institution would be destroyed if private persons were free to take one's property whenever they judged that it was being hoarded wrongfully. This justified legal right is a covering right that extends to the right of wrongfully hoarding one's legally recognized property. But such a right, not being a moral right, does not bar one's government from transferring one's lottery winnings through its power of taxation.

The remaining cases that Waldron mentions involving the right to speak freely, to vote freely and to associate freely present additional complications. These rights also serve the common good of a society, but they ground limits to government interference as well as the interference of private persons. Accordingly, to understand them, and the rights to do wrong that they purportedly cover, we need a fuller analysis of their structure. The next chapter pursues this task by focusing specifically on the right to free expression.

---

[42] It is threatened by excessive taxation that amounts to confiscation of property, but it is not threatened by taxation as such.

9

Free Expression

The right to free expression is of special importance for any discussion of the legal and social enforcement of morality. This is true for two principal sets of reasons. First, the free expression and communication of ideas in a political society profoundly affects its ethical environment. The right to free expression, or more precisely the social condition that is brought about by the adequate recognition and protection of the right, is itself a public good.[1] As such, the recognition and protection of the right to free expression is an important component of the common good of a society. Further, the extent to which this right is exercised well or poorly by those who are afforded it in a society substantially affects the ethical character of the society. As we saw in the previous chapter, the right to free expression is a prime candidate for a right to do wrong, a right to engage in wrongful speech. The tension between the public good aspect of the right and the need for a society to guard against its potential abuse lies behind many of the hard cases of free speech jurisprudence. Second, the free expression and communication of ideas, especially ideas relevant to politics, is widely considered to be a condition of government legitimacy. Governments that wrongly deny their subjects the right to freely express their ideas, on this view, forfeit a claim to rule over them. They lose the right to be obeyed, or, more perspicuously, the normative power to give orders and impose political duties.[2] To the extent that this claim is true, the adequate protection and recognition of the right to free expression conditions legitimate law, including legal measures that are designed to enforce morality.

This chapter engages with both sets of reasons, which I will refer to as the *public good consideration* and the *legitimacy consideration*, respectively, with an eye toward clarifying the grounds of the right to free expression and the limits to its scope. This chapter will pay special attention to an argument, or set of arguments, that I will refer to as the classic argument for free expression. Along the way, we will consider whether the right to free expression extends to so-called dangerous speech; that is,

---

[1] Raz, "Free Expression and Personal Identification," in *Ethics and the Public Domain*, pp. 146–169.
[2] Dworkin, "Foreword" to *Extreme Speech and Democracy*, p. viii.

speech that advocates for violence against the government and/or certain targeted groups. Before discussing these matters, however, it is necessary to say a few words about the nature of the right we are considering and to rebut some preliminary reasons for doubting its existence.

9.1 A SPECIAL RIGHT?

The previous chapter distinguished moral rights from justified legal rights. As explained there, the latter can differ from the former for a host of reasons. Is free expression best understood as a basic moral right or instead as a right that would be recognized and protected by a well-ordered legal system in a modern democratic society? To be sure, if it is a basic moral right, then there would be a strong case for extending legal protection to it, but our question here concerns its fundamental character.[3]

One way to argue for the claim that free expression is a basic moral right is to imagine a situation under which the right to free expression is perfectly legally recognized and protected. Would this perfect legal arrangement suffice for the establishment of the right? Here is a reason to think not. The right to free expression protects our interest in free expression, and that interest can be frustrated as much by social penalty as by legal penalty. That was why Mill insisted that free speech is a matter of culture as well as law. If people are afraid to speak their minds out of fear of social ostracism, then the legally recognized right to speak freely will not adequately serve the interests that ground the right. This is not to deny that there are some considerations that support the right to free expression that apply only to the government and to its law. It is to say merely that not *all* of the considerations that ground the right are of this kind.

The considerations that support the right to free expression are a mix of values, with some applying to governmental officials specifically and others applying to members of society generally. Consider the legitimacy consideration. If a legitimate government must be responsive to the views and wishes of those over whom it rules, then it must allow its subjects to express their views and wishes. Further, it must not try to manufacture or manipulate these views and wishes in such a way that would make its pledge to be responsive to them a charade. Thus, the legitimacy consideration grounds duties on the part of governmental officials to respect the free expression of their subjects. Ronald Dworkin explains:

> People who believe in democracy think that it is fair to use the police power to enforce the law if the law has been adopted through democratic political proced-
> ures that express the majority's will. But ... [democratic legitimacy] requires,

---

[3] A basic moral right, as I am understanding it, need not be a universal human right. Some basic moral rights may only come into existence under certain background conditions; and the content of basic moral rights is dependent on contingent social facts.

further, that each citizen have not just a vote but a voice: a majority decision is not fair unless everyone has had a fair opportunity to express his or her attitudes or opinions or fears or tastes or presuppositions or prejudices or ideals, not just in the hope of influencing others (though that hope is crucially important), but also just to confirm his or her standing as a responsible agent in, rather than a passive victim of, collective action.[4]

The "fair opportunity" to express one's views that Dworkin invokes, however, can be compromised by factors that are not addressed by governmental duties. Think of the argument standardly given for secret ballots. If votes were public, then people might be reluctant to vote for the candidate that they favored out of fear of reprisal, not from the government but from their fellow citizens. For the same reasons, those who hold unpopular views may be reluctant to express them in public. Given sufficient social intolerance, the legally protected freedom to express one's views can become merely formal. If democratic legitimacy demands a more than merely formal fair opportunity for citizens to express their views, then it grounds social, as well as governmental, duties to ensure it.

Free expression, then, is a social condition. The value of the social condition, whether it is explained by the legitimacy consideration or by the public good consideration, grounds duties on the part of the members of a society to secure and protect it. The duties apply to ordinary subjects as well as legal officials, and the content of the duties helps to fix the content of the right of free expression. This analysis leaves something crucial about free expression unexplained. If government officials prevent a citizen from passing out political pamphlets that express condemnation of the government, then, on the legitimacy consideration, the legitimacy of the government is compromised. This is bad for everyone in the society, on the plausible assumption that all have an interest in being ruled by a legitimate government. But is it not especially bad for this citizen? Have they not been wronged in a way that other members of their society have not? To say that *their* right to free expression has been violated is to say that they in particular have been wronged.

Writers on free expression often distinguish different interests at stake when considering its regulation and restriction. These interests divide roughly into three broad categories: speaker, audience and bystander interests.[5] The public good and legitimacy considerations strongly implicate audience and bystander interests. However, to explain why free expression is a right, and not merely a valuable social condition, we must advert to the interests of the speaker (or expresser). Stated very generally, each member of a society has an interest in being able to convey their attitudes and opinions to others, not just in private communication but to a wider audience. For many people, the interest in being able to communicate to audiences outside their circle of family, friends and associates may be quite small. They may

4   Dworkin, "Foreword" to *Extreme Speech and Democracy*, p. vii.
5   Scanlon, "Freedom of Expression and Categories of Expression," in *The Difficulty of Tolerance*, pp. 84–112.

have little to contribute to larger social discussions. But their interest in free expression here is augmented by another interest, which is alluded to in the passage earlier from Dworkin. They have an interest in being recognized as a full member of their society. This is not simply a matter of having the vote. It is, as Dworkin rightly emphasizes, a matter of having a voice.[6] And, even if one is not inclined to contribute to the social and political debates in one's society, one has an interest in being recognized as someone who is entitled to participate in these debates.[7] It is these twin interests, the interest in being able to contribute to wider debates in one's society if one has something to contribute and the interest in being recognized as someone with standing to contribute to such debates, that explain why a speaker (or someone engaged in expression) is wronged if their right to free expression is infringed. The setbacks to the interests of audiences and bystanders when an individual's right to free expression is wrongly infringed upon augment the harm that is done, thereby making the infringement of their right a more significant or serious matter from the point of view of the public.

I have been seeking to clarify the right to free expression on the assumption that such a right exists. But its existence can be challenged. The sophisticated version of the challenge holds not that people never have rights to speak freely but only that these rights can be adequately explained without invoking a special right to free expression.[8] For example, so-called free speech rights could be understood to be specific members of the more general set of rights to engage in behavior that does not cause harm to others. On this proposal, there is no need to single out speech or expression for special protection, since expressive acts that do not cause harm to others are already protected. It is for this reason that some writers claim that for there to be a significant free speech right, the right must cover expressive acts that cause harm to others that "normally would be sufficient to justify the imposition of legal sanctions."[9]

We need not here assess the merits of this proposal or the response to it. In previous chapters I have rejected the claim that the harm principle, on any of its variants, provides the only basis for restricting liberty. I have also rejected the claim that there is a general right to liberty. If I was right to reject these claims, then defenses of particular rights are required, since there is no background general right from which to derive them. In this respect, the right to free expression is special in the same way that other rights, such as the right to free association or the right to private property, are special.

---

[6] The right to have a voice, so understood, is more fundamental than the right to have a vote. On the assumption that nondemocratic governments can be legitimate, they must find a way to afford full membership to their members. Securing their right to free expression is part of how this can be accomplished.

[7] To use a helpful term from Anderson, each member of a society has an interest in "respectability," which is a form of "social status constituted by others' recognition of one's entitlements to have a say in what is going on" (*The Imperative of Integration*, p. 14).

[8] See Greenawalt, *Speech, Crime and the Uses of Language*, pp. 9–12 and Schauer, "Free Speech on Tuesdays."

[9] Scanlon, "A Theory of Freedom of Expression," p. 6.

The right to free expression may still be thought to be superfluous. If there is a right to free expression, then there must be some explanation for this fact. The explanation will need to advert to values that are served by the right. But, if so, then the skeptic can press their case. Why is it necessary to highlight the right to free expression, if everything that it protects can be explained by the background values? To be sure, there may be pragmatic reasons for invoking "the right of free expression" in this or that context, but the right itself should not be thought of as having independent importance. Further, the content or character of the right to free expression plausibly will vary across societies, as the interests it serves will be partially dependent on social practices and conventions.

One should not be too impressed by this line of skepticism. The right to free expression is supported by a plurality of considerations, some of which apply only to certain subcategories of expression, others of which apply to expressive as well as non-expressive behavior. Taken together, the supporting values and the standards they inform establish the scope and stringency of a plausible right to free expression, demarcating what interferences with expression are most worrisome and what types of expression deserve special support.[10] In addition, we need to distinguish the right to free expression from the institutional arrangements that best realize or protect it.[11] The established practices and traditions of different societies plainly affect how the right ought to be secured in different places. Thus, we need to distinguish the following two claims:

(1) Societies, or at least societies that meet certain conditions (more on this later), should establish or sustain an institutionalized practice that recognizes the right to free expression for its members.

(2) The stringency and scope of the right to free expression in a society is dependent on the best understanding of the institutionalized practice in that society that has been established to recognize it.

The first of these claims expresses the idea that the right to free expression is a basic, albeit not universal, moral right. The second reflects the dependence of this right on established practice. Given that the right to free expression is justified in part by the public good consideration and the legitimacy consideration, and given that both of these considerations depend on social facts that vary from place to place, we have antecedent reason to expect there to be legitimate variation across societies on how the right to free expression is delineated and secured. If both claims are accepted, then it would be a mistake to think that there is a universal right to free expression applicable to all societies, or even all societies that meet certain

---

[10] The approach adopted here is similar to that proposed by Greenawalt in *Speech, Crime and the Uses of Language*, pp. 12–34.

[11] Scanlon, "Content Regulation Reconsidered," p. 153 ("the exact content of such moral rights depends on an institutional context").

conditions.[12] But for free expression to be a basic moral right, it need not also be a universal right.

Perhaps in light of these points it would be more apt to speak of *rights* of free expression rather than the right to free expression. But our concern in this chapter is with relatively general considerations that bear on the value of free expression in modern societies, not with the considerations that explain why it appropriately takes the shape that it does under different circumstances. So long as it is remembered that there is wide scope for legitimate variation, no harm should be done by our continuing to speak of the right to free expression.

9.2 THE EXPRESSION/ACTION ASYMMETRY

The right to free expression can assume different forms. But on all forms of the right a distinction must be drawn between expression and other types of action. Part of the challenge of making sense of and vindicating the right to free expression is explaining why the expressive acts that the right protects differ from other unprotected acts that have similar effects or are supported by similar concerns. The notion of an "expressive act" is generally understood to be one done with the intention to communicate some proposition or idea to others. So defined, expressive acts cast a wide net, one that is much too wide to be of much help in distinguishing expression from action. The petty thief who threatens their victim and demands that they give them their wallet engages in an expressive act, but no one seriously thinks that this kind of expression merits protection. We want to say that the thief is engaged in an action, not speech or expression. Yet their threat is unambiguously an expressive act.

The thief's expression is not intended to communicate a social or political idea to their victim. Nor are they trying to communicate a view to the public, or significant portions of it. The interests served by the right to free expression apply primarily to expressive acts that aim to communicate some proposition or idea of interest to a general audience. Accordingly, the expressive acts covered by a right of free expression could be winnowed down to exclude private communications with no such content, such as the threat made by our thief. This maneuver would be controversial among proponents of free speech, but it could explain why harassment, face-to-face verbal abuse and so-called fighting words are excluded from free speech protection.[13]

---

[12] Free expression is not special in this regard. There are, I believe, very few, if any, universal rights. This is not to deny that some of the interests that ground the right to free expression may be universal, such as the interest human beings have in being able to communicate their thoughts to others. For the dependence of rights on established practice, see my "Political Morality and the Authority of Tradition," *Journal of Political Philosophy* 24/2 (2016): 137–161.

[13] This maneuver invites the objection that it excludes ordinary private communications from protection under the right of free expression and such communications plausibly merit protection. In reply, it could be said that private communications do not fall under the right to free expression but there are plenty of other reasons for not interfering with them.

Still, even if this controversial maneuver were adopted, many troublesome cases would remain. Consider the following:

(1) Incitement
(2) Defamatory speech
(3) False advertising
(4) Criminal solicitation

Each of these examples has attracted a fair amount of discussion from philosophers of law and legal scholars interested in free speech. They invite us to further narrow down the class of expressive acts that are properly protected by a right of free expression.

Many have thought that these examples can be harmonized with the right of free expression in a fairly straightforward way. There is, it is held, a vital distinction between communication-independent misconduct and communication-dependent misconduct. Restriction of the former, but not the latter, is consistent with full respect for the right of free expression.[14] On inspection, the troublesome cases just mentioned are not really troublesome at all, since they all instantiate communication-independent misconduct.

This persuasiveness of this response plainly rests on the sustainability of the distinction between communication-independent and communication-dependent misconduct. Characterizing that distinction has proven to be a challenging task. A first proposal holds that when harm or wrongdoing can result from both a communicative act and a non-communicative act, restrictions on the communicative act can be justified by reference to the need to address the harm or wrongdoing associated with the non-communicative act. The example of the threat issued by our petty thief nicely illustrates the idea. The thief commits assault by communicative means. But assault "as a general type of misconduct is communication-independent because it can be instantiated by non-communicative actions as well as by communicative actions."[15] After all, the thief can commit assault by brandishing a knife to their victim without saying a word. Generalizing from the example, we can say that when a communicative act belongs to "a genus of wrongdoing" that includes both communicative and non-communicative instances, we can appeal to its membership in that genus to justify its restriction.[16]

This proposal has an unsettling consequence. The legitimacy of prohibiting an act of expression, on the grounds that it is harmful, seems to turn on the availability of non-communicative means of bringing about that same harm. Speech with an offensive message, such as speech that denies that the Holocaust occurred, can produce mental distress in those who are subjected to it. Offensive speech of this kind is widely regarded as expression that merits free speech protection.

[14] See Kramer, *Freedom of Expression as Self-Restraint*, especially pp. 66–68.
[15] Ibid., p. 101.
[16] Ibid., p. 68.

Yet technology could emerge that enables us to cause the identical mental distress in others in a non-communicative way, such as by bombarding them with special gamma rays that produce the exact phenomenological state in them. The offensive speech would now belong to a genus that cuts across the communicative and non-communicative, which, in turn, would allow the would-be restrictor of offensive speech to justify restriction by adverting to the "genus of wrongdoing" that it shares with non-communicative acts. The legitimacy of restricting offensive speech should not turn on the availability or non-availability of such technology, however.

The first proposal for characterizing the distinction between communication-independent and communication-dependent wrongdoing is unpromising. A second proposal has more promise. It seeks to draw a line between the expression of a message and direct involvement or participation in a non-communicative act of wrongdoing. Sometimes the expression of a message crosses that line and becomes a direct element of the non-communicative wrongdoing, thereby making it an appropriate object of restriction. The thief's threat crosses the line from expression to assault. False advertising crosses the line from the expression of a message to participation in commercial fraud, for instance. To assess this proposal, it will be helpful to return to the case of incendiary speech. Recall Mill's memorable discussion: "An opinion that corn-dealers are starvers of the poor, or that private property is robbery, ought to be unmolested when simply circulated through the press, but may justly incur punishment when delivered orally to an excited mob assembled before the house of a corn-dealer, or when handed about among the same mob in the form of a placard."[17] For Mill, opinions published in the press should be treated differently from those uttered before excited mobs. Since both types of speech can cause harm to others, some explanation is needed for why they should be treated differently.

The second proposal maintains that published opinions in the press are instances of mere advocacy, while incendiary exhortations to an excited mob cross the line into participation in violence. Following the 1969 United States Supreme Court decision in *Brandenburg* v. *Ohio*, writers who aim to distinguish mere advocacy from incitement point to three distinguishing factors: the intention of the speaker, the imminence of the harm or wrong that is brought about and the likelihood that the harm or wrong will be brought about by the expression. These factors, it is claimed, explain why incitement to violence crosses the line into participation in the violence, whereas mere advocacy of violence does not. The first factor does not sharply distinguish mere advocacy of violence from incitement to violence, however. The speaker in front of the angry mob in Mill's example might not intend to incite violence. They might just be reckless or negligent in their failure to consider the likely consequences of their fiery speech. Likewise, the author of the published message in the press in Mill's example might fully intend for their message to

---

[17] Mill, *On Liberty*, p. 260.

motivate others to cause harm to the corn-dealers.[18] The third factor also fails to sharply distinguish the two kinds of expressions. Incitement, it may be said, cannot occur unless there is a high likelihood that the expressed message (in the context at issue) will bring about the contemplated harm or wrong, whereas mere advocacy of the expressed message does not as such pose a high likelihood of producing the harm. Yet, granting this, there surely are non-standard cases in which mere advocacy does present a high likelihood of causing the harm or wrong in question, and in these cases mere advocacy would resemble incitement.

The second factor of imminence, then, is the crucial one. It does sharply distinguish mere advocacy from incitement, but its normative significance for the regulation of expression is less clear. To be sure, imminence is correlated with likelihood of resultant harm, which is plainly normatively significant. Other things being equal, the more time that elapses between the expression of a message and the occurrence of the harm associated with it, the more likely it is that some intervening event will prevent the harm from occurring, reducing its likelihood of occurrence. For this reason, the second factor could be viewed as redundant. The normative significance of imminence is already captured by the third factor of likelihood of harm.

To assess whether imminence is a normatively significant factor on its own, we need to consider cases where the likelihood of harm or misconduct is held constant. However, appropriately isolated, imminence is not always a factor that is relevant to the regulation of expression. Imminence is not a necessary feature of communicative acts of criminal solicitation, for example. One can appropriately be subject to criminal penalty for soliciting a crime that is intended to take place a year from the act of solicitation. Why then does imminence assume normative significance in some contexts, such as those presented by advocacy that is likely to cause violence or harm to victims, but not others, such as those presented by acts of criminal solicitation?

Criminal solicitation is focused on or oriented toward specific or concretely particularized courses of criminal action, whereas the mere advocacy of wrongdoing is not similarly focused.[19] This fact can explain why criminal solicitation, whether imminent or not to the contemplated crime, involves direct participation in criminal wrongdoing while mere advocacy does not. Yet acts of incitement can resemble mere advocacy in not being oriented toward specific acts of wrongdoing. Speaking in front of the excited mob, Mill's orator may have no specific harms or wrongs in mind. They may just be trying to stir up mischief of some sort. So, an appeal to the specificity or lack of specificity of the wrongdoing at issue cannot explain why

[18]   Cause here should be understood to be a necessary, but not sufficient, condition for the harm in question. Incitement causes harm only in the sense that it is necessary for the harm to occur, not that it suffices for the harm to occur.
[19]   Kramer, *Freedom of Expression As Self-Restraint*, p. 72 (citing Wechsler, Jones and Korn, "The Treatment of Inchoate Crimes in the Model Penal Code of the American Law Institute: Attempt, Solicitation and Conspiracy (Part One)," *Columbia Law Review* 61 (1961): 571–628).

incitement, but not mere advocacy, of violence is appropriately subject to restriction. The upshot is this. To distinguish incitement from mere advocacy, the normative significance of imminence must be played up, but to distinguish criminal solicitation from mere advocacy, its normative significance must be downplayed.[20]

The cases I have been discussing are troublesome in that they challenge the sustainability of the distinction between communication-independent and communication-dependent harm or wrongdoing. Reflection on the cases also reveals the limitations of two commonly invoked principles to delimit the class of expressive acts protected by the right to free expression. The two principles are the "persuasion principle" and the "content-neutrality principle." The first of these principles expresses the appealing thought that free expression is fundamentally about persuasion, especially persuasion that does not bypass our rational or deliberative faculties. It protects our efforts to persuade others of what we believe. The second principle, the content-neutrality principle, expresses the appealing demand that restrictions on speech should not be designed to favor some ideas over others.[21]

The persuasion principle holds that the bad consequences that result from persuasive speech should not be taken to contribute to the case for restricting it.[22] This principle is often applied to governments, but it can be extended to apply to other institutions with the power to restrict speech. The persuasion principle neatly explains Mill's example. Opinions published in the press should be treated differently from those uttered before excited mobs. As we have noted, provocative expressions before excited mobs in general are more likely to result in harm than the same expressions published in the press. But this observation fails to capture Mill's point in presenting the example. Mill's idea is not that we should weigh the benefits of expression against the risks it poses and then restrict the expression when the costs exceed the prospective benefits. His point rather is that contexts of expression matter. In contexts of persuasion, opinions deserve special protection from restriction, whereas in contexts of non-deliberative instigation, as we might put it, they do not. The members of the excited mob are not in a state of mind receptive to deliberative persuasion.

[20] One might hold that either imminence or orientation toward specific acts of wrongdoing is necessary for a communicative act to cross the line from expression to participation in the wrongdoing. In the incitement case, imminence does the work; in the criminal solicitation case, orientation toward specific acts of wrongdoing does the work; but with mere advocacy, neither factor is present. (This analysis is suggested by, albeit not explicitly stated in, Kramer, *Freedom of Expression As Self-Restraint*, pp. 69–72.) The relevance of imminence in cases of incitement, on this analysis, would still call out for some explanation. Here is one possibility. Incendiary speech imminently causes violence and achieves its effects not by persuasion but by bypassing the deliberative faculties of its audience. The normative significance of imminence, on this view, would implicate the persuasion principle discussed in the text.

[21] A little more precisely, the content-neutrality principle excludes favoring some categories of expression over others, as well as, and more fundamentally, favoring some views over others.

[22] Straus, "Persuasion, Autonomy and Freedom of Expression," *Columbia Law Review* 91/2 (1991): 334–371, at 335 (describing the persuasion principle as it applies to governmental action).

Invoking the persuasion principle, the friend of Mill can say that it is appropriate to consider the harmful or wrongful effects of expression in deciding whether to restrict it when the expression does not occur in a context of persuasion. However, when the expression occurs in a context of persuasion, these effects should not play any role in justifying its restriction. In Mill's example, the two contexts of expression are sharply contrasted. Opinions published in the press are read in a calm state of mind by people with the time to think about their merits. Opinions expressed before excited mobs present little to no opportunity for such reflection. But many contexts of expression – think of internet chat rooms – involve an unholy mixture of efforts at deliberative persuasion and non-deliberative instigation. Further, the line between deliberative persuasion and non-deliberative instigation is not sharp. What we might think of as a genuine context of persuasion in which all or most parties are sincerely committed to rational discussion and deliberation is the exception, not the norm, in modern forums of communication.[23]

The persuasion principle also confronts problems when it is applied to some of the examples listed earlier. Defamatory speech harms its victims by persuading others to believe false statements about them. Possibly this can be addressed by holding that defamatory remarks about private persons do not concern matters of general interest and so fall outside the ambit of the right of free expression, whereas defamatory remarks about public figures or celebrities are of general interest and are appropriately subject to special protection. But even if this were granted, the same cannot be said of false advertising or criminal solicitation. These expressive acts accomplish their mischief through persuasion, sometimes concern matters of general interest and are appropriately subject to legal restriction in ways that would be improper for other kinds of persuasive speech.

The persuasion principle thus needs to be qualified. Not all, but only some, kinds of persuasive expression fall under it. Here the second principle mentioned earlier, the content-neutrality principle, is often invoked to provide the requisite qualification. In restricting the expression associated with false advertising and criminal solicitation, it can be said, the content of the expression is not being targeted. Fraud and the crime solicited are being targeted. Generalizing from these examples, the proposal holds that the bad consequences of persuasive expression can be grounds for restriction and regulation of the expression, providing there is a cogent content-neutral justification for doing so. So-called time, manner and place restrictions on speech illustrate the idea. If a group opposing capital punishment is denied the opportunity to hold a rally in the public square because it has not applied for a permit to do so, then this restriction of expression is content-neutral, so long as the same permit requirement is imposed on other groups with different messages, such

---

[23] Habermas famously articulates a context of communication that is a context of persuasion par excellence: "the ideal speech situation." (See Habermas, *The Structural Transformation of the Public Sphere.*) In it the only force that prevails is "the force of the better argument." But nearly all actual contexts of communication fall short of this ideal.

as a group supporting capital punishment. The permit restriction does not target the message of the speech, and if there is good content-neutral reason for the restriction, such as the need to avoid disruption of traffic, then it can be justified.

The two principles – persuasion and content-neutrality – can be viewed as complementary sides of a larger account of the scope of the right to freedom of expression. The right protects the interest of the expresser in having a fair opportunity to persuade others of their beliefs and sentiments. If they are held accountable for the harms that result from their persuasive efforts, while others are not similarly held accountable for the harms that result from their expression, then their right is infringed upon. Restrictions on expression that are applied evenhandedly,[24] by contrast, do not target the ideas of the expresser and so do not deny them the fair opportunity to persuade others of their ideas. It does not follow that content-neutral restrictions could never infringe on the right of free expression. A city government that denied permits to all political groups would treat the different political groups evenhandedly, but in so doing it would deny them all the opportunity to persuade others of their views.[25] So, even if the two principles were sound, they would not provide the whole story about the scope of the right to free expression. Still, they would go far in delimiting the domain of protected expression.

The content-neutrality principle is subject to an important challenge, however. And, if it is rejected, then the persuasion principle will remain vulnerable to the problem of qualification that the content-neutrality principle was introduced to address. The challenge with the content-neutrality principle concerns whether it should be applied in a content-neutral way, or whether it should be applied differently depending on the value of the expression in question. To illustrate the issue here, consider these examples:

(1) A politician who "brands" themself as a champion of the underdog makes false statements about their past and their record of helping those in need.
(2) A marketing firm hired by a company makes false statements about the products that the company is selling and has sold in the past.
(3) A death with dignity activist urges people who desire to end their lives to break or circumvent laws that prohibit euthanasia and offers advice for how to do so. They object to these laws and hope that disobedience to them will lead to their repeal.
(4) An accounting firm urges its clients to not pay taxes and offers strategies for avoiding detection.

---

[24] The content-neutrality principle will likely need to advert to the distinction between communicative-independent and communicative-dependent misconduct discussed in the text. Restrictions that target communicative-independent harms do not seek to favor the expression of some messages over others. If so, the difficulties in drawing that distinction in a satisfactory way will carry over to the task of formulating the principle.

[25] Stone, "Content-Regulation and the First Amendment," *William and Mary Law Review* (1983): 189–252, at 197.

In principle, the restriction of speech in all four examples could be defended on content-neutral grounds. After all, (1) and (2) involve false representations about one's brand and (3) and (4) involve assistance in criminal behavior. But (2) and (4) seem importantly different from (1) and (3). Restrictions on commercial speech, as in (2), should be easier to justify than restrictions on political speech, as in (1); and restrictions on expression that aims to facilitate the commission of ordinary crimes, as in (4), should be easier to justify than restrictions on expressions that aim to facilitate the commission of crimes that are controversial and not considered to be crimes at all by many in the society. It is tempting to say that the speech in (1) and (3) merits protection because it is of high value, while the speech in (2) and (4) does not because it is of low value. But if we say this, then we have abandoned content-neutrality and have apportioned the protection of expression to the perceived value of the speech that is protected.

A defender of the content-neutrality principle can grant the force of the examples we have just reviewed, but then hold that the principle applies evenhandedly within categories of expression, even if not across categories of expression. On this view, it is permissible to make content-based distinctions between categories of expression, such as that between political speech and commercial speech, but not permissible to make content-based distinctions within a category of speech, such as by providing strong protection to political speech that is judged to have high value and weak protection to political speech that is judged to have low value. In short, the content-neutrality principle is sound, providing that its sphere of application is appropriately defined.

This last-ditch effort to defend content-neutrality must steer between two hazards. On one side, if the categories of expression are too broad, then the same concerns that motivated moving from uniform application of the principle to application within categories of expression will resurface. There will be pressure to subdivide broad categories of expression in order to track compelling differences in the value of expressive acts. On the other side, if the categories are carved in a manner that is too fine-grained, then it will be difficult to distinguish the view from one that simply abandons content-neutrality altogether and urges us to apportion protection of speech to its perceived value.

In discussing the persuasion principle and the content-neutrality principle, I have wanted to call attention to their limitations. It does not follow that they do not have a role to play in articulating the right to free expression. What does follow, I think, is that these principles cannot be foundational. They are downstream from the more fundamental concerns that justify the right to free expression. If they are accepted as sound principles, then their content and range of application must be fixed by these more fundamental concerns.

9.3 THE CLASSIC ARGUMENT

The range of concerns relevant to the protection of free expression is broader than those that can be grouped under either the public good consideration or the legitimacy consideration. One such concern speaks to the trust that it is reasonable to grant to those who are in a position to restrict expression – a trust that they will exercise this power fairly and wisely. I will return to this concern at the end of this chapter. Yet even adding it to the public good and legitimacy considerations will not give us a complete account of the fundamental concerns that underlie the right to free expression. The discussion that follows, accordingly, is not intended to be complete. Its more modest purpose is to show how certain fundamental concerns can guide the specification of the right of free expression.

It is time now to revisit the classic argument for free expression, which is the argument (or series of arguments) advanced most forcefully by Mill in *On Liberty*.[26] We reviewed this argument in Chapter 2 and noted some preliminary challenges to it. Here I aim to give the argument a better run for its money, discussing it more fully and relating it to the public good and legitimacy considerations. In doing so, I will go beyond Mill's explicit arguments and claims, adding supplements and making modifications.

It is commonly thought that Mill based the case for free expression on truth discovery. The free and open discussion of ideas leads over time to the discovery of important truths. Efforts to suppress false, offensive or dangerous ideas often do more harm than good, as the historical record confirms. Yet, as we saw in Chapter 2, Mill was concerned not only with the discovery of truths but also with the conditions under which people form their beliefs. You can have a true belief about an important matter but not adequately understand it or adequately grasp the reasons or evidence for affirming it. "Dead dogma," as Mill termed it, can be either true or false. And the free and open discussion of ideas, he thought, is the only corrective to it.

"Dead dogma" contrasts with "living truth." The latter can be understood in terms of justified belief in a proposition that one understands. The fundamental concern behind the classic argument, accordingly, concerns the generation of justified true beliefs, or knowledge,[27] and not merely the discovery of truths. But this is still not quite right, for it leaves out of the account false views that are justified. These are neither living truths nor dead dogmas. They are, to use a term that Mill does not employ, "living falsehoods." The thrust of Mill's discussion is that false justified beliefs can have value in terms of their contribution to truth discovery and knowledge generation. "Truth gains more even by the errors of one who, with due study and preparation, thinks for himself, than by the true opinions of those who only hold

---

[26] In addition to Mill, the classic argument is associated with Milton, *Areopagitica* (1817) and with the First Amendment decisions of two influential US Supreme Court Justices, Holmes and Brandeis.

[27] Knowledge requires more than having justified true beliefs for reasons pointed out famously by Gettier in his 1963 paper "Is Justified True Belief Knowledge?" I pass over this complication in what follows.

them because they do not suffer themselves to think."[28] "Living falsehoods" can be instrumentally valuable in generating "living truths." But I want to suggest that on the classic argument they have intrinsic value as well. Mill argued that beliefs that are arrived at and held in justified ways contribute to the mental development of those who hold them, and this mental self-development is itself intrinsically valuable. Indeed, the mental powers that are realized and exercised by those who acquire justified beliefs, whether true or not, are partly constitutive of the self-development or self-perfection of human beings.

The classic argument for free expression thus rests on two pillars. One concerns its value to society in terms of its purported contribution to the generation of knowledge. The other concerns its value to the individual in terms of its purported contribution to self-development, which itself is intrinsically good.[29] Optimistically, Mill believed that free expression, or, as he put it, "the complete liberty of thought and discussion," serves both of these pillars in complementary ways. It is likely that Mill was too optimistic on this point.[30] One regime of free expression might serve one pillar best, while a different regime of free expression serves the other best. Optimistically, Mill also thought that the regime of free expression that best serves the interests of the intellectual elite also best serves the interests of the non-elite. No balancing of conflicting interests is required. But, again, it is possible that he was mistaken on this point as well.

Let us define a regime of free expression as a set of legal and social practices that regulate the expression of ideas in a society. No actual regime matches Mill's description of "complete liberty of thought and discussion," but regimes can approximate it, and they can be assessed in terms of how robust they are in protecting the expression of ideas. The classic argument appeals to knowledge generation and personal self-development to make the case for a very robust regime of free expression. I turn now to some of the more specific claims that Mill pressed in articulating his argument. In perhaps his most uncompromising statement on free expression, Mill proclaimed that "all silencing of discussion is an assumption of infallibility." No doubt this statement is an exaggeration, and it was immediately recognized as such by Mill's contemporary critics. James Fitzjames Stephen in 1873 shrewdly observed that "an opinion may be suppressed, not because it is false, but because it is true, or because it is doubtful whether it is true or false, and because it is not considered desirable that it should be discussed."[31]

---

[28] Mill, *On Liberty*, pp. 242–243.
[29] To speak more precisely, our well-being is intrinsically good, and self-development is an essential component of our well-being.
[30] Or perhaps Mill's optimism was well justified, given the social conditions of his time and place. "It is worth remembering that Mill himself thought of his essay as aimed almost wholly at an English audience; it was the intellectual and social oppressiveness of Victorian England that was his target" (Ryan, "Mill's Essay on Liberty," reprinted in *The Making of Modern Liberalism* (Princeton, NJ: Princeton University Press, 2012), pp. 257–278, at 257).
[31] Fitzjames Stephen, *Liberty, Equality, and Fraternity*, p. 27.

Mill's claim can be made more plausible by stripping it of its exaggeration. Silencing of opinions, on this softened version, characteristically, if not invariably, rests on unwarranted assumptions of their being correct. Is this softened claim compelling? Mill seemed to have the following idea in mind. Suppose you have a favorite thesis, perhaps it is a scientific hypothesis or a claim about some historical event, and you want this thesis to be widely believed because, as you think, it is both true and important for people to know it. To protect your thesis, and to facilitate its transmission to others, you seek to suppress claims that purport to provide a case against it. You seek to protect your thesis from what you consider to be misleading evidence. To the extent that you succeed in suppressing these claims, however, you lose something important in the process. You lose the warrant, or justification, for holding that your thesis is correct. And you need that warrant, for without it your insistence that you simply know that your thesis is correct is an unjustified presumption.[32]

The line of argument obviously rests on an account of warrant. Roughly, for any proposition that has a truth value, one is justified in believing it only if it has been exposed to refutation by others. In Mill's words, "There is the greatest difference between presuming an opinion to be true, because, with every opportunity for contesting it, it has not been refuted, and assuming its truth for the purpose of not permitting its refutation."[33] The former opinion can be believed with warrant, whereas the latter cannot. Or, to put the point more cautiously than Mill did, the degree to which a proposition can be justifiably believed increases as it confronts and overcomes attempts at its own refutation. Complete liberty of thought and discussion, accordingly, is necessary for a belief to be maximally justified. Assuming that there is a link between justification and truth discovery, complete liberty of thought and discussion would also be necessary for a society to do maximally well in terms of discovering new and important truths.

Mill's argument on this matter has been rejected by many, including both friends and opponents of a robust regime of free expression. We will address some of the criticism in the next section, but first I want to flesh out how the argument relates to the public good and legitimacy considerations. If sound, the classic argument would go far in establishing that free expression is a public good. The members of a society have an interest in living under social conditions that are conducive to knowledge generation and truth discovery. These social conditions, as we have stressed, are not secured merely by government action, or the refusal of the government to use its power to suppress opinions deemed to be false or dangerous. The social conditions, in addition, require a tolerant public culture, one that welcomes, or at least does not seek to penalize, controversial or heterodox opinions. Further, the interest that any

---

[32] "Infallibility" connotes perfect reliability, an incapacity for error. But Mill, I believe, has in mind a slightly different thought in using this word. The feeling that one is certain that one is correct, and that one does not need justification for this feeling of certainty, is what he is targeting.

[33] Mill, *On Liberty*, p. 231.

particular member of a society has in having beliefs with a greater degree of justification likely would not be significant enough to justify the establishment of these conditions, given that free expression brings its own costs and dangers. Yet the cumulative interests of all the members of a society plausibly are great enough to do so. So, if sound, the argument can show that the social conditions of robust free expression are a presumptive public good.

The argument, if sound, can also forge a link between free expression and legitimate government. The link in question is primarily not one of fairness, as Dworkin asserted, but rather one that draws on the conditions of justified government authority.[34] Governments claim a right to rule us and they demand obedience from us. But we can rationally submit to their rule only if we can have justified confidence in their reliability in making reasonable decisions. We must be able to judge that our government merits our obedience. But if we are not free to question it or challenge it, then we cannot have confidence in its reliability. It may be countered that legitimate governments demand obedience from their subjects for content-independent reasons.[35] The right to rule is not the right to request, but the right to command, and commands bind even when those to whom they are directed reject them. This may be correct but it does not undermine the point in question. For it is plausible to hold that a government can only acquire the right to rule, and hence the right to issue binding content-independent commands, if its subjects can reasonably believe that it is generally reliable in responding to the reasons that justify its establishment.[36] And to have a warranted judgment about its general reliability, a government's subjects need to be free to debate its competence and to debate matters that bear on its competence, at least on the assumption that the Millian argument regarding warrant is broadly correct.

The classic argument thus engages the legitimacy consideration insofar as the robust free expression of ideas that it supports contributes to the case for judging with warrant that governments are to be obeyed. If free discussion reveals that a government is not competent, then its claim to legitimacy will be undermined. So, incompetent governments have a strong interest in suppressing discussion of ideas that call their competence into question. To maintain de facto legitimacy, they have an interest in preventing the establishment of conditions that are necessary for their de jure legitimacy. Competent governments need not have the same concern.

---

[34] The idea I have in mind here is closer to the idea expressed by Scanlon when he claims, in defense of what he terms the "Millian Principle," that a person, to be autonomous and rational, "must see himself as sovereign in deciding what to believe in weighing competing reasons for action." And that, as a consequence, such a person "cannot rely on the judgment of others, including the judgment of those who command him, unless he has independent reason for thinking that they are likely to be correct" (Scanlon, "A Theory of Freedom of Expression," pp. 15–16).

[35] Hart, "Commands and Authoritative Reasons," in his *Essays on Bentham* (Oxford: Oxford University Press, 1982).

[36] Raz, "The Service Conception of Authority Revisited," in his *Between Authority and Interpretation* (Oxford: Oxford University Press, 2009).

Still, they might worry that their subjects will be misled by free discussion and falsely conclude that their commands do not merit obedience. But the proposal I am advancing holds that competence is not sufficient for legitimate rule. Legitimate governments need to be both competent and justifiably regarded as competent by those over whom they rule, and this requires the establishment of a regime of free expression that makes this possible.

It is true that when the classic argument is interpreted in light of the legitimacy consideration, its reach is limited. Not every proposition that subjects take an interest in bears on the assessment of the competence of the government that rules them. I might believe that Shakespeare was not the playwright who wrote *Hamlet*, and I might think that it is important for people to know this, but the justifiability of my belief on this matter likely has no bearing at all on the judgment that I need to make about the competence of those who claim a right to rule over me. Granting this point, we should not conclude that the argument here extends only to political speech, narrowly construed. Speech and expression on matters that are of general interest to the public can indirectly bear on assessments of the competence of political officials. So, the classic argument, as it bears on the legitimacy consideration, may extend a good deal further than it initially appears. Still, the limitation remains. Rather than viewing this as a defect of the classic argument, we can view it as a virtue. For it is plausible to think that political speech and expression merits an extra degree of protection over and above the protection merited by other forms of expression.[37] By appealing to the legitimacy consideration, the classic argument can account for this.

A second concern about the line of argument we are now considering is more challenging. Those who invoke the legitimacy consideration often speak in categorical terms. Dworkin, in the article from which the passage quoted earlier is taken, claims that a government that restricts political speech "forfeits" its moral title to rule.[38] And Scanlon suggests, a bit more carefully, that when governments restrict the kind of speech that is covered by the legitimacy consideration, they give up a great deal, including the "claim to be obeyed which goes beyond the relative advantages of obedience and disobedience."[39] On the classic argument, these claims are difficult to defend. For on the argument as I have reconstructed it, the legitimacy of government turns on warranted judgments about its competence, and these judgments are not all or nothing but judgments of degree. Suppose, for example, that an exemplary government restricts speech that bears on its competence with regard to one domain of decision-making, such as its handling of public health

---

[37] Scholars of the free speech clauses of the US Constitution often argue that these constitutional protections apply with special force to political speech. For an influential statement of this view, see Meiklejohn, *Political Freedom: The Constitutional Powers of the People*.

[38] Dworkin, "Foreword" to *Extreme Speech and Democracy*, p. viii.

[39] Scanlon, "A Theory of Freedom of Expression," p. 25. (Scanlon backs away from this more absolutist position in his later work on the topic.)

matters. This restriction would not plausibly undercut its right to rule on all matters on which it claims authority. At most, it would undercut its claim to be obeyed on matters pertaining to public health. Yet even in this domain, if the restrictions on speech that it imposed were modest, allowing significant criticism of its efforts despite the restrictions, its subjects might be able to reasonably judge that it was competent to rule on public health matters, even if their judgments had less warrant than they would have had without the restrictions. However, if this is correct, then restrictions on political speech do not necessarily destroy or undermine the legitimacy of governments. They may just diminish their legitimacy. And now it would seem to be an open matter whether the goods secured by the restrictions could be sufficiently important to justify the diminishment in legitimacy that is incurred.

To appreciate the significance of the point here, consider two much-discussed examples: pornography and hate speech. Regarding these forms of speech, Dworkin grants that "pornographic images hardly supply 'ideas' to any marketplace of thought; and history gives us little reason for expecting racist speech to contribute to its own refutation."[40] Nonetheless, he insists that these forms of expression merit strong protection, and that when governments suppress them, they compromise their legitimacy. But if it is also granted that these forms of expression bring real costs – they degrade the ethical environment of a society and/or contribute to harmful or discriminatory treatment of women and targeted groups – then why not conclude that the value of suppression overbalances the diminishment in legitimacy that is incurred? Even if pornographers and hate speech purveyors could now view their governments as having a weaker claim to their obedience, even if they could plausibly claim that they have not been given a fair opportunity to be heard and, to that extent, are not being treated as full members of their society, why not judge that this is a price worth paying?

It is tempting, Dworkin agrees, to make some exceptions to the right of free expression. It is tempting to allow that "those whose opinions are too threatening or base or contrary to the moral or religious consensus have forfeited any right to the concern on which the right rests." But such a reservation, he warns, "would leave room only for the pointless grant of protection for ideas or tastes or prejudices that those in power approve, or in any case do not fear."[41] There is a slide here from (1) the thought that if those in power make exceptions to protecting expression, then (2) they will protect only expression that they approve of or do not fear. That conclusion would indeed make a mockery of free expression, but the notion that it follows inexorably from the former thought is not at all obvious. Dworkin's assertion here is charitably interpreted as appealing to the trust it is reasonable to extend to those with the power to restrict expression. Understood in these terms, he may be largely correct. We will return to this concern. But there is another line of argument that

---

[40]   Dworkin, "Foreword" to *Extreme Speech and Democracy*, p. vii.
[41]   Ibid., p. ix.

bears on this matter that we now need to discuss, a line of argument that emanates from the classic argument for free expression.

The argument I have in mind rests on the second pillar of the classic argument, the pillar that invokes self-development rather than knowledge generation. When people are confronted with ideas that they find offensive or disturbing or immoral, they often experience some measure of discomfort. They may feel "hurt" or threatened by the expression of such ideas, for example. But, as we noted in Chapter 2, it is possible that they will also benefit from exposure to the disturbing ideas. This surprising possibility – that one can benefit by being offended or disturbed – depends on how one reacts to the disturbing expression. For being confronted with ideas that challenge one's convictions can impel one to reexamine them in the light of the challenge. To the extent that this occurs, exposure to disturbing ideas, whether in words or imagery, can contribute to the mental self-development that occurs when one's beliefs become living convictions.[42] Even if exposure to offensive ideas had no effect at all on truth discovery, it could still be valuable to those offended. For it could serve as a corrective to the common tendency of the human mind to fall asleep and stagnate when there is no enemy in the field.

I have expressed these claims in modest terms. Exposure to offensive and disturbing ideas, such as those found in pornography and hate speech, could benefit people by leading them to reexamine the grounds for rejecting them. But it may not, and for many it would not. Further, for all that I have said, the costs generated by the offensive expression may be greater than any benefit that exposure to it could provide. Still, the argument looks compelling when pushed to the limit. Imagine a society that tried to protect its members from any speech or expression that they found distressing, and largely succeeded. This would not be a society conducive to the mental development of its members. People in this society might learn many truths but they would not understand the challenges that could be brought against them. And, of course, some truths would need to be suppressed. For people find true as well as false ideas threatening and disturbing.

Societies sometimes try to get the benefits from the expression of offensive ideas while minimizing the costs. Expression deemed to be offensive is confined to special spaces. Today many universities mark out "free speech zones" on their campuses. In these zones, all expression is permitted, but members of the university can easily avoid exposure to the messages that are voiced within them. Indeed, one can view the internet as providing a plethora of free speech zones, virtual spaces that it is easy for people to avoid if they fear being offended. But these zones of free speech probably do very little to further the mental self-development that Mill was championing. As it has become common to point out, people have a strong tendency to self-segregate, preferring to communicate with people with whom they largely share an outlook.

[42] For more discussion of the point advanced here, see Waldron, "Mill and the Moral Value of Distress," a paper from which the discussion in the text draws.

Mental self-development, on Mill's view, requires confrontation between conflicting views and perspectives. Moreover, the confrontation must be conducted in the right spirit. One must be open to hearing the other side if one is going to learn from it. Securing a robust right of free expression by no means guarantees the benefits of self-development that Mill envisioned. Even if Mill is right about these benefits, they require for their realization a certain type of character, one that manifests a willingness to expose one's commitments to challenge, even when the challenge is painful.[43] It is far from clear whether a society in which this type of character predominates is a realistic possibility for human beings.

9.4 TENSIONS AND CHALLENGES

The classic argument is a set of arguments. For Mill, the different lines of argument complement one another, establishing a powerful case for free expression. But, as I alluded to earlier, the arguments can pull in different directions. There are tensions in the classic argument, and by attending to them we can appreciate some forceful challenges that can be raised against it.

Mill's idea of "living truths" assumes a link between justification and truth discovery. That there is such a link seems plain. We value justified beliefs because we think they are more likely to be correct than unjustified beliefs. But it is not at all plain that Mill's understanding of justification is the best understanding if our concern is with knowledge generation and truth discovery. On inspection, the notion of "living truths" contains a tension. Are the truths "living" because they represent the thinker's own take on the matter or because they are epistemically justified? I will refer to the first option as *independence* and the second as *well-groundedness*. A person can make up their own mind, thinking for themselves and forming independent judgments, and yet arrive at beliefs that are not well grounded. Conversely, a person can form well-grounded beliefs, accepting claims on the say-so of others, without exercising independent judgment. The tension here matters. Independence serves self-development; well-groundedness serves knowledge and truth discovery. To decide what regime of free expression would be best for a society, we may need to balance these two values against each other. And the classic argument, having not confronted the tension, does not tell us how to do this.[44]

---

[43] Ibid., p. 123.

[44] The field of social epistemology aims to distinguish better from worse social environments for truth discovery and knowledge generation. "[S]ocial epistemology is, in the first instance, an enterprise concerned with how people can best pursue the truth (whichever truth is in question) *with the help* of, or *in the face* of, others" ("Social Epistemology," *Stanford Encyclopedia for Philosophy*, https://plato .stanford.edu/entries/epistemology-social). We can interpret Mill as offering a proposal about the kind of social environment that does best in this regard, namely one that encourages open and free discussion of any matter on which people disagree. But there are a host of reasons for thinking that people would do better in arriving at true beliefs if expression in their society were restricted in various ways. For discussion, see Goldman, *Social Epistemology*, pp. 209–217.

We have already alluded to a second tension in the argument. It is evident that people differ in their capacities and their willingness to engage in the kind of discussion conducive to self-development and/or knowledge. Revealingly, as we have noted before, Mill indexed his argument to societies that had reached a level of development in which people were "capable of improvement by free and equal discussion." He claimed that the principle of liberty, of which the liberty of thought and discussion was a central component, did not apply to "backward states of societies."[45] This claim suggests that societies need to reach a threshold level of development before the argument for liberty kicks in; but, even so, the degree to which a regime of robust free expression serves the interests of its members plausibly varies with their capacities for improvement by discussion. And these capacities almost certainly will be unequally distributed among their members, either because they differ in natural abilities, or because they have received different kinds of education, or both. Once this point is given its due, it becomes harder to maintain that there is one regime of free expression that best serves the interests of all those who are subject to it. A robust regime of free expression of the sort that Mill championed may be best for some members of a society and suboptimal for others. Once again, some balancing may be in order to ensure that the interests of different classes of people are advanced fairly.

A third tension in the classic argument, while always present, has become more pressing with the development of modern technologies of communication. Free expression, I have emphasized, is a social condition. It can be set back by nonlegal as well as by legal means. The classic argument seeks to protect expression from both of these threats. But now consider the possibility that effective efforts to combat social restrictions on free expression call for legal restrictions on free expression. Start with a simple example. Imagine that a town has only one newspaper, and that if one is to reach a large audience in this town, one needs to publish in this paper. Imagine further that the paper refuses to publish any opinion critical of the timber industry, which is a major funder of the newspaper. Frustrated by this situation, suppose that the members of the town pass a measure that requires the paper to publish a certain number of pieces that are critical of the timber industry. By so doing, they would combat the nonlegal social restriction on expression, thereby promoting free expression, but, at the same time, they would restrict the expression of the paper's editors, thereby setting back free expression.

The problem the example illustrates may not seem very compelling. After all, rather than restrict the expression of the newspaper, could not the town instead support a rival newspaper that gives a platform to the anti-timber industry views? That indeed might be the right response to the problem, but only if having a second newspaper in the town were an economically viable possibility.

---

[45] Mill, *On Liberty*, p. 224.

The simple example is quaint. Newspapers are no longer as important as they once were as platforms for expression. The internet has rendered speech "cheap," making it possible for anyone with access to a computer and an internet connection to reach a large audience.[46] But this fact in its own way supports the very tension we are now considering. For if speech is cheap, then we can expect there to be more of it, all competing for our limited spans of attention. This, in turn, makes possible new ways for powerful actors to control the spread of ideas.[47] They can design platforms and infrastructure for communication to privilege some ideas over others. To combat this kind of speech control, the government may need to restrict the persuasive efforts of the powerful actors. The restriction of expression, once again, is the remedy for the restriction of expression. The classic argument is split against itself.

These three tensions – that the values behind the classic argument can conflict, that different regimes of free expression can serve different members of society differently and that some restrictions of expression may be needed to combat other restrictions of expression – will suggest to some that the classic argument must be rejected. Critics of the argument often charge that it rests on empirical claims that are difficult to defend, contending that there is little reason to think that Mill was right that an expressive environment of complete liberty of thought and discussion would best serve the values he championed.

Are the critics right? Our discussion has suggested that the classic argument can be viewed at different levels. There is, first, a set of claims about the fundamental values that a regime of free expression serves. There is, second, a picture or image of the kind of expressive environment that furthers these concerns; and there is, finally, a proposal about the institutions and policies that constitute or help to bring about the requisite expressive environment. It is possible to accept some of these parts of the argument and reject others. The claim that legal restrictions on free expression are sometimes necessary to counteract various kinds of speech distortion is often taken as a critique of the classic argument. But a friend of the classic argument should be open to the idea that the institutions and practices of a regime of free expression need to be evaluated in light of their contribution to the expressive environment that serves the fundamental concerns it highlights. Indeed, Mill himself was likely more open to various restrictions on expression than his bold phrase "complete liberty of thought and discussion" suggests.[48]

Shifting attention from institutions and policies to the expressive environment that serves the fundamental concerns greatly complicates empirical assessment of the classic argument, however. The classic argument presents an image of an expressive environment in which all ideas worth debating are given a fair hearing.

---

[46]   Volokh, "Cheap Speech and What It Will Do," *Yale Law Journal* (1995).
[47]   Wu, "Is the First Amendment Obsolete?" *Michigan Law Review* (2018).
[48]   See Brink, *Mill's Progressive Principles*, pp. 165–171 (arguing that Mill's arguments support a modest form of "deliberation-enhancing" censorship). But see Jacobson, "Mill on Liberty, Speech, and the Free Society," *Philosophy and Public Affairs* 29/3 (2000): 276–309.

But it is controversial what conditions must be in place for ideas to be given a fair hearing. A popular left-wing critique of the classic argument holds that ideas cannot be given a fair hearing under conditions of social and economic inequality. The critics favor various restrictions on speech to level the playing field.[49] This critique itself rests on contestable empirical claims.[50] It invites us to think about which expressive environment, one that permits inequality-favoring expression or one that restricts it, would best serve the values of knowledge generation, truth discovery and mental self-development. Notice, moreover, that the critique largely accepts the image of the expressive environment provided by the classic argument. Indeed, one way to read the left-wing critique is to interpret it as holding that modern democratic societies have not yet reached the point of development that Mill posited for the application of the argument. On this reading, so-called free societies are not yet ready to be free.[51]

Whatever truth there is in this critique, it inherits the tensions in the classic argument. It leaves unaddressed the fundamental tension between promoting independence of mind and well-grounded belief. We need to think for ourselves and we need to defer to reasonable authorities and experts. In discussing submission to governmental authority, I suggested that subjects need to be able to form warranted beliefs about the reliability of those who claim a right to rule them. But this just pushes the tension back one step. Independence of mind and reasonable trust in the judgments of others are both important, but the celebration of the former can erode the basis of the latter.

I have not said anything so far about the role of the government in supporting expression as opposed to restricting it, or combating its restriction. Governments can take steps to favor high-value or deliberative expression over low-value expression, striving to support intellectual authority without restricting freedom of expression.[52] Government speech and government support for expression can be viewed as enlarging and improving public debate over important matters.[53] An ideal expressive environment might require a government that supports intellectual authority by providing funds for scientific research, universities, libraries, museums and so on and it might require a public culture that is broadly respectful of expertise. Since most of what we think rests in the end on the testimony of others, we need to be able to

---

[49] Marcuse, "Repressive Tolerance."

[50] Under the egalitarian social conditions imagined by the critic, the issue of what restrictions on speech, if any, would best serve the fundamental concerns identified by the classic argument would itself have to be addressed.

[51] This reading is strongly suggested by Marcuse, who both calls attention to Mill's claim about development and holds that all actual societies are still in the process of creating the conditions of freedom: "freedom is still to be created even for the freest of the existing societies" ("Repressive Tolerance").

[52] Sunstein, "A New Deal for Speech," *Hastings Communications and Entertainment Law Journal* 137 (1994). Admittedly, the issue here is delicate. Drawing the line between government restriction of an idea and government failure to support it, while supporting the expression of other ideas, is a challenging task. See Alexander, *Is There a Right of Freedom of Expression?*, pp. 82–102.

[53] This will be more plausible the more the government can be viewed as one speaker among others, and not as the arbiter of acceptable speech. See Fried, *Modern Liberty*, p. 119.

distinguish reliable from unreliable sources of testimony if we are to form warranted beliefs. In *On Liberty* Mill highlighted the contribution of the critique and contestation of ideas to their justification, but the other side of the coin – reasonable trust in others – remained unexplored. Not that Mill was blind to the problem here. In an essay on the conservative writer and poet Samuel Taylor Coleridge, published nineteen years before the publication of *On Liberty*, Mill endorsed the idea of a National Church. This was not to be a religious institution but one whose purpose would be "the advancement of knowledge, and the civilization and cultivation of the community." This "church" was to be supported by public funds and would establish an endowed class whose function was to cultivate and enlarge "the knowledge already possessed" and to watch over "the interests of the physical and moral sciences."[54]

The Mill of *On Liberty* saw suppression of ideas as the major threat to the "living truths" of the mind. By contrast, the Mill who wrote the essay on Coleridge saw the leveling character of modern democracy as the major threat to respect for authority in the cultivation and dissemination of knowledge. The classic argument for free expression, as I have presented it, must be alive to both kinds of threats. It must find a way to celebrate independence of mind without undermining rational trust in expertise.

9.5 WRONGFUL SPEECH

The third tension in the classic argument mentioned earlier is that the protection of free expression sometimes requires the restriction of free expression. Legal restrictions on campaign financing are often presented as an example of this tension. But, as we noted in Chapter 2, such restrictions need not be designed to favor some views over others. The more challenging examples concern expression that purportedly "silences" the voices of others in virtue of the content of the message it sends. Here the restriction of one view is deemed necessary to protect the expression of others. Expression that "silences" others is an example of wrongful speech. There are other examples of such speech, but expression that silences others directly engages the very considerations that justify the right to free expression. It is, accordingly, a good place to start an examination of wrongful speech.

Those who engage in wrongful expression do wrong. As we saw in Chapter 8, one can consistently maintain that it is wrong for a person to do something and that the person has a right – a justified legal right – to do it. But consistency is one thing; plausibility is another. Our focus here is on whether expression that silences the expression of others could plausibly fall under the right of free expression. We confront an initial difficulty. To put it mildly, it is not immediately clear how

---

[54] Mill, "Coleridge," in *John Stuart Mill and Jeremy Bentham: Utilitarianism and Other Essays*, ed. Ryan (New York: Penguin Books, 1987). Here Mill sympathetically summarizes Coleridge's view of the Church of England and its importance. He then comments: "On this subject we are entirely at one with Coleridge" (p. 212).

an act of expression could silence the expression of others. Some examples are clear, to be sure. Suppose that Jack and Jill are at a company board meeting. Every time Jill tries to speak, Jack interrupts her and speaks so loudly that no one can hear what she is saying. Jack's expression silences Jill insofar as it prevents her from being heard. Everyone agrees that this kind of silencing can be restricted without infringing on anyone's right of free expression. But this is not the kind of example that people typically have in mind when they talk about speech or expression that silences others.

A better example brings silencing expression close to harassment and intimidation. A white supremacist group burns a cross in front of the home of a black civil rights leader, sending the message that they had better keep quiet if they know what is good for them. But while this example brings us closer to the phenomenon we want to investigate, it still does not get us there. For expression can be restricted on the grounds that it constitutes harassment or intimidation, and this type of restriction need not target the content of the message in question.[55] What kind of expression, then, silences in virtue of its content or the message that it expresses? Recently, some feminists have proposed an answer. "[P]ornography and its protection," they claim, "have deprived women of speech, especially speech against sexual abuse."[56] The idea here is that pornographic speech conditions what women can do with their words. It can disable their refusal to have sex. When refusals by women are disabled, they are prevented "not from speaking, but from achieving the effects that they want to achieve" with their words.[57] For example, if pornography makes rape look sexy, and if consumers of pornography in virtue of this message come to believe that when women refuse sex they are actually expressing a desire for sex, then pornography will silence women.

The power attributed to pornography here, if indeed it had this power, would be an important fact about the effects of pornographic expression. But this power is not aptly characterized in terms of the silencing of expression. Being ignored or not listened to when one speaks can be very bad, but freedom of expression does not include a claim that one be effective in "achieving the effects" that one wants to have in speaking. When I engage in persuasive speech, my aim is to persuade others, but if I convince absolutely no one, I cannot plausibly complain that I have been silenced.

Feminists have a more subtle point to make about the silencing power of pornographic expression, however. They invite us to imagine that pornography could make it the case that a woman's refusal to have sex did not even count as a refusal. Try as she may, she could not refuse. If pornographic expression had this

---

55 They need not, but they still could. As Scalia's memorable opinion in *RAV* v. *City of Saint Paul* pointed out, if these viewpoint-neutral restrictions are applied in a non-neutral manner, then they will in fact favor some messages over others.

56 Mackinnon, *Only Words*, p. 9. See also Langton, *Sexual Solipsism*, especially pp. 47–62.

57 Langton, *Sexual Solipsism*, p. 56.

kind of power, then it would silence women not by preventing them from speaking, and not by contributing to a culture that leads men to ignore them when they do speak, but by depriving them of an important linguistic power – the power to say no.[58] This argument threatens to prove too much. If women cannot refuse to have sex, then they cannot claim to be raped in virtue of their rapist's refusal to honor their refusal. But, of course, they can be raped in this way; and the pornographers with their expression do not have the power to change this moral and legal reality.

The feminists' argument against pornography, I have been suggesting, is not well expressed in terms of the silencing power of pornographic expression.[59] But their concerns can be and often are expressed in a different idiom. Recall the dignity-based defense of hate speech restrictions that we encountered in Chapter 2. Hate speech, or at least certain forms of it, undermines the equal social standing of its victims, or so the argument here alleges. By the same token, pornography, or at least certain forms of it, may be held to undermine the equal social standing of women. These facts, if they were facts, would bear directly on the values that ground the right of free expression. For if people have contributions to make to public debate, then they need to be heard. If their contributions are systematically ignored or given less weight for reasons that have nothing to do with the quality of what they have to say, then truth discovery, knowledge generation and the cultivation of "living" beliefs will all be served less well. The claim we are now considering holds that this is precisely what happens when hate speech and pornography are given free rein in a society. Moreover, if these forms of expression undermine the equal standing of their victims, then they would engage the legitimacy consideration as well. For, as Dworkin emphasized in the passage quoted near the beginning of this chapter, legitimate government demands that each citizen have not only a vote but also a voice and that their "standing as a responsible agent" in politics be confirmed.

Expressed in these terms – the terms of equal standing and equal voice – the case for restricting the free expression of hateful and degrading forms of expression splits the classic argument against itself. For here the restriction of expression is the remedy for its restrictive impact on other expression. The idea that expression by its communicative impact can undermine the standing of others is plausible in the abstract, but hazardous to apply in practice. Recall from Chapter 2 Waldron's discussion of the Danish cartoon that depicted the prophet Muhammad as a bomb-throwing terrorist. Is this hate speech of the social standing-denying kind? Waldron is unsure. It is "a question of judgment whether this was an attack on Danish Muslims as well as an attack on Muhammad."[60] The same "question of judgment" will arise

---

58   In Langton's words, this is "illocutionary disablement."
59   There is much more to be said on this matter. For an extended critical discussion of the feminist claim that pornography constitutes a form of silencing, see Kramer, *Freedom of Expression As Self-Restraint*, pp. 160–243.
60   Waldron, *The Harm in Hate Speech*, p. 126.

with respect to most of the cases concerning hateful and degrading expression that is not also harassment or intimidation. The question of judgment concerns the social meaning of the expression in question.

The social meaning of expression is a function of what it is taken to represent. The Danish cartoon was widely perceived by Muslims as an attack on them, not just an attack on their religion, as if the two could be neatly separated in their minds. Muslim leaders raised the ante. Legal systems that protect the expression of messages like that conveyed in the cartoon are themselves complicit in its message. This can seem preposterous. If I protect your right to say Y, then it does not follow that I endorse Y. But social meanings have their own logic. Here the feminist argument against pornography seems to get matters right. It is a mistake to focus attention on the best interpretation of a film that celebrates rape. One should look to its effects on the standing of women who live in the society in which the film, and others like it, are freely expressed and consumed. But once this line is taken, it becomes hard to discern any limit on expression that could be taken to be degrading and standing-denying. Could the publication of a book like *The Bell Curve*[61] undermine the social standing of blacks in the USA? The answer would turn not on the quality of the arguments in the book or on the intentions of the authors but on the message its publication was taken to express.

Writers like Waldron try to distinguish dignity-denying expression from expression that is offensive to one's group. Part of the trick here is to insist on a picture of the person that can stand apart from the values, beliefs, commitments and prejudices it affirms. No one can demand to live in an expressive environment in which others are not permitted to contest or ridicule one's deepest beliefs and commitments. Such a demand would spell the end of free expression. Freedom from offensive expression is a false freedom. Better, Waldron argues, to target only expression that attempts "to denigrate or eliminate" the social standing of others.[62] It is doubtful that the distinction Waldron needs can be sustained in practice, however. Consider the Danish cartoon again. Suppose the social meaning of the cartoon is that Muslims in virtue of their religious commitments are predisposed to violence and terrorism. Is this an attack on Muslims or on their religious convictions? A Muslim should not be identified with their religious commitments. The disparagement of their convictions may be painful to them, but it is not an attack on them. Suppose next that the publication of the cartoon encourages others in their society to view Muslims as a menace to their society as opposed to members of it. Does this undermine their social standing? Yes, but only to the extent that their social standing is bound up with their religious commitments.

The point here is not that the distinction between offensive and dignity-denying expression is a false one, or one that cannot be drawn. The point is that offensive

---

[61] Hernstein and Murray, *The Bell Curve*. The book sparked much public controversy as it contained, among other things, very sensitive discussions of race and intelligence.

[62] Ibid., p. 135.

expression about race, gender, religion and culture will often be experienced as dignity-denying expression that attacks the standing of the members of the targeted group. The difficulty is that the maxim "restrict offensive expression when it is experienced as dignity-denying" is not a generalizable maxim for a regime of free expression. The protection it seeks to provide cannot be extended to all groups who would demand it without excessive restriction of expression.

A tempting response to this problem is to lean heavily on the distinction between deliberative or high-value expression and low-value expression. Waldron is especially concerned with hate speech and pornography on the internet. It is "the enduring presence of the published word or the posted image that is particularly worrying."[63] Much of this expression is decidedly of low value. The persuasion principle discussed earlier, which animates many defenses of the classic argument, is not engaged by displays of neo-Nazi symbols or depictions of violent rape. To be sure, efforts to restrict the expression of offensive and degrading low-value expression can backfire.[64] But in principle such an approach would fit well with the ethical environmentalism I have been defending in this book.

Another tempting response to the problem of distinguishing wrongful expression that is appropriately subject to restriction from wrongful expression that is not involves an appeal to the intent or motive behind the expression. The Nazis who marched in Skokie, Illinois were not trying to contribute to public debate. By all accounts, their intention was to cause offense and to wound the Jewish residents in this town. Their expression in this march can be fairly described as intentionally injurious.[65] Likewise, some expression, including political expression, on the internet is motivated entirely by the desire to confuse or mislead others. Propaganda funded by international actors is a political weapon, not an effort to engage others in argument. Narrowly tailored restrictions on wrongful expression could target expression that was judged to be both of low value and intentionally injurious or intentionally deceptive in these ways.

These are helpful pointers. They are both challenging to apply in practice. Some expression plainly has low value, but it will be difficult for us to judge expression that we abhor as having high value. Some expression is plainly motivated by an intent to harm or promote confusion, but we will be inclined to find a bad motive behind expression whenever we find it to be deeply offensive or wrongheaded. And, of course, much expression results from multiple motives, with some being more respect-worthy than others.

Let us assume these problems of application can be managed. Then we could hold that the right of free expression does not cover expression that is of low value and is

---

[63] Ibid., pp. 37–38.

[64] For evidence of the counter-productiveness of such efforts, see Strossen, *Hate Speech*.

[65] In discussing the propriety of campus speech codes, some writers appeal to the intent of the speakers. "Campus speech codes, if they must exist, should be directed primarily at the intentionally injurious use of speech" (Greenawalt, *Fighting Words*, p. 77).

motivated by a desire to offend, promote hatred of particular groups or sow confusion.[66] Such expression is not expression whose primary aim is to persuade by engaging the deliberative faculties of its audience. What about high-value expression with a bad motive? Writers who argue that the Holocaust did not occur or that some racial groups are more intelligent than others may have bad motives, but their expression aims to persuade by argument. Expression of this kind serves the underlying values of the classic argument. Some matters, it can be said in reply, are settled. There is nothing to be learned from the writings of members of the Flat Earth Society. But there is this complication. The matters that are settled is not itself a matter that is settled.

Mill held that so long as there were some people who wanted to contest a claim, then it should not be considered to be settled. Indeed, Mill went further. When people contest a widely held view with evidence and argument, they perform a public service: "If there are any persons who contest a received opinion, or will do so if law and opinion will let them, let us thank them for it, open our minds to listen, and rejoice that there is someone to do for us what we otherwise ought, if we have any regard for ... the vitality of our convictions."[67] Some expression is wrongful. If people nonetheless have a right to engage in it, then they have a right to do wrong. But if we follow Mill here, then those who contest received doctrines, including of course true doctrines, perform a public service and do no wrong. That implication will be very hard to accept when applied to expression that, whatever its other motivations, wrongfully stigmatizes or degrades members of targeted groups.[68]

Expression that does not serve the common good of a society and imposes costs on others is wrongful. If it merits protection, then this will be for reasons of distrust. We may feel that governmental efforts to distinguish expression that is on balance bad and unworthy of protection from expression that merits protection are too liable to error and abuse. The better policy is to avoid making these discriminations, when possible.

This may be good counsel in some circumstances, even in most circumstances. But reasons of distrust threaten to extend beyond free expression to other areas of governmental action. Recall Mill's discussion of polygamous marriage discussed in Chapter 2. This institution, in Mill's eyes, was close to slavery for the women in it, but it merited protection nonetheless. The liberty protected by the harm principle extended to it. Such a view makes sense if one believes, as Mill apparently did, that the rights to liberty protected by the principle must be nearly absolute.[69] But most proponents of the classic argument do not follow Mill in this regard. They cleave to

---

[66] We might want to add as well that the expression has some reasonable probability of achieving its purpose.

[67] Mill, *On Liberty*, p. 252.

[68] Waldron, *The Harm in Hate Speech*, p. 194.

[69] Gray, *Mill on Liberty: A Defence*, p. 60 (arguing that Mill believed that "utility itself demands the adoption of a weighty (but not infinitely weighty) side-constraint principle about the protection of moral rights").

a near absolutist line when it comes to free expression but a relaxed line when it comes to other governmental regulations of action. Is this position coherent? Perhaps not. Still, it does seem plausible to hold that the justificatory bar for restricting expression with a persuasive purpose should be significantly higher than that for restricting action that is not primarily expressive. It is one thing for a society to restrict the practice of polygamous marriage to protect women but another thing for it to prevent people from even making the case for it.

The legal moralism defended in the second part of this book takes seriously the responsibility of legal officials to bring about and sustain an ethical environment informed by sound judgments of critical morality. This is a challenging responsibility. Even under the best of conditions, judgments of critical morality are prone to error, and changing circumstances continually require the members of a society to rethink the morality that is appropriate for them. To be defensible, the practice of ethical environmentalism must facilitate critical reflection on the judgments that inform it. It must not strive to ossify current understandings of right and wrong conduct and of good and bad ways of living, but instead be open to its own reform and improvement. The right of free expression serves this critical function, but it can do so only if a society is willing to tolerate the costs and harms that result from the persuasive impact of wrongful expression.

10

Pragmatism and the Perils of Enforcement

This book has foregrounded general arguments and fundamental principles that purport to justify or limit the enforcement of morality. Many of the arguments and principles examined cannot do the work that their proponents hoped they could do, but we have seen that a critical investigation of them nonetheless brings into view important considerations that bear on the questions we have been investigating. Still, the moral considerations we have been analyzing, even if properly characterized and adequately balanced against one another, do not tell us what actual societies, or more precisely those in actual societies who are well positioned to enforce morality, ought to do when it comes to the enforcement of morality. To reach answers on these more practical questions, we must apply the moral considerations to the facts at hand, and when we do so we may find that an enforcement proposal that looked attractive in the abstract would be a disaster in practice.

The "war on drugs" that has been undertaken by many societies serves as a compelling example of this possibility. Even if it is granted, as the discussion in this book suggests, that laws proscribing the use of dangerous recreational drugs can be justified as serving the common good of the societies in which they are undertaken, and that no fundamental principles rule them out, one might sensibly conclude not only that these "wars" have failed in practice but also that the dangers and risks associated with their execution made it highly unlikely that they could have succeeded. The war on drugs often does not work, and has been too costly, even when it does work. Resources spent on drug enforcement could have been spent on other things, including drug prevention and drug rehabilitation programs. Further, in the process of conducting the legal campaign against drugs, liberties, other than those involved in the production, sale, consumption and possession of the targeted drugs, have been infringed upon. And to add insult to injury, objectionable inequalities between different ethnic and racial groups have been exacerbated by the way in which the drug war has been conducted.

With examples like the drug war in mind, this chapter shifts the focus from principle to pragmatic concerns. Given the importance of the pragmatic concerns, some may wonder whether the order of inquiry pursued in this book is misguided.

Better to start with what is practically feasible, they might be tempted to say, and then structure the inquiry in light of this feasibility constraint. Section 10.1 indirectly defends the approach adopted here by outlining what would be lost if this rival feasibility-first approach were pursued. Section 10.2 continues this critical discussion by considering two examples of indirect constraints on the enforcement of morality that are worked up from pragmatic considerations. It argues that the considerations, while valid, cannot support the constraints. Both examples illustrate the tendency on the part of pragmatists to overgeneralize from compelling cases. Section 10.3 discusses the problem of overcriminalization, to which the ethical environmentalism defended in this book may seem to be especially vulnerable. This problem points to the importance of identifying alternative enforcement methods to the criminal law, and the importance of comparative assessments of legal and social enforcement mechanisms, which is explored in Section 10.4. The concluding section discusses the social fact of intractable disagreement over the content of morality in modern societies, and the limits, as well as the benefits, this fact presents to the project of ethical environmentalism.

10.1 REVERSING THE ORDER OF INQUIRY

Generalizing from the "war on drugs" example, we might try to formulate a series of pragmatic maxims that apply to the enforcement of morality in general, or to the legal enforcement of morality in particular. Such maxims – to name just a few – would include the following:

Competence. Do not entrust the enforcement of morality to those who are not competent to do it well.

Efficacy. Do not attempt to enforce morality if doing so is likely to be ineffective or counter-productive.

On Balance Beneficial. Do not attempt to enforce morality if doing so would engender costs that exceed the prospective benefits of enforcement.

Proportionality. Do not attempt to enforce morality if the severity or harshness of the enforcement measure, as experienced by some, is excessive in relation to the prospective good secured, or the prospective evil adverted, by the measure.

Fairness. Do not enforce morality if doing so would engender unfair treatment between individuals or groups.

These maxims are crisply stated. No doubt they would require elaboration, refinement and qualification to serve as plausible guidelines. After all, each person, whether competent or not, must be entrusted to enforce morality insofar as doing so is necessary for their own self-defense. So, the competence maxim must be qualified. Further, any enforcement measure risks engendering unfair treatment, since even the most reliable procedures for enforcing morality can misfire. We should not forswear efforts to criminally enforce the moral prohibition on rape because there is some chance that some will be unfairly treated in the process. So, the fairness maxim must be qualified as well.

Let us put these complications aside and suppose that we have in hand fully specified and adequately qualified pragmatic maxims of the sort adverted to here. We could now reframe our inquiry. The maxims could be put first, and they could be used to filter the in-principle enforcement proposals to be investigated. For example, our discussion in this book has taken seriously the idea that people have self-regarding duties that could in principle justify legal restrictions on self-regarding conduct. But if all such proposals run afoul of the pragmatic maxims, then the import of our discussion of them is called into doubt. The friend of the maxims-first approach, accordingly, will view the order of inquiry that has been pursued in this book as back to front. We have started with principle and then turned to pragmatic considerations, but the better approach starts with pragmatic considerations and turns to principle only when doing so is necessary to help us determine the best option that has not been excluded by the maxims.

There is no need to reject the maxims-first approach out of hand. Different methods of inquiry are appropriate for different purposes. Those who wish to advise policymakers may have little need to consider far-fetched possibilities to test the soundness of various principles. But this book is not meant to be a guide for policymakers. It is meant to be a contribution to our understanding of justified enforcement in law and morality. As such, the maxims-first approach would be unsatisfactory for a number of reasons. First, in addition to wanting to know what we should do, we may also want to know what we should think.[1] Thus, one might grant that no drug war is going to succeed, and that all legal efforts to restrict the use of targeted drugs for recreational purposes are doomed to failure, at least in the world in which we live. Yet one might want to know whether drug wars could be justified if the world were different than it is. Imagining better enforcement technology and wiser people in charge, one might want to know whether drug enforcement policies could be permissible or required. This question may not exercise everyone, but just as it can be good for one to know truths about morality generally, it can be good for one to know truths about the enforcement of morality.[2]

Second, principles and abstract discussions of those principles that seem to have no practical application can surprise us. The practical upshot of the principles may not be straightforward or easy to appreciate. Recall an example from Chapter 3, Section 3.4. We imagined there a choice we could make that concerned two separate worlds with no communication between them, a world of saints and a world of sinners. Our choice was whether to intercept and destroy a bundle of life-enhancing resources that was on its way to the world of sinners. Confronted with this example,

---

[1] See Cohen's discussion of justice in *Rescuing Justice and Equality*, p. 268 ("the question for political philosophy is not what we should do but what we should think, even when what we should think makes no practical difference").

[2] For further defense of the value of impractical knowledge, see Estlund, *Utopophobia*, pp. 304–315.

some will protest immediately that the issue it poses is idle. We have no need for a principle, they will say, to help us to decide what to do in circumstances we will never encounter. But this reaction is too quick. As we saw, the example and the retributive principle that contravenes the person-affecting restriction that it brings into focus bear on choices that we do confront in ordinary life, such as the justification of punishment in cases of pure legal moralism. The connection between the far-fetched example, and the somewhat arcane principle it engages, and the enforcement of morality that we confront in our own lives is not obvious or straightforward, but it is real.

Third, the pragmatic maxims are not invariant across social contexts. The claim that a particular enforcement proposal will do more harm than good can be true in some contexts and false in others. We might respond by confining our inquiry to this or that social context. But there would be costs to such an approach. As I noted in Chapter 1, we seek a general understanding of the moral limits of the enforcement of morality. Society-specific inquiries cannot provide that understanding. They tell us only what enforcement proposals it would be advisable to undertake in the society under consideration.

Fourth, the pragmatic maxims tie the legitimacy of enforcement measures too tightly to the competence and moral sensitivity of those in charge of the enforcement. Not only do these factors vary across societal contexts; they also distort our inquiry in the following way. We want to know what it is permissible for legal officials to do if they are disposed to act well. The pragmatic maxims, by contrast, invite us to think about how the legal officials in our society are likely to behave if this or that enforcement proposal were undertaken. If the legal officials likely would do more harm than good if they were directed to enforce a certain measure, then we should not direct them to do so. In this spirit Mill claimed that the strongest argument of all against interference with "purely personal conduct" is that the interferers will, in all likelihood, interfere "wrongly and in the wrong place."[3] Better to not give people permission to do something they will not do well. This claim sweeps too broadly, however. Surely some people can sometimes interfere rightly and in the right place, as Mill concedes in his own discussion of the bridge case. And, even if Mill's claim were generally true, it would be a mistake to conclude from this that the problem lies with the principle that permits the interference. The fault may lie instead with the people who could, but will not, apply it correctly.

We seek to understand the permissible enforcement of morality, not just what it would be expedient to tell others to do, given their evident shortcomings. Still, there are difficult complications to consider here. For the enforcement of morality itself presupposes that people are not acting as they should. Imagine someone inviting us to consider a society in which every member was resolutely disposed to comply fully with the legal and moral norms of the society, and imagine further that the legal and moral norms of the society in question were all sound. The issues we have been

---

[3]   Mill, *On Liberty*, p. 283.

discussing in this book would not arise for such a society. No enforcement of morality would be necessary.[4] We might imagine instead a social world in which ordinary subjects could not be relied on to act as they should (and hence there is a need to consider enforcement measures), but legal officials could be relied on to act as they should. Of course, legal officials are also subject to the laws that they enforce, and so in their capacity as ordinary subjects they too would be appropriately subject to the enforcement measures, but in their capacity as legal officials they would remain faultless. That world is not our world, of course. But it is a world in which we could say of any contemplated enforcement proposal that was misguided that the fault lay with the proposal itself, and not with those who were charged with administering it.

A world in which legal officials entrusted with the task of enforcing morality could be relied on to behave faultlessly will strike many as too far-fetched to be of much interest. Moreover, or so it might be thought, principles for the enforcement of morality formulated for that world could be dangerous for our world. Responsible inquiry must tailor principles to realistic expectations about the conduct of legal officials.

How might this be done? In his discussion of the moral limits to the criminal law, Feinberg invites us to take up the perspective of an advisor to a legislative body. Although Feinberg does not emphasize the point, good advisors must be cognizant of the limitations of their advisees. The basic question to answer, Feinberg writes, is: "What criminal legislation would be morally legitimate (justified in principle) for a democratic parliament to enact in a world populated by people like us (where 'us' includes virtually *all* of us, including Third World countries) in circumstances like those that prevail in our modern period."[5] Presumably, an answer to Feinberg's basic question will need to abstract from differences in the character and competence of the members of different democratic parliaments. We answer his question by thinking about what it would be morally legitimate for a democratic parliament to do, not by thinking about what it would be reasonable to tell this or that parliament to do, given its infirmities.

Working with Feinberg's advisory perspective, it will be helpful to distinguish two levels of inquiry. The primary level, as I will call it, addresses a non-actual ideal parliament. This parliament consists of members who are competent, conscientious, well informed and committed to the common good of their society. Such a parliament makes laws for people like us in circumstances like those that prevail in the modern period. The secondary level, by contrast, addresses actual parliaments that make laws for people like us in circumstances that prevail in the modern period. This level is sensitive to the differences between actual parliaments, including their varying competences. The secondary level is less fundamental than the primary level

---

[4] This possibility has also been taken to show that it is not necessary or essential to a legal system that it contain enforcement mechanisms. See Hart, *The Concept of Law*.

[5] Feinberg, *Harmless Wrongdoing*, p. 332.

in the following sense. Competent inquiry at the secondary level requires some knowledge of the results of inquiry from the primary level, but the converse does not hold. A good advisor to an actual parliament would not only need to know what it would be morally legitimate for them to do in principle but also what would be the best advice to give them in light of their particular infirmities.[6]

In this book our discussion in the main has taken place on the primary level. We have noted the importance of tradition-dependent social facts, and such facts must be taken into account at the secondary level, but on the whole we have abstracted from societal conditions that differentiate societies in the class of those that Feinberg had in mind by the modern period. Our inquiry has been broader than Feinberg's, however, for we have been concerned with the legal enforcement of morality and not just that part of it that engages the criminal law. We also have been concerned with the nonlegal social enforcement of morality. Given this broader focus, the perspective of an advisor to a parliament, whether ideal or actual, is inapposite. We must take up the perspective of an advisor to other state officials and of citizens quite generally, distinguishing primary and secondary levels of inquiry.

A philosophical discussion of the enforcement of morality need not start with the primary level. A bottom-up approach would start at the secondary level and ascend to the primary level only when doing so was necessary to address a problem or answer a question. But such a discussion, I have suggested, could not ignore the primary level. The indispensability of attending to the primary level, if correct, thus provides a further measure of support for the approach adopted here.

10.2 INDIRECT ARGUMENTS

Pragmatic considerations of the sort expressed by the maxims could inform principles formulated at the primary level. The pragmatic maxims, I claimed earlier, are not invariant across social contexts. But is this always the case? Might there be pragmatic maxims that are robust across societal contexts? If this were so, then one could formulate pragmatic principles to supplement the non-pragmatic principles. An ideal advisor at the primary level could then recommend these principles to any enforcer of morality.

We cannot rule out this possibility. The pragmatic principles in question here would need to appeal to facts over and above those about human nature or the social conditions that prevail in the modern period. For these facts have been presupposed in the articulation of the in-principle principles that this book has considered. The facts at issue would need to be of a different sort, reflecting general truths about value for people like us. But, while we cannot rule out the possibility that there are such pragmatic principles, we can consider attempts to establish their existence. If these

---

[6]   Compare this claim with Smith's discussion of an ideal rational advisor for an imperfectly rational agent in the circumstances that they find themself in. See Smith, "Internal Reasons," reprinted in *Ethics and the A Priori* (Cambridge: Cambridge University Press, 2004), pp. 17–42.

attempts fail, then we have some reason to think that the general strategy they instantiate is unpromising.

This section considers two indirect arguments against the enforcement of morality. Both of these arguments aim to establish that otherwise sound enforcement proposals would be inefficacious and therefore inadvisable or illegitimate to undertake. The arguments seek to show that the means of enforcement frustrate the ends that purport to justify it. Both arguments draw inspiration from Locke's famous argument against the enforcement of religious practice. That argument holds that religious salvation requires sincere belief on the part of the believer and that this belief cannot be induced by force. The means of the religious persecutor – force and threats of force – cannot achieve the end at which they aim – the salvation of the persecuted. Invoking a medical metaphor, Locke writes: "However likely and generally accepted a medicine may be, it is administered in vain if the stomach rejects it as soon as it is taken, and it is wrong to force a remedy on an unwilling patient when his particular constitution will turn it to poison."[7] Locke's argument was effectively rebutted by his contemporary critic Jonas Proast. A structurally similar rebuttal, I will argue, can be pressed effectively against both of the indirect arguments considered here that draw inspiration from Locke.

The first indirect argument targets enforcement with regard to character-centered legal moralism. As explained in Chapter 5, the improvement, or protection, of a person's character can be a justifying ground for interfering with them. Perhaps having a good character is conducive to their well-being, and so the contemplated interference would qualify as an instance of moralistic legal paternalism, or perhaps the person has no such well-being interest in having a good character, but it would be good if they had such a character, even if it was not good for them. Either way, or so we claimed, the interference could be justified under the aegis of ethical environmentalism, providing the judgments of good character that informed it were sound.

Still, the contemplated interference would be justified only if it could be reasonably expected that it would achieve its end. And, certainly sometimes at least, the contemplated interference could not meet this burden. Laws criminalizing or otherwise discouraging prostitution or gambling, for example, might succeed in deterring people from engaging in these activities, and engagement in these activities, it might be granted, is detrimental to good character; but the laws might do nothing to improve people's character, for good character requires that one act on the right motives. Here is Feinberg again: "Genuine excellence . . . consists in acting or forbearing with genuine understanding of the ground for reasonable restrictions on one's conduct, and a commendable motive for it, not just out of prudent fear of sanctions or the desire for respectability."[8] So far, the point pressed here is a mere reminder of the importance of the pragmatic maxim that we labeled efficacy. If good

---

[7] Locke, *A Letter Concerning Toleration*, p. 41.
[8] Feinberg, *Harmless Wrongdoing*, p. 286.

character requires good motives, and if the means of interference in question frustrate good motives, then insofar as the interference is justified by appeal to its effects on the character of those subject to it, it will be inefficacious and therefore wrong. The indirect argument, however, generalizes from specific cases to a blanket judgment that character-centered legal moralism will always be inefficacious because it will invariably engender the wrong motives for compliance.

If sound, the indirect argument would establish a general limit on the enforcement of morality, and not merely a limit that was sound in this or that circumstance or in this or that society. It thus would be the kind of pragmatic argument that could be pressed at the primary level of inquiry concerning the enforcement of morality.

To assess the argument, start by noting Feinberg's appeal to "genuine excellence" in the passage just quoted. Two people might be equally good insofar as they forbear from participation in an objectionable activity, but one could be better than the other with regard to the activity in question in virtue of their motivation for avoiding it. Granted, the former's forbearance from the activity is more excellent than the latter; yet it does not follow that the latter gains nothing from their forbearance. Less excellent as their forbearance may be, their forbearance might be good for their character insofar as it is good for them to avoid participation in the activity.[9] We might say this. Best of all is to forbear for the right reasons. Worst of all is not to forbear, and in between is to forbear for the wrong reasons. (Example: it is best for one's character to refrain from murder and to do so out of proper respect for human life; it is much less excellent for one to refrain from murder out of fear of criminal sanction; but it is much worse for one's character to commit murder.)

The proponent of character-centered legal moralism, accordingly, can concede Feinberg's point about genuine excellence but hold that the appropriate focus of such moralism must lower its sights. The law can safeguard people's character by preventing them, or dissuading them, from engaging in character-damaging activities, even if excellent people would not need the law's assistance. This response can be resisted. Someone might hold that our character is nothing more than a set of dispositions to act across a range of circumstances, actual and possible. Our dispositions to act, and not our actions themselves, constitute our character. On this view, the person who refrains from murder out of fear of criminal sanction is not made better by their forbearance. They simply reveal the limits of their propensity to murder.

Acceptance of this view of character does not rule out the evident possibility that our actions affect our dispositions to act. The person who forbears from engaging in an objectionable activity for the wrong reasons might not get credit for their forbearance, but their forbearance may be good for their character in that if they had engaged in the activity, their dispositions to do so would have been changed for the worse. Legal measures that succeed in dissuading them from engaging in the activity may protect their character by preventing them from corrupting it even further.

[9]   George, *Making Men Moral*, p. 46.

Let us now put these points aside. The target of the indirect argument that character-centered legal moralism must fail can be narrowed. Not all such moralistic measures are its concern – only measures designed to elevate people's character by getting them to appreciate the value of acting (or forbearing to act) in various ways. This inner appreciation of value, like "the inward persuasion of the mind" that Locke insisted was necessary to benefit from engagement with true religious practice,[10] cannot be compelled or induced by outward force.

There is little question that this argument has force. The appreciation of why one should act virtuously or avoid acting viciously and the motivation to act in ways guided by that appreciation cannot itself be brought by force, threats or incentives. To this extent, the law cannot improve people's character. At most, it can induce them to act as they should.[11] Notwithstanding this point, the law may be able to play an indirect role in improving the character of those who are subject to it. This was, in brief, Proast's point against Locke. Let us consider it in a little more detail. Outward force, or other forms of inducement, cannot act on the mind directly, but they can, Proast claims, "bring men to consider those Reasons and Arguments which are proper and sufficient to convince them, but which, without being forced, they would not consider" and thus "indirectly and at a distance" outward force can assist people in embracing the truth.[12]

Proast's concern was with appreciation of religious truths. The law can help to bring about or sustain a context or environment that is conducive, or more conducive than it would otherwise be, to the formation of true beliefs, religious or otherwise. Stated in these terms, Proast's point is very hard to deny. As we saw in the previous chapter on free expression, debates over the limits of free speech often center on what types of restrictions or regulations on speech would contribute to an epistemic environment that does well in terms of truth or knowledge promotion. No one thinks that you can directly compel a person to believe a truth they will not accept, but most people think that the law could – whether or not it should – regulate, for better or worse, what ideas people are exposed to, and that this regulation can affect what they come to believe.

[10] Locke, *A Letter Concerning Toleration*, p. 20.
[11] This is a plausible claim, but it needs qualification. Consider the following remarks from Hurka, who reports that he is rehearsing an argument that Hastings Rashdall pressed against T. H. Green: "The criminal law forces us, or at least gives us a strong self-interested reason, to do things we should do for their own sakes, such as not killing, not stealing, and not committing sexual assault. Yet most of us continue to do these things partly for a moral reason. We refrain from killing partly to avoid punishment but partly because we think that killing is morally wrong. Here the presence of state coercion does not interfere with endorsement; we can be forced and, simultaneously, act from a worthy motive. And it is arguable that the coercion encourages endorsement. By attaching a severe punishment to killing, society expresses its conviction that this act is seriously morally wrong, and by doing so reinforces our own moral beliefs" (Hurka, "Indirect Perfectionism: Kymlicka on Liberal Neutrality," *Journal of Political Philosophy* 3/1 [1995]: 36–57, at 46; Rashdall, *The Theory of Good and Evil*, vol. I, pp. 297–300).
[12] Proast, "The Argument of the Letter Concerning Toleration, Briefly Consider'd and Answer'd," in *The Reception of Locke's Politics*, vol. V, ed. Goldie (London: Pickering and Chatto, 1999), pp. 25–37, at 27.

Our concern here is not in the first instance with true beliefs, but with character more broadly. How then does Proast's point carry over to this context? Consider an example. So-called bad Samaritan laws penalize people for failing to help or rescue others in grave peril, when they could do so at little cost or danger to themselves. These laws are sometimes justified, in part, on grounds of legal moralism.[13] The primary point of such laws is to protect the interests of those in need in the circumstances in which the laws have application, but a subsidiary point is to help people appreciate that they have a moral duty to provide assistance in these circumstances.[14]

The rescue situations envisioned by bad Samaritan laws are not likely to be recurring events in the lives of those who are subject to them. Since character develops over time, not in one-off events, these laws likely would not do much to improve the character of those who were subject to them. Rescuing another out of fear of penalty on one occasion is not likely to do much in helping one to appreciate the moral reasons to do so. The indirect argument has considerable force when applied to this example.

Consider next the case of national service. National service programs are government-run programs to provide community work. They can be either voluntary or compulsory. A compulsory national service program, for example, might require all young adults to spend one year of service in the program. For national service programs to be justified, they must do valuable work. But the production of the valuable work on its own is hardly a compelling argument for the programs. After all, the work can be done in other ways, and often in more efficient ways. Those who propose and defend the programs, however, standardly point to an important additional reason to support them. Participation in the programs is good for the participants in the sense that it makes them better people. Participants come to have a keener appreciation of the value of the work that they do and the significance of its impact on those who benefit from it. These claims in defense of the programs are clear instances of character-centered legal moralism. Further, the character-centered claims in defense of national service provide a reason to favor compulsory over voluntary versions of the programs. By requiring everyone to participate in the programs, the law can strive to improve the character of many who would otherwise avoid the work in question.[15]

---

[13]   Burgess-Jackson, "Bad Samaritanism and the Pedagogic Function of Law," *Criminal Justice Journal* 8 (1985).

[14]   Discussing the justification of bad Samaritan statutes, Feinberg reports that he was relieved to discover that they could be justified by the harm principle. These statutes appear to be justified, but if they were justified solely on grounds of legal moralism, then they could not be justified on his view (*Harmless Wrongdoing*, p. 296). Feinberg allows that such statutes might improve the character of those who were subject to them but insists that this possibility should be considered to be merely "a fringe benefit" and not a justifying ground for their enactment.

[15]   In discussing hard, dangerous and dirty labor, Michael Walzer observes that these negative goods often match the low status of those who provide them. Negative people for negative goods, in short (*Spheres of Justice*, pp. 165–183). National service programs that supply the labor associated with negative goods might be effective at counteracting this association. When all are involved in the

If the indirect argument we have been considering is sound, then that striving will be futile and should not be undertaken. Those who would have their character improved by participation in national service programs are already inclined to value the work. Better to leave it to them than to require people who do not wish to participate to participate only out of fear of penalty. But the indirect argument, when applied to this example, has considerably less force, at least on its face. The possibility that some, or even most, of those who participate in national service only because it is legally required will come in time to appreciate the value of the work that they are doing and hence value it for the right reasons is not far-fetched. At the very least, the matter invites empirical investigation.

To have one's character improved by engaging in right action, the indirect argument holds, people must appreciate and be moved by the reasons for engaging in the action. Force or threats of penalty cannot bring about this appreciation. But it is not implausible to think that while one's initial participation in a national service program might be motivated by the desire to avoid penalties for failing to do so, over time one could come to appreciate the value of engaging in the work provided by the program. Those who protest that legal threats can never get people to see the point or value of the actions that they require overlook the possibilities for this type of moral improvement.[16]

Let us turn now to a second, and related, indirect argument that seeks to establish a general principle – worked up from the pragmatic maxims – for limiting the enforcement of morality. The argument I have in mind shifts from character enforcement to prudential benefit. As such, it targets legal paternalism quite generally. The argument rests on a contrast between living a life "from the inside" and living a life that is informed by values that one does not accept. Here is a representative statement of the idea: "[N]o life goes better by being led from the outside according to values the person doesn't endorse. My life only goes better if I am leading it from the inside, according to my beliefs about value."[17] Three clarifications of this idea are in order. First, the notion of a life going better for a person is best construed in first-personal terms. My life goes better *for me* if I lead it from the inside, even if it might be better for others or in some impersonal sense if I did not lead my life from the inside. Second, the claim that a life only goes better if led from the inside states only a necessary, not a sufficient, condition. Leading a life from the inside does not ensure that it will be good for one to do so. Third, the notion of a better life here should be understood to include all the component parts that

provision of this kind of labor, none are viewed as inferior in virtue of their association with it. If so, there is an egalitarian character-based reason to support national service programs of this kind.

[16] The point here, to some degree, likely would have been accepted by Mill, who is widely considered to be a resolute opponent of coercive legal moralism. Mill thought it was very important for citizens in modern societies to be called upon to serve the public in some capacity. Participation in public functions was vital for their intellectual and moral development. See *Considerations on Representative Government*, pp. 399–412.

[17] Kymlicka, *Liberalism, Community and Culture*, p. 12.

make it better. Someone who leads their life from the inside, pursuing aims and projects that reflect their own assessment of what is worth doing, might on occasion be forced or induced to do something that they do not value. On the argument we are now considering, this forced or induced component could not benefit them.

We briefly considered a version of this indirect argument in Chapter 6 under the heading of the endorsement constraint. There we argued that the argument is ineffective against defenses of legal paternalism that rest on considerations of fairness. If I am compelled to do something that I do not value, I may not benefit from it, but it may be fair nonetheless to require me to do it if others would benefit substantially from the general imposition of the requirement. This points to a limitation of the indirect argument, but the argument, if sound, would still have considerable force. It would be an important truth, if it were indeed true you could never benefit a person by getting them to do something the value of which they do not accept.

In the philosophical literature on well-being this purported truth is standardly referred to as the resonance requirement. Take any purported good, such as any item that might appear on an objective list of prudential goods, and ask whether its possession or instantiation in the life of a person would benefit them if they found nothing of value in it. An affirmative answer would seem to license an unsettling consequence: "[F]riends of an objective account of well-being seem forced to accept the unappealing claim that I could be extremely well off, provided that I have the right objective goods in my life, even though these things hold no appeal for me, and I am, in fact, utterly miserable."[18] The resonance requirement blocks the unappealing conclusion. This is not to say that accepting it is the only way to block the conclusion. You might think that pleasure is an objective good and that any life that is good for a person must contain a decent amount of pleasure. On this view, it does not follow from the rejection of the resonance requirement that a person could be extremely well off and yet be miserable. Still, the thought that pleasure could be good for someone, even though they did not like it, is hard to credit. We are inclined to think that a sensation is not pleasurable if one does not like it.

Grant the resonance requirement then, at least for the sake of argument.[19] For some good or participation in some valuable activity to benefit me, it must resonate with me. What exactly does it mean to say that a good or activity resonates with me? One view – the actualist view – holds that I, given my actual psychological profile, must value it, or have some favorable attitude toward it. If I do not enjoy, and fail to see the point of, playing the piano, then doing so will not benefit me, however valuable the activity of playing the piano might otherwise be. Still, I might value

---

[18] Kagan, "Well-Being As Enjoying the Good," *Philosophical Perspectives* 23 (2009): 253–272, at 254.

[19] A weaker, and I believe more plausible, version of the resonance requirement is defended in Wall and Sobel, "A Robust Hybrid Account of Well-Being." This weaker version holds that resonance affects the prudential value of the thing that benefits the agent but is not a strict condition for its being a benefit to the agent.

playing the piano if I were more rational or more attentive to the good-making features of the activity than I currently am. If so, then playing the piano, some will say, does resonate with me. Call this the counterfactual view.

There are good reasons to reject the actualist view of the resonance requirement. The actualist view would imply that playing the piano would not benefit me, even if it served one of my central projects. I might consider self-development to be an important component of a good life, and I might believe that the development of my capacities to engage with music was an integral part of that development, but then fail to see the connection between my playing the piano and my self-development. My rational mistake here does not plausibly block the conclusion that playing the piano benefits me. I might go to my grave thinking that playing the piano was a waste of time for me, but I would be mistaken about that.

The counterfactual view avoids these problems; but, by so doing, it diminishes the force of the resonance requirement as an argument against legal paternalism. Once the issue is framed in terms of what *would* resonate with people, if they were *rational*, then many instances of legal paternalism would likely satisfy the resonance requirement. Much here will turn on how much idealization of actual attitudes and valuings is countenanced on the counterfactual view.[20] Likewise, the counterfactual view opens the door to legal interventions that aim to transform people's actual attitudes so that they come to value what they do not currently value. This legal strategy has been described as "coercive habituation to the good."[21] The law, on this strategy, compels people to engage in a valuable activity that they do not currently value so as to get them to appreciate its merits and come to value it for its own sake.

Coercive habituation to the good is an apt label for the strategy Proast urged in response to Locke's argument that religious persecution must always fail in its aim. Proast's concern was habituating people to accept what he took to be the true religion. On matters of such supreme importance as eternal salvation or damnation, the costs imposed by this strategy – the costs of religious persecution, in Proast's case – pale into insignificance. How could setbacks to human interests outweigh the transcendent good of acquiring true belief on such matters?[22] However, applied to secular goods that are implicated in assessments of human welfare, the costs against pursuing the strategy weigh heavily against it. Even if the strategy succeeds, there is the standing cost of employing coercion, which may on many occasions do more harm to the intended beneficiaries of the strategy than the good that is secured. This valid concern rightly speaks in favoring of pursuing noncoercive strategies, such as government subsidies for goods and activities, that could secure the uptake necessary for resonance without incurring the costs of coercion, at least when such strategies are available and likely to be effective. (On the broad understanding of legal

---

[20]   I discuss this issue in more detail in my "Subjective Perfectionism," *American Journal of Jurisprudence*.

[21]   The phrase is taken from Hurka, "Indirect Perfectionism: Kymlicka on Liberal Neutrality," p. 44.

[22]   Christiano, "Does Religious Toleration Make Sense?"

enforcement that we have been working with in this book, these noncoercive strategies qualify as instances of legal enforcement.)

We need not here explore the full range of policies that could be undertaken under the noncoercive strategy of habituating to the good. Our modest aim has been to highlight how the indirect argument against legal paternalism that invokes the resonance requirement sweeps too broadly. The good points it identifies speak against some, but not all, of the measures that it targets. Like the argument that legal coercion cannot protect or elevate the character of those who are subject to it, the argument that you cannot make someone's life go better for them by inducing them to engage in an activity that they do not value is best viewed as an overgeneralization from cases where it is most plausible. Pragmatic-minded critics are right to call attention to the prudential significance of resonance. They err when they present it as grounds for a general limit to legal paternalism.

10.3 OVERCRIMINALIZATION

The pragmatic maxims, and the indirect arguments considered in the previous section, by no means exhaust the pragmatic case against the legal enforcement of morality. Rather than focusing exclusively on particular legal interventions to enforce this or that component of morality, we also need to consider the enforcement measures as a whole. Possibly, each legal intervention taken on its own, and viewed in abstraction from other legal interventions undertaken in the system of enforcement of which it is a part, could be fully justified, while the system as a whole was not. Too much legal enforcement overall could bring problems that are not glimpsed when considering each intervention singly. Let us refer to this as the problem of overcriminalization.[23]

To appreciate the problem, it will be helpful to distinguish the content of a criminal measure from its application. A criminal measure that is unjustly applied is objectionable even if it would not be objectionable were it justly applied. For example, critics of the death penalty in the USA often argue that the problem with it is not its content per se but rather the discriminatory manner in which it is administered.[24] The problem with the death penalty, on this argument, is that its

---

[23] My characterization of the problem of overcriminalization differs from that commonly found in the literature. As I describe it, the problem is not that the law criminalizes trivial offenses or criminalizes activities that are not appropriately subject to criminalization. (See Sun Beale, "The Many Faces of Overcriminalization: From Morals and Mattress Tags to Overfederalization," *American University Law Review* 54/3 [2005]: 747–782.) The problem rather concerns too much criminalization of activities that otherwise would be appropriately subject to criminalization.

[24] No doubt the constitutional context of the USA shapes this response. The "equal protection under the laws" clause of the Fourteenth Amendment to the US Constitution provides a way to argue for the unconstitutionality of capital punishment without resolving the issue of whether the punishment in the abstract could be justified. For discussion of this issue, compare van den Haag, "The Ultimate Punishment: A Defence," *Harvard Law Review* 99/7 (1986): 1662–1669 with Nathanson, "Should We Execute Those Who Deserve to Die?"

application is not consistent with basic rule-of-law values. Like cases should be treated alike, but if the death penalty is imposed on some but not others for arbitrary reasons, then it offends against this value. The injunction to treat like cases alike expresses a basic demand of fairness. The fair treatment of individual persons, accordingly, demands that rule-of-law values be honored in the application of criminal statutes.

The distinction between the content and the application of a criminal measure does not by itself suggest a problem with overcriminalization. It points only to the need to consider both the content and the application of any particular criminal measure. Defenders of the death penalty in the USA have pushed for reforms, such as mandatory sentencing guidelines, in an effort to reduce the arbitrariness of its administration. We need not here consider the degree to which such reforms have been successful in addressing the problem. The point is just to illustrate a strategy available to those who wish to defend a particular criminal measure against this kind of rule-of-law objection.

How then might rule-of-law values relate to the problem of overcriminalization? Imagine a society in which every criminal measure on the books could be given an independent justification. Further imagine that legal officials in this society, including prosecutors and police, were all committed to the fair administration of the measures. This imaginary world is ideal in many respects, but it is not a world in which there are infinite resources available for the detection, prosecution and punishment of offenders. In this world, decisions would need to be made about which offenses should be prioritized and how many resources should be expended on enforcing particular measures. Call this the demands of discretion. If there are few criminal measures on the books in the society in which we are imagining, then the demands of discretion may not present much of a problem at all. The resources available for the administration of the criminal measures may be adequate to ensure the fair and uniform application of all the criminal laws in the system. But when the level of criminalization in the society increases, the demands of discretion become more pressing. Even if each additional offense were justified on its own, its contribution to the aggregate of criminalization in the society could become problematic, as legal officials were forced to focus on some crimes and downplay the enforcement of others.

To sharpen the point, we can distinguish the law on the books from what one commentator has referred to as "the real law."

> The *real* law – the law that distinguishes the conduct that leads to punishment from the conduct that does not – cannot be found in criminal codes. Even those police and prosecutors who pledge fidelity to the rule of law could not hope to honor their commitment because they receive almost no guidance from legislators about what they are expected to do. The number and scope of criminal laws guarantee that neither police and prosecutors will enforce statutes as written.[25]

25 Husak, *Overcriminalization*, p. 27.

The demands of discretion drive a wedge between the law on the books and the "real law." As the wedge widens, rule-of-law values are compromised.[26]

The ethical environmentalism defended in this book might seem to be especially vulnerable on these grounds. Its case for criminalization is too easy to make, or so it might be feared. By contrast, limiting the criminal enforcement of morality to that which contravenes the harm and sovereignty principles, it might be thought, would be preferable, since at least doing so would put barriers in the path to overcriminalization. But, in actuality, any plausible view about the legal enforcement of morality will confront a version of the overcriminalization problem.[27] Further, as I will now explain, ethical environmentalism provides a promising way to address the problem.

The rule of law, and the values it serves, are an integral component of the common good of a society. But it would be a mistake for a society to attempt to maximize the realization of this component by striving to close the divide between the law on the books and the real law. The reason this would be a mistake is that discretion itself serves important values. For one thing, uncompromising adherence to the rule of law would prove too costly in terms of other legitimate legal aims. Speed limits on driving are surely justifiably enforced, even if some measure of discretion concerning enforcement should be left to police officers. No reasonable policy on speed enforcement could aspire to reduce offenses to zero and efforts to specify with precision in the law on the books exactly when speeding offenses should be penalized and when they should not would be foolish. The better course of action calls for balancing the values served by the rule of law, predictability and fair notice, for example, and the values served by discretion, flexibility in the pursuit of reasonable legal aims, for example.[28] With this in mind, it will be instructive to consider a striking example of drug enforcement that was undertaken by the city of New York in the 1980s. Here is a brief description of the example: "When serving as a federal prosecutor in New York, Rudolph Giuliani sought to keep drug dealers 'off balance' by instituting 'federal day': one day each week chosen at random in which street-level drug dealers arrested by local police were prosecuted in federal rather than state court, where sentences are far more severe."[29] The motivation for this "Russian roulette" style of drug enforcement was twofold: state courts were overwhelmed with a backlog of drug prosecutions and "federal day," in effect, stiffened the penalties for drug crimes over those provided by state law, thereby purportedly increasing the deterrent to engage in such crimes.[30]

[26] As one writer observes: "Generally speaking, the more room there is for choice in the application and enforcement of law, the more room there is for non-rational social factors to operate." Shiner, "Crime and Criminal Law Reform: A Theory of the Legislative Response," *Critical Review of International Social and Political Philosophy* 12/1 (2009): 63–84, at 67.
[27] One of the examples that Husak uses to illustrate the problem of overcriminalization concerns the enforcement of traffic rules. *Overcriminalization*, pp. 30–31.
[28] Hart, *The Concept of Law*, pp. 129–136.
[29] Husak, *Overcriminalization*, p. 28.
[30] Labaton, "New Tactics in the War on Drugs Tilt Scales of Justice Off Balance," *The New York Times* (December 29, 1989), p. A1.

Giuliani's policy runs counter to basic rule-of-law values. As one commentator observes, "no person would contend that the same criminal behavior becomes more serious and should be punished more harshly because it happens to be perpetrated on a Tuesday rather than on a Wednesday – especially when notice is deliberately withheld about the date on which the longer sentences will be imposed."[31] Now suppose, for the sake of argument only, that the harsher sentences imposed in the federal courts had "fit" the crime. Then no drug offender would have been given a sentence that was disproportionately severe. Still, the policy is objectionable on grounds of evenhanded treatment. Like cases should be treated alike, and the day on which an offense is committed is not a variable that reasonably distinguishes cases.[32]

Imagine next a different drug enforcement policy, one also designed to reduce the total number of drug prosecutions. This policy, like the Giuliani policy, also leaves punishment to chance but does not impose stiffer sentences on the unlucky. Instead, under the imagined policy, the police randomly step up drug enforcement on some days rather than others. Would this enforcement policy objectionably violate rule-of-law values? It might be said in parallel with the earlier-quoted response to the Giuliani policy that "no person would contend that the same criminal behavior becomes more liable to punishment because it happens to be perpetrated on one day rather than another – especially when notice is deliberately withheld about the day on which the punishment will be imposed." But this claim is not nearly as compelling as the first one. A measure of police discretion seems appropriate and reasonable when it comes to the timing of enforcement measures.

Rule-of-law values, while important, are not the only considerations that matter. They must be balanced against the values of efficiency and the flexibility and adjustment to particular circumstance that discretion makes possible. One might propose that the rule of law is not offended when reasonable discretion is exercised, but it is better to view the rule of law as one virtue among many that can be realized by legal systems. Being one virtue among others it is not a master value that always takes precedence over the others or incorporates them into its formulation.[33]

So long as the rule of law is not taken to be a master value that takes precedence over all other values, it can be understood to be a component part of the common good that the project of ethical environmentalism seeks to secure. Concerns about overcriminalization thus can find their place within the project of ethical environmentalism. Still, the problem of overcriminalization is not just a problem of too much criminalization. A society might criminalize very few activities but have

---

[31] Husak, *Overcriminalization*, p. 28.
[32] Might it be said in response that each offender faced an equal expected chance of receiving the same punishment, under the policy, thereby securing fair treatment via the equality of expected punishment? The reply will be that just punishment should not be designed to turn on chance. But see Lewis, "The Punishment That Leaves Something to Chance," *Philosophy and Public Affairs* 18 (1989): 53–67 (attempting to rationalize the practice of punishing successful criminal offenses more harshly than unsuccessful attempts).
[33] Raz, "The Rule of Law and Its Virtue," in *The Authority of Law* (Oxford: Oxford University Press, 1979).

difficulty enforcing the criminal prohibitions in a fair and predictable manner because of the uncooperativeness of the public in assisting the police and prosecutors.[34] We can ask two questions of any proposed criminalization measure. To what degree would the measure be justified on its merits? And how much public support would the measure enjoy? Suppose a proposed measure scored well on the first question but poorly on the second. Then, while the measure might be in-principle justified, it might be wrong to pursue it in practice. The lack of public support for the measure could prevent it from being enforced in a way that respected rule-of-law values, as citizens might be reluctant to report crimes or cooperate with law enforcement officials in bringing offenders to justice. To the extent that this were true, the society would have reason to look for alternatives to the criminal law in enforcing the measure. Overcriminalization here would be more a matter of the mismatch between the views of legal officials and the views of ordinary citizens than the excess number and range of offenses subject to criminal punishment.

10.4 COMPARATIVE ASSESSMENTS

The enforcement of morality, as this book has stressed, is not confined to the criminal law. Given that the criminal law deliberately imposes hard treatment on offenders, and is thereby especially difficult to justify, and given that the criminal justice system is, by all accounts, a very costly practice of enforcement, it is often said that criminalization should always be considered a last resort. On this view, state punishment, whenever possible, should be avoided. With this in mind, one might propose general pragmatic guidelines of the following sort.

> **Incremental Coercion.** Enforcement strategies should "begin with interventions that invite voluntary compliance, if appropriate add in minimally coercive measures, and adopt more fully coercive measures only when compliance is not secured by more voluntary means."[35]

This guideline excludes all unnecessary coercion. If appropriate enforcement can be secured without resort to criminal penalty, then no such resort would be justified.

To follow the *Incremental Coercion* guideline, one would need to specify what qualifies as "appropriate" enforcement. Interventions that "invite voluntary compliance" might be effective but too costly in terms of other values. The idea behind the guideline is reasonably clear. When it comes to legal enforcement, always prefer the less coercive intervention to the more coercive intervention, providing both could be effective at securing or improving compliance with the norm in question. Yet the state can harm people in various ways without coercing them. Suppose the norm against drunk driving could be effectively enforced either by (1) imposing a short prison sentence and substantial fine on offenders or (2) subjecting them to public

---

[34]   Husak, *Overcriminalization*, p. 32.
[35]   Shiner, "Crime and Criminal Law Reform: A Theory of the Legislative Response," p. 76.

and officially sanctioned shaming. Option (2) could be less coercive but more harmful. Offenders might lose their jobs or experience depression as a result of the shaming, for example. With this kind of possibility in mind, one might shift to a different enforcement guideline:

> **Incremental Harm.** Enforcement strategies should begin with interventions that invite voluntary compliance, if appropriate add in minimally harmful measures and adopt increasingly harmful measures only when compliance is not secured by less harmful means.

This new enforcement guideline, like *Incremental Coercion*, would need to be qualified in various ways to be at all plausible. On their face, both guidelines would justify excessive or disproportionate cost on offenders if doing so were necessary to achieve an appropriate level of norm enforcement. But, even duly qualified, *Incremental Harm* looks suspect. Sometimes values other than harm minimization, such as ensuring fair treatment across individuals, are more important than minimizing harm in enforcement. Return to the drunk driving example. Option (2), even if it proved less harmful, might be more likely to offend rule-of-law values than option (1). The amount of harm experienced by those convicted of drunk driving from the public shaming might be hard to predict in advance and might vary considerably across offenders for arbitrary reasons.

In any event, the enforcement strategies that minimize the coercion and harm imposed by legal means leave the law behind entirely and rely on social penalties or sanctions. Social enforcement of a norm (without legal enforcement) occurs when the members of a society acting collectively, even if not in coordination, express their commitment to the norm by publicly criticizing norm violators and subjecting them to various social penalties, ranging from pointed rebuke, to ostracism and humiliation, to loss of employment or livelihood.[36] These social enforcement strategies raise their own set of concerns, which have been amplified with the development of mass communication on social media and the internet. We have already touched on some of these concerns in Chapter 9. When "social penalties" are systematically imposed on those who express disfavored views, the values served by free expression can be seriously compromised, even when the legal framework is exemplary with regard to free expression. But here the issue is with the social enforcement of norms of conduct, as opposed to speech. Are there general pragmatic factors that favor the social over the legal enforcement of morality, or vice versa?

Some moral wrongdoing is not appropriately enforced by law. Suppose that every September 11 a person celebrates the anniversary of the September 11 attacks on the Twin Towers in New York. This celebratory activity is clearly wrong[37] but it should

---

[36] For general discussion of social enforcement strategies, see Billingham and Parr, "Enforcing Social Norms: The Morality of Public Shaming."

[37] If the celebratory activity were purely private, then its wrongness might not be plain. The issue is contentious. See Sher, *The Wild West of the Mind*. So, let us assume here that the celebratory activity in question is not purely private.

not be subject to criminal sanction. The law should not police our celebrations for a variety of reasons. However, it might be appropriate for those who know this person to rebuke them for their actions, turning a cold shoulder to them as a form of informal punishment.[38] Yet even if this were justified, it would not follow that it would be appropriate for those who know them to go further and organize a campaign against them on social media, one that aimed to publicly vilify them. There are two principal reasons for this. First, and most obviously, such campaigns have a tendency to spiral out of control and result in penalties that are disproportionate by any standard.[39] Second, those on social media who do not know the offender are not well positioned to assess their conduct and their degree of culpability in engaging in it.

The example of a wrongful celebration does not involve the infringement of the rights or justified claims of others. Perhaps the family members and friends of the victims of the September 11 attacks have a claim on others not to publicly celebrate the event, but it is hard to credit the thought that they have a claim that people not celebrate the attacks in private.[40] But other cases present issues of justice. Consider unjust practices of discrimination in hiring among certain businesses. In principle, a society has a choice in pursuing a justice enforcement strategy against these companies. It could either use the law, criminal and civil, to target the injustice or it could leave the enforcement to private individuals and groups. For example, individuals and groups might be able to organize consumer boycotts that would be effective in pressuring the offending companies to change their practices. Suppose it were known that the two strategies would be equally effective in combating the discrimination. One might argue then that the social enforcement strategy would be preferable. It would be less coercive and less costly to the state. In line with *Incremental Coercion* and *Incremental Harm*, and in keeping with the maxim that criminalization should be a last resort, one might urge the society to adopt the social enforcement strategy. But effectiveness is, of course, not the only desideratum. General considerations against leaving the enforcement of justice to private persons would apply here as well. While the offending companies are engaged in wrongful business practices, they, or those who own or run them, retain a claim to be treated fairly in the process of enforcement.

Generally speaking, legally sanctioned punishment, at least in well-ordered legal systems, can be expected to do better than vigilantism in at least two key respects. It is less likely to make errors and it is more likely to allow potential offenders a reasonable opportunity to avoid disproportionate penalties. Prior to the boycott, offending companies may not know what business practices would trigger it, or how effective the

[38] See Radzik, *The Ethics of Social Punishment* (defending the concept of informal social punishment).
[39] For documentation of how such shaming campaigns have spiraled out of control, see Ronson, *So You've Been Publicly Shamed*.
[40] Mounting a public shaming campaign against someone who celebrates the September 11 attacks could have the consequence that the celebratory activity is brought to the attention of the victims of the attacks, thereby causing them distress. This provides an additional reason against organizing the campaign.

boycott would be if it were triggered, and hence how much cost they would incur from it. A general concern with the fair imposition of costs over and above the concern with effectiveness, then, likely favors the legal enforcement strategy over the social enforcement strategy in this kind of case.

We can go further. We can say that it would be wrong to employ the social enforcement strategy in this case, given the availability of the preferable legal enforcement strategy. Given that the latter strategy is as effective as the former, and given that it is fairer to potential offenders, it becomes the required strategy, assuming it would not be prohibitively costly to undertake. Still, the legal enforcement strategy may not always be available. It might not be a viable option in the circumstances we are imagining in virtue of the fact that it will not be undertaken, even though legal officials could undertake it, if they were appropriately motivated to do so. From one perspective, the social enforcement strategy would remain unjustified. The society ought to enforce anti-discrimination through the law, even though it is not disposed to do so. But, from another perspective, the social enforcement strategy now might be justified. The citizens in our imagined society who are in a position to organize the consumer boycott of the offending company are different actors from the legal officials who refuse to enforce anti-discrimination through law. These citizens can reason that, given that legal officials will not do what they ought to do, they ought to take up the slack.[41] The second-best option of social enforcement is better than no enforcement, and given that the best option of legal enforcement is not an option that *they* can undertake, they are justified in pursuing the social enforcement of the anti-discrimination norm. Whether this is so will depend not only on the justice of the cause, in this case the justice of the enforcement of the anti-discrimination norm, but also on the fairness of the expected costs imposed on the offending companies, as well as the expected costs incurred by others who are not responsible in any way for the discriminatory practices. These matters would obviously require a contextual investigation into the circumstances at hand.

One last variant of the example is worth discussing. Imagine the anti-discrimination laws of the society in question to be as good as they could be. No improvement is possible. Yet the discriminatory practices persist. To achieve justice, there must be a change in social norms and attitudes, and the law, we are assuming, cannot bring about that change. In this situation, the social enforcement strategy would be the only game in town. The defects of the social enforcement strategy would still be fully present, but now it might be judged that the unfair or disproportionate costs imposed on the offending companies would be justified, given the importance of the goal of ending discrimination in hiring practices. But while justified, the unfairness of the disproportionate costs would not simply vanish. Those who lost their jobs as a result of a successful boycott of the offending

---

[41] Many questions of political and moral justification involve multiple agents. What some agents should do depends on what other agents are doing, or can be expected to do. See Enoch, "Against Utopianism: Non-Compliance and Multiple Agents," *The Philosopher's Imprint* 18/6 (2018): 1–20.

companies, and who had done nothing themselves to perpetuate the discriminatory practices, could object that their interests were unfairly set back in the process of achieving a morally necessary goal. The force of that objection, and the remedial measures it might support, are not matters that can be investigated here. But they remind us of the point stressed in Chapter 5 on the aspirational nature of the common good that is pursued by the project of ethical environmentalism. The common good is a state of affairs in which the fair treatment of all does not frustrate the good of any member. In practice, transitions that move a society closer to the realization of this aspirational state can further its common good, but not because, or in virtue of the fact that, they thereby further the good of each member of the society.

10.5 THE FACT OF DISAGREEMENT

Political theorists sometimes object that political philosophy should not be understood to be a branch of moral philosophy, one that applies to political and legal topics. Such an approach, it is said, ignores or downplays the salient fact of political and legal disagreement.[42] A radical version of this view holds that there is no common good in modern political societies. There is only a variety of perspectives or conceptions of the common good. A moderate version of the view holds that while there may be a determinate common good for such societies, politics is not the art of securing it but rather the art of respectfully managing disagreement about it.

The objection behind both the radical and the moderate views is important, and it cuts deep. In response, it can be said that political morality consists of two parts. There is the fundamental part that articulates the content of the common good, which includes, as we have seen, an account of the rights and duties of the members of the society; and there is a supplementary part that articulates how those with mistaken views in the society, as seen from the perspective of one who adheres to the fundamental part, are to be treated. The supplementary part, in the words of one writer, can be viewed as political morality's "foreign office."[43] With the distinction between these two parts of political morality in mind, the proponent of one who views political philosophy as a branch of moral philosophy can reply to the objection in the following way.

> Yes, it is plainly true that we disagree over the common good. We have competing conceptions of the common good of the societies in which we live. And it is also true that, in light of that ongoing disagreement, we must view politics as in part the art of respectfully managing it. But what exactly it means to respectfully manage disagreement over the common good is itself a question of political morality, one that is covered by the supplementary part of a complete account of political morality.

[42]   Waldron, *Law and Disagreement.*
[43]   Raz, "Facing Diversity: The Case of Epistemic Abstinence," *Philosophy and Public Affairs* 19/1 (1990): 3–46, at 25.

This reply might seem to underestimate the force of the objection. After all, it can be pointed out, the members of modern societies can be expected to disagree not only over the common good of their societies but also over what would count as respectful management of that disagreement. The problem posed by disagreement would just resurface at a different point. For example, if it were urged that, in the face of disagreement over the common good, and the shape of the ethical environment that best serves the common good, the respectful response is to submit the disagreement to a fair procedure, then a new question would emerge. What about disagreement over the status and character of the proposed fair procedure? Does not that disagreement demand a respectful response as well?

A regress threatens. Any proposed respectful response to disagreement can be expected to provoke disagreement over itself. At some point, the spade will be turned. One must assert that the proposed response to disagreement is the correct response, and that disagreement over it does not undercut its claim to be the correct response. Political morality, like morality generally, bottoms out in the first-person perspective.[44]

None of this implies that the fact of disagreement is insignificant at the bar of morality, or that political philosophers have done well in taking the full measure of its significance. But it does suggest that disagreement is more of a pragmatic than a moral problem. Political morality instructs us to treat our opponents with respect. Beyond that, the significance of disagreement for politics is that it limits what can be done in the pursuit of the common good. Several truisms follow. Compromise is central to political decision-making. To build support for common-good measures, one will often need to settle for less than ideal proposals so as to win sufficient support from others. One also will need to work within established political procedures, even as one judges them to be defective in various ways.[45]

Do these pragmatic factors make the enforcement of morality a largely conservative enterprise? Devlin-style enforcement, a version of which we have defended in Chapter 6, has a conservative dimension. The morality to be enforced is established morality. But, as our discussion in the previous section suggested, the enforcement of morality can be a progressive undertaking as well, one that seeks to change established norms.[46] To be sure, the line between enforcing established morality and using the law, and other social mechanisms, to improve established morality is not a sharp one. A society's established morality is always in flux and subject to competing understandings. Those who seek to enforce this or that moral norm in their society often seek to further some strands of the social morality of their societies

[44] On this point, compare my "On Justificatory Liberalism," *Philosophy, Politics and Economics* 9 (2010): 123–150 with Gaus, *The Order of Public Reason*, pp. 225–232.
[45] In saying this, I do not mean to imply that revolutionary political action is never justified. Established frameworks are a collective achievement. They enable a society's members to act in concert, despite their differences and disagreements. Given the difficulty of establishing them, they should not be abandoned lightly.
[46] See Green, "Should Law Improve Morality?" *Criminal Law and Philosophy* 7 (2013): 473–494.

over others. Indeed, one might deny that there is a single social morality in each society, preferring instead to speak of the social moralities of different segments of the populations of the society. Social moralities, one might say, compete within a society for dominance, and efforts to enforce and/or improve the social morality of a society reflect this competition.

Ethical environmentalism is a project animated by critical morality but constrained by social morality. Those who reject the social morality of their society can seek to transform and improve it, but if their views are not shared by others, they will have little prospect of success. That is why the enforcement of morality naturally takes place at the intersection of social morality and (what is taken to be) critical morality. In societies marked by pluralism and deep disagreement, the size of that intersection is contracted, and the project of ethical environmentalism is effectively limited to sustaining widely valued practices and furthering widely shared values and seeking to further some prevalent strands of the established social morality over others.

The fact of disagreement is not all a matter of pragmatic constraint, however. Assuming that value pluralism is true and that it is good for people to realize autonomy in their lives, the fact of disagreement can serve a positive ethical function. The core idea of value pluralism, and its relevance to self-determination, was well expressed by Nozick in his discussion of what he termed "creative pluralism." This obtains when there is not

> one uniquely correct objective ranking of [objective values], one optimal (feasible) mix of them, one fixed desirable schedule of tradeoffs among them. There is some open range within whatever partial rankings of value are objectively correct. Individuality is expressed in the interstices of the objective rankings of value, in the particular unified patterning chosen and lived; this itself will be objectively valuable.[47]

The reality of creative pluralism would provide a further measure of support for the tradition-dependent goods of different societies discussed in Chapter 6. Societies can navigate their way through the "interstices of the objective rankings of value" and express their ethical character by the traditions that they establish and sustain. Likewise, individuals within societies can do so as well. They can fashion their own valuable lives by the patterned choices that they make within the constraints of objective value. But creative pluralism is a thesis about the nature of value. It does not speak to the sociological conditions that facilitate the achievement of individuality. The truth of creative pluralism, after all, is consistent with a society in which there is a broad consensus on what is and what is not of value. In such a society people would not be exposed to a wide range of different patterns of living, reflecting different mixes of objective goods. They would not confront in their daily lives what Mill termed "a variety of situations." By contrast, in a society that contained numerous rival conceptions of the good life, all competing with one another to

---

[47] Nozick, *Philosophical Explanations*, p. 448.

gain adherents, each member of the society would be made vividly aware of the wide range of materials open to them in deciding how to live.

No doubt a society that contained a plurality of competing conceptions of the good life would experience more conflict and disagreement than one united by a consensus on objective value, but it would be, as a consequence, a freer society in the sense that its members would be more alive to the diverse possibilities for leading valuable autonomous lives. The contestation over what shape the shared ethical environment of a society should assume is itself an ethically significant feature of that environment. Political and social disagreement over morality, given the truth and general acceptance of creative pluralism, becomes not merely an obstacle to achieving the goal of sustaining an ethical environment that furthers the flourishing of those within it but also an important factor that contributes to the realization of that goal.

Bibliography

Alexander, L. 2005. *Is There a Right to Freedom of Expression?* (Cambridge: Cambridge University Press).

    2013. "Voluntary Enslavement," in *Paternalism: Theory and Practice*, eds. C. Coon and M. Weber (Cambridge: Cambridge University Press), pp. 231–246.

Arneson, R. 1982. "Fairness and Free Rider Problems," *Ethics* 92/4: 616–633.

    1989. "Paternalism, Utility and Fairness," *Revue Internationale de Philosophe* 43/170: 409–437.

    2000. "Luck Egalitarianism and Prioritarianism," *Ethics* 110/2: 339–349.

    2005. "Joel Feinberg and the Justification of Hard Paternalism," *Legal Theory* 11/3: 259–284.

    2007. "Cracked Foundations of Liberal Equality," in *Dworkin and His Critics*, ed. J. Burley (London: Blackwell), pp. 79–98.

    2018. "Egalitarian Perspectives on Paternalism," in *The Routledge Handbook of the Philosophy of Paternalism*, eds. K. Grill and J. Hanna (New York: Routledge), pp. 194–205.

Austin, J. 1832 [1995]. *The Province of Jurisprudence Determined*, ed. W. E. Rumble (Cambridge: Cambridge University Press).

Beale, S. 2005. "The Many Faces of Overcriminalization: From Morals and Mattress Tags to Overfederalization," *American University Law Review* 54/3: 747–782.

Beauchamp, T. 1977. "Paternalism and Biobehavioral Control," *The Monist* 60/1: 62–80.

Berger, F. 1984. *Freedom, Morality and Happiness* (Berkeley: University of California Press).

Bickel, A. 1975. *The Morality of Consent* (New Haven, CT: Yale University Press).

Billingham, P. and Parr, T. 2020. "Enforcing Social Norms: The Morality of Public Shaming," *European Journal of Philosophy* 28/4: 997–1016.

Bork, R. 1990. *The Tempting of America* (New York: Simon & Schuster).

Brink, D. 2008. "Mill's Liberal Principles and the Freedom of Expression," in *Mill's On Liberty: A Critical Guide*, ed. C. Ten (Cambridge: Cambridge University Press).

    2013. *Mill's Progressive Principles* (Oxford: Oxford University Press).

Burgess-Jackson, K. 1985. "Bad Samaritanism and the Pedagogic Function of Law," *Criminal Justice Journal* 8: 1–27.

Burke, E. 1774. "Speech to the Electors at Bristol," *The Works of The Right Honourable Edmund Burke in Twelve Volumes: Volume the Second* (London: John C. Nimmo).

Christiano, T. 1996. *The Rule of the Many* (Boulder, CO: Westview).

    2008. "Does Religious Toleration Make Any Sense?" in *Contemporary Debates in Social Philosophy* (London: Blackwell).

Cohen, G. A. 1995. *Self-Ownership, Freedom and Equality* (Cambridge: Cambridge University Press).

2006. "Casting the First Stone: Who Can and Who Can't Condemn the Terrorists?" *Political Philosophy*, ed. A. O'Hare. Royal Institute of Philosophy supplement 58.

2008. *Rescuing Justice and Equality* (Oxford: Oxford University Press).

2011. "Rescuing Conservatism: A Defense of Existing Value," in *Reasons and Recognition: Essays on the Moral Philosophy of T. M. Scanlon*, eds. R. Jay Wallace, R. Kumar and S. Freeman (Oxford: Oxford University Press).

Darwall, S. 2006. *The Second-Person Standpoint* (Cambridge, MA: Harvard University Press).

Devlin, P. 1959. "The Enforcement of Morals," *Proceedings of the British Academy* 45: 1–25.

1965. *The Enforcement of Morals* (Oxford: Oxford University Press).

Dworkin, G. 1982. "Is More Choice Better Than Less?" *Midwest Studies in Philosophy* 7: 47–61.

1988. *The Theory and Practice of Autonomy* (Cambridge: Cambridge University Press).

2012. "Harm and the Volenti Principle," *Social Philosophy and Policy* 29/1: 309–321.

Dworkin, R. 1976. *Taking Rights Seriously* (Cambridge, MA: Harvard University Press).

1986. *Law's Empire* (Cambridge, MA: Harvard University Press).

1996. *Freedom's Law* (Cambridge, MA: Harvard University Press).

2000. *Sovereign Virtue* (Cambridge, MA: Harvard University Press).

2008. *Is Democracy Possible Here?* (Princeton, NJ: Princeton University Press).

2009. "Foreword," in *Extreme Speech and Democracy*, eds. I. Hare and J. Weinstein (Oxford: Oxford University Press), pp. v–ix.

2011. *Justice for Hedgehogs* (Cambridge, MA: Harvard University Press).

Edmundson, W. 2004. *An Introduction to Rights* (Cambridge: Cambridge University Press).

Enoch, D. 2002. "A Right to Violate One's Duty," *Law and Philosophy* 21: 355–384.

2018. "Against Utopianism: Noncompliance and Multiple Agents," *The Philosopher's Imprint* 18/6: 1–20.

Estlund, D. 2020. *Utopophobia* (Princeton, NJ: Princeton University Press).

Eyal, N. 2017. "How to Keep High Risk Studies Ethical: Classifying Candidate Solutions," *Journal of Medical Ethics* 43/2: 74–77.

Feinberg, J. 1965. "The Expressive Function of Punishment," *The Monist* 49/3: 397–423.

1974. "Noncomparative Justice," *Philosophical Review* 83/3: 297–338.

1984. *Harm to Others* (Oxford: Oxford University Press).

1986. *Harm to Self* (Oxford: Oxford University Press).

1988. *Harmless Wrongdoing* (Oxford: Oxford University Press).

Finnis, J. 1985. "Human Rights and Their Enforcement," reprinted in *Human Rights and the Common Good* (Oxford: Oxford University Press, 2011).

1996. "Limited Government," reprinted in *Human Rights and the Common Good* (Oxford: Oxford University Press, 2011).

2003. "Describing Law Normatively," reprinted in *Philosophy of Law* (Oxford: Oxford University Press, 2011).

Frankfurt, H. 2004. *Reasons of Love* (Princeton, NJ: Princeton University Press).

Frey, B. and Jegen, R. 2001. "Motivating Crowding Theory: A Survey of Empirical Evidence," *Journal of Economic Surveys* 15: 589–611.

Fried, C. 1981. *Contract As Promise* (Cambridge, MA: Harvard University Press).

2007. *Modern Liberty* (New York: Norton).

Fuller, L. 1964. *The Morality of Law* (New Haven, CT: Yale University Press).

Galston, W. 1993. "On the Alleged Right to Do Moral Wrong," *Ethics* 93/2: 320–324.

Gardner J. and Shute, S. 2007. "The Wrongness of Rape," in *Offences and Defences* (Oxford: Oxford University Press).

Gardner, J. and Tanguay-Renaud, F. 2011. "Desert and Avoidability in Self-Defense," *Ethics* 122/1: 111–134.

Gaus, G. 2011. *The Order of Public Reason* (Cambridge: Cambridge University Press).

George, R. 1993. *Making Men Moral* (Oxford: Oxford University Press).

Gettier, E. 1963. "Is Justified True Belief Knowledge?" *Analysis* 23/6: 121–123.

Gibbard, A. 1990. *Wise Choices, Apt Feelings* (Oxford: Oxford University Press).

Goldman, A. 1996. *Social Epistemology* (Oxford: Oxford University Press).

Goldman, A. and O'Connor, C. 2021. "Social Epistemology," *The Stanford Encyclopedia of Philosophy* (winter edition), Edward N. Zalta (ed.). https://plato.stanford.edu/archives/win2021/entries/epistemology-social.

Gray, J. 1983. *Mill on Liberty: A Defence* (London: Routledge and Kegan Paul).

Green, L. 2013. "Should the Law Improve Morality?" *Criminal Law and Philosophy* 7/3: 473–494.

Green, S. P. 1997. "Why It's a Crime to Tear the Tag Off a Mattress: Overcriminalization and the Moral Content of Regulatory Offenses," *Emory Law Journal* 46/4: 1553–1616.

Greenawalt, K. 1992. *Speech, Crime and the Uses of Language* (Oxford: Oxford University Press).

1995. *Fighting Words* (Princeton, NJ: Princeton University Press).

Habermas, J. 1989. *The Structural Transformation of the Public Sphere* (Cambridge, MA: MIT Press).

Haidt, J. 2001. "The Emotional Dog and Its Rational Tail: A Social Intuitionist Approach to Moral Judgment," *Psychological Review* 108/4: 814–834.

Hart, C. L. 2021. *Drug Use for Grown Ups: Chasing Liberty in the Land of Fear* (New York: Penguin Press).

Hart, H. L. A. 1955. "Are There Any Natural Rights?" *The Philosophical Review* 64/2: 175–191.

1959. "Immorality and Treason," *The Listener*, July 30.

1961 [1994]. *The Concept of Law*, ed. L. Green, 3rd ed. (Oxford: Oxford University Press).

1963. *Law, Liberty and Morality* (Stanford, CA: Stanford University Press).

1982. "Commands and Authoritative Reasons," in *Essays on Bentham* (Oxford: Oxford University Press), pp. 243–268.

Hernstein, O. J. 2014. "A Legal Right to Do Legal Wrong," *Oxford Journal of Legal Studies* 34/1: 21–45.

Hohfeld, W. 2001. *Fundamental Legal Conceptions As Applied in Judicial Reasoning* (New York: Ashgate).

Honore, A. 1961. "Ownership," in *Oxford Essays in Jurisprudence*, ed. A. G. Guest (Oxford: Oxford University Press), pp. 107–147.

Hooker, B. 2000. *Ideal Code, Real World* (Oxford: Oxford University Press).

Humboldt, W. von. 1969. *The Limits of State Action*, trans. J. W. Burrow (Cambridge: Cambridge University Press).

Hurd, H. 2009. "Paternalism on Pain of Punishment," *Criminal Justice Ethics* 28/1: 49–73.

Hurka, T. 1987. "Why Value Autonomy?" *Social Theory and Practice* 13/3: 361–382.

1995. "Indirect Perfectionism: Kymlicka on Liberal Neutrality," *Journal of Political Philosophy* 3/1: 36–57.

Husak, D. 1983. "The Presumption of Freedom," *Nous* 17/3: 345–362.

2008. *Overcriminalization* (Oxford: Oxford University Press).

2013. "Penal Paternalism," in *Paternalism: Theory and Practice*, eds. C. Coon and M. Weber (Cambridge: Cambridge University Press), pp. 39–55.

Jacobson, D. 2005. "Mill on Liberty, Speech and the Free Society," *Philosophy and Public Affairs* 29/3: 276–309.

Kagan, S. 1991. *The Limits of Morality* (Oxford: Oxford University Press).

2009. "Well-Being As Enjoying the Good," *Philosophical Perspectives* 23: 253–272.

2011. "Do I Make a Difference?" *Philosophy and Public Affairs* 39/2: 105–141.

2019. *How to Count Animals* (Oxford: Oxford University Press).

Kahneman, D. 2011. *Thinking, Fast and Slow* (New York: Farrar, Straus and Giroux).

Kant, I. 1775–80 [1997]. *Lectures on Ethics*, eds. P. Heath and J. B. Schneewind (Cambridge: Cambridge University Press).

Kramer, M. 2003. *The Quality of Freedom* (Oxford: Oxford University Press).

2021. *Freedom of Expression As Self-Restraint* (Oxford: Oxford University Press).

Kristol, I. 1971. "Pornography, Obscenity, and the Case for Censorship," *The New York Times Magazine*, March 28.

Kronman, A. 1983. "Paternalism and the Law of Contracts," *Yale Law Journal* 92/5: 763–798.

Kymlicka, W. 1989. *Liberalism, Community and Culture* (Oxford: Oxford University Press).

Labaton, S. 1989. "New Tactics in the War on Drugs Tilt Scales of Justice Off Balance," *The New York Times*, December 29, p. A1.

Langton, R. 2009. *Sexual Solipsism* (Oxford: Oxford University Press).

Larmore, C. 1986. *Patterns of Moral Complexity* (Cambridge: Cambridge University Press).

Locke, J. 1685 [1983]. *A Letter Concerning Toleration* (Indianapolis, IN: Hackett).

Lyons, D. 1979. "Liberty and Harm to Others," *Canadian Journal of Philosophy* supp. vol. V: 1–19.

Mackinnon, C. 1996. *Only Words* (Cambridge, MA: Harvard University Press).

Marcuse, H. 1965. "Repressive Tolerance," in *A Critique of Pure Tolerance* (Boston, MA: Beacon Press), pp. 81–123.

Marneffe, Peter de. 2010. *Liberalism and Prostitution* (Oxford: Oxford University Press).

2013. "Self-Sovereignty and Paternalism," in *Paternalism: Theory and Practice*, eds. C. Coon and M. Weber (Cambridge: Cambridge University Press), pp. 56–73.

Meiklejohn, A. 1960. *Political Freedom: The Constitutional Powers of the People* (New York: Harper and Brothers).

Mill, J. S. 1840 [1987]. "Essay on Coleridge," reprinted in *John Stuart Mill and Jeremy Bentham: Utilitarianism and Other Essays*, ed. A. Ryan (New York: Penguin), pp. 177–227.

1859 [1977]. *On Liberty*, in *The Collected Works of John Stuart Mill*, vol. XVIII, ed. J. Robson (Toronto: University of Toronto Press), pp. 213–310.

1859 [1978]. *On Liberty*, ed. E. Rapaport (Indianapolis, IN: Hackett).

1861 [1969]. *Utilitarianism*, in *The Collected Works of John Stuart Mill*, vol. X, ed. J. Robson (Toronto: University of Toronto Press), pp. 203–260.

1861 [1977]. *Considerations on Representative Government*, in *The Collected Works of John Stuart Mill*, vol. XIX, ed. J. Robson (Toronto: University of Toronto Press), pp. 371–578.

Milton, J. 1644. *Areopagitica* (Will Jonson).

Moore, G. E. 1903. *Principia Ethica* (Cambridge: Cambridge University Press).

Moore, M. 1997. *Placing Blame* (Oxford: Oxford University Press).

Murphy, M. 2006. *Natural Law in Jurisprudence and Politics* (Cambridge: Cambridge University Press).

Murray, C. and Hernstein, R. 1994. *The Bell Curve* (New York: The Free Press).

Nagel, T. 1991. *Equality and Partiality* (Oxford: Oxford University Press).

Nathanson, S. 1985. "Does It Matter if the Death Penalty Is Arbitrarily Applied?" *Philosophy and Public Affairs* 14/2: 149–164.

Nozick, R. 1974. *Anarchy, State and Utopia* (New York: Basic Books).

1981. *Philosophical Explanations* (Cambridge, MA: Harvard University Press).

1993. *The Nature of Rationality* (Princeton, NJ: Princeton University Press).

Parfit, D. 1984. *Reasons and Persons* (Oxford: Oxford University Press).

Patton, A. 2014. *Equal Recognition* (Princeton, NJ: Princeton University Press).

Pereboom, D. 2001. *Living without Free Will* (Cambridge: Cambridge University Press).

Perry, S. 1997. "Risk, Harm and Responsibility," in *Philosophical Foundations of Tort Law*, ed. D. Owen (Oxford: Oxford University Press), pp. 321–346.

Pettit, P. 2001. *A Theory of Freedom* (Oxford: Oxford University Press).

Pitkin, H. 1967. *The Concept of Representation* (Berkeley: University of California Press).

Postema, G. 1994. "Public Faces and Private Places: Liberalism and the Enforcement of Morality," in *Harm and the Law*, ed. G. Dworkin (Boulder, CO: Westview Press), pp. 76–90.

Proast, J. 1999. "The Argument of the Letter Concerning Toleration, Briefly Consider'd and Answer'd," in *The Reception of Locke's Politics*, vol. V, ed. M. Goldie (London: Pickering and Chatto), pp. 41–116.

Radzik, L. 2020. *The Ethics of Social Punishment* (Cambridge: Cambridge University Press).

Rashdall, H. 1907. *The Theory of Good and Evil*, vol. I (London: Oxford University Press).

Rawls, J. 1971. *A Theory of Justice* (Cambridge, MA: Harvard University Press).

　　1993. *Political Liberalism* (New York: Columbia University Press).

Raz, J. 1975. *Practical Reason and Norms* (Oxford: Oxford University Press).

　　1979. "The Rule of Law and Its Virtue," in *The Authority of Law* (Oxford: Oxford University Press), pp. 210–229.

　　1982. "Right-Based Moralities," in *Theories of Rights*, ed. J. Waldron (Oxford: Oxford University Press), pp. 182–200.

　　1986. *The Morality of Freedom* (Oxford: Oxford University Press).

　　1988. "Liberalism, Skepticism and Democracy," *Iowa Law Review* 74: 761–786.

　　1990. "Facing Diversity: The Case of Epistemic Abstinence," *Philosophy and Public Affairs* 19/1: 3–46.

　　1994. "Free Expression and Personal Identification," in *Ethics and the Public Domain* (Oxford: Oxford University Press), pp. 146–169.

　　2009. "The Problem of Authority: Revisiting the Service Conception," in *Between Authority and Interpretation* (Oxford: Oxford University Press), pp. 126–165.

Ripstein, A. 2006. "Beyond the Harm Principle," *Philosophy and Public Affairs* 34/3: 215–245.

　　2009. *Force and Freedom* (Cambridge, MA: Harvard University Press).

Ronson, J. 2015. *So You've Been Publicly Shamed* (London: Picador).

Ryan, A. 2012. "Mill's Essay on Liberty," in *The Making of Modern Liberalism* (Princeton, NJ: Princeton University Press), pp. 257–278.

Scalia, A. 1997. *A Matter of Interpretation* (Princeton, NJ: Princeton University Press).

Scanlon, T. M. 1998. *What We Owe to Each Other* (Cambridge, MA: Harvard University Press).

　　2003. "A Theory of Freedom of Expression," in *The Difficulty of Tolerance* (Cambridge: Cambridge University Press), pp. 6–25.

　　2003. "Content Regulation Reconsidered," in *The Difficulty of Tolerance* (Cambridge: Cambridge University Press), pp. 151–168.

　　2003. "Freedom of Expression and Categories of Expression," in *The Difficulty of Tolerance* (Cambridge: Cambridge University Press), pp. 84–112.

Schauer, F. 1993. "The Phenomenology of Speech and Harm," *Ethics* 103/4: 635–653.

　　2015. "Free Speech on Tuesdays," *Law and Philosophy* 34: 119–140.

　　2015. *The Force of Law* (Cambridge, MA: Harvard University Press).

Scheffler, S. 1982. *The Rejection of Consequentialism* (Oxford: Oxford University Press).

　　1992. *Human Morality* (Oxford: Oxford University Press).

　　2011. "Valuing," in *Reasons and Recognition: Essays on the Moral Philosophy of T. M. Scanlon*, eds. R. J. Wallace et al. (Oxford: Oxford University Press), pp. 23–42.

Shafer-Landau, R. 1996. "The Failure of Retributivism," *Philosophical Studies* 82: 289–316.

Sher, G. 2021. *A Wild West of the Mind* (Oxford: Oxford University Press).

Shiffrin, S. 2000. "Paternalism, Unconscionability Doctrine, and Accommodation," *Philosophy and Public Affairs* 29/3: 205–250.

Shiner, R. 2009. "Crime and Criminal Law Reform: A Theory of the Legislative Response," *Critical Review of International Social and Political Philosophy* 12/1: 63–84.

Simmons, A. J. 1979. "The Principle of Fair Play," *Philosophy and Public Affairs* 8/4: 307–337.

1996. "Philosophical Anarchism," in *For and Against the State*, eds. J. T. Sanders and J. Narveson (Lanham, MD: Rowman & Littlefield), pp. 19–39.

Skorupski, J. 2006. *Why Read Mill Today?* (London: Routledge).

Smith, M. 2004. "Internal Reasons," in *Ethics and the A Priori* (Cambridge: Cambridge University Press), pp. 17–42.

Stephen, J. Fitzjames. 1873. *Liberty, Equality and Fraternity* (New York: Holt & Williams).

Stone, G. 1983. "Content-Regulation and the First Amendment," *William and Mary Law Review* 25/2: 189–252.

Straus, D. 1991. "Persuasion, Autonomy and Freedom of Expression," *Columbia Law Review* 91/2: 334–371.

Strawson, P. F. 1961. "Social Morality and Individual Ideal," *Philosophy* 36/136: 1–17.

Strossen, N. 1990. "Regulating Racist Speech on Campus: A Modest Proposal," *Duke Law Journal* 39: 484–573.

2018. *Hate Speech* (Oxford: Oxford University Press).

Sunstein, C. 1994. "A New Deal for Speech," *Hastings Communications and Entertainment Law Journal* 17: 137–160.

Tadros, V. 2016. *Wrongs and Crimes* (Oxford: Oxford University Press).

Temkin, L. 1995. "Justice and Equality: Some Questions about Scope," *Social Philosophy and Policy* 12/2: 72–104.

2000. "Equality, Priority, and the Leveling Down Objection," in *The Ideal of Equality*, eds. M. Clayton and A. Williams (London: Macmillan), pp. 126–161.

Titmus, R. 1970. *The Gift Relationship* (London: George Allen and Unwin, Ltd.).

Tocqueville, Alexis de. 1805–59 [1838]. *Democracy in America* (New York: G. Dearborn & Co.).

Valdman, M. 2010. "Outsourcing Self-Government," *Ethics* 120/4: 761–790.

van den Haag, E. 1986. "The Ultimate Punishment: A Defence," *Harvard Law Review* 99/7: 1662–1669.

Volokh, E. 1995. "Cheap Speech and What It Will Do," *Yale Law Journal* 104: 1804–1850.

Waldron, J. 1981. "A Right to Do Wrong," *Ethics* 92/1: 21–39.

1987. "Mill and the Value of Moral Distress," *Political Studies* 35/3: 410–423.

1999. *Law and Disagreement* (Oxford: Oxford University Press).

2014. *The Harm in Hate Speech* (Cambridge, MA: Harvard University Press).

Wall, S. 1998. *Liberalism, Perfectionism and Restraint* (Cambridge: Cambridge University Press).

2009. "Self-Ownership and Paternalism," *Journal of Political Philosophy* 17/4: 399–417.

2010. "On Justificatory Liberalism," *Politics, Philosophy and Economics* 9/2: 123–150.

2015. "Introduction," in *The Cambridge Companion to Liberalism*, ed. S. Wall (Cambridge: Cambridge University Press), pp. 1–18.

2016. "Autonomy As a Perfection," *American Journal of Jurisprudence* 16/2: 175–194.

2016. "Political Morality and the Authority of Tradition," *Journal of Political Philosophy* 24/2: 137–161.

2018. "Subjective Perfectionism," *American Journal of Jurisprudence* 63/1: 109–131.

2019. "Rooted Reciprocity," *Journal of Moral Philosophy* 16/4: 1–23.

Wall, S. and Klosko, G. 2003. *Perfectionism and Neutrality: Essays in Liberal Theory* (Lanham, MD: Rowman & Littlefield).

Wall, S. and Sobel, D. 2021. "A Robust Hybrid Account of Well-Being," *Philosophical Studies* 178: 2829–2851.

Wallace-Wells, B. 2021. "Is There a Case for Legalizing Heroin?" *The New Yorker*, August 29.

Walzer, M. 1983. *Spheres of Justice* (New York: Basic Books).

Watson, G. 2004. "Two Faces of Responsibility," in *Agency and Answerability* (Oxford: Oxford University Press), pp. 260–288.

Williams, B. 1981. "Internal and External Reasons," reprinted in *Moral Luck* (Cambridge: Cambridge University Press), pp. 101–113.

Wu, T. 2018. "Is the First Amendment Obsolete?" *Michigan Law Review* 117/3: 547–581.

Index

For EU product safety concerns, contact us at Calle de José Abascal, 56–1°,
28003 Madrid, Spain or eugpsr@cambridge.org.

www.ingramcontent.com/pod-product-compliance
Ingram Content Group UK Ltd.
Pitfield, Milton Keynes, MK11 3LW, UK
UKHW020353140625
459647UK00020B/2445